The Business Value of Software

The Business Value of Software

By
Michael D.S. Harris

CRC Press
Taylor & Francis Group
Boca Raton London New York

CRC Press is an imprint of the
Taylor & Francis Group, an **informa** business

AN AUERBACH BOOK

CRC Press
Boca Raton and London
CRC Press
Taylor & Francis Group
6000 Broken Sound Parkway NW, Suite 300
Boca Raton, FL 33487-2742

Printed on acid-free paper

International Standard Book Number-13: 978-1-4987-8286-9 (Hardback)

Library of Congress Cataloging-in-Publication Data

Names: Harris, Michael D. S., author.
Title: The business value of software / Michael Harris.
Description: Boca Raton : Taylor & Francis, a CRC title, part of the Taylor & Francis imprint, a member of the Taylor & Francis Group, the academic division of T&F Informa, plc, [2017]
Identifiers: LCCN 2017006007| ISBN 9781498782869 (hb : acid-free paper) | ISBN 9781498782906 (e)
Subjects: LCSH: Business--Data processing. | Computer software--Development.
Classification: LCC HF5548.2 .H374 2017 | DDC 005.068--dc23
LC record available at https://lccn.loc.gov/2017006007

Visit the Taylor & Francis Web site at
http://www.taylorandfrancis.com

and the CRC Press Web site at
http://www.crcpress.com

Contents

Preface

As president and owner of a consulting company that for over 20 years has specialized in helping our clients measure and improve their software development processes, I have met many frustrated leaders of software development. Our conversations are often about their struggle to explain why software development is so challenging and how they are delivering value to their often aggravated business colleagues who struggle to understand. Struggling is a reasonable place to be, because it implies dissatisfaction with the status quo. This is fair because the status quo in the software development industry is to pretty much ignore the business value of software. This book is for all those "strugglers"—both information technology (IT) leaders and business executives alike.

Unfortunately, for every frustrated leader of software development that I meet, I meet two or three comfortable software development leaders who are satisfied with their software development and the metrics they use to measure it. What's interesting is that most are not measuring the business value of their software and don't want to measure it. Their reasons for avoiding quantifying software value are understandable—it's too hard, the business won't understand it, and (maybe) they don't want to know if it might be bad news. Some of our clients—major international companies—have moved or are moving beyond this. Hence, this book is for these leaders too—time to move out of your comfort zone before somebody pushes you out of it.

This book is not about business–IT alignment, although it does emphasize the benefits of business–IT collaboration. To me, alignment too often implies "agreeing to disagree" on the areas in which we are supposed to be working together. If readers can use even half of the ideas in this book, then I know that the business–IT alignment will improve as a result of a common understanding of how to improve the business value delivered by the organization's software development initiatives.

Acknowledgments

It is not possible to recognize all those individuals who have ultimately made this book a reality. The ideas in this book come from articles and books read, webinars and seminars attended, and many conversations with colleagues and clients. To all of those unnamed individuals who have influenced the ideas in this book, thank you.

I am grateful to John Wyzalek at Taylor & Francis Group for having the confidence in me to support this second book.

One particular set of conversations provided the spark that lit the fire that became this book, and I'm grateful to Howard Watson and John Nevins of BT for asking the questions that got me thinking several years ago.

I am very fortunate to work with a great bunch of people at the Premios Group. These individuals are the collective "face" of Premios to the world. Their care for our clients and continuing professionalism have made Premios and continue to keep us at the forefront of software development measurement and process improvement. Harrison Zipkin was very helpful with words and thoughts on Chapter 11. I am especially indebted to Tom Cagley for his willingness and ability to argue with me about the big picture and the finer points, and, in particular, for his extensive contributions to Chapter 10. My thanks are due to Capers Jones for privately sharing his lucid explanation of the differences between Waterfall and Agile, which formed the basis of the Appendix.

I must thank my reviewers who helped me with improving the content and text of the chapters as I went along: Maria Bassegio, Karen Higgins, and Sarah Weddle. Any remaining errors are mine alone.

Once again, I must acknowledge my eternal thanks for the love and support of my wife, Jane. My muse.

Author

Michael D.S. Harris brings to this book a wide range of IT perspectives, specifically in the area of delivering business value. His international career has taken him from production management, through research and development (R&D), project management, and academia, to consulting, before planting him firmly in charge of a large software engineering group for a public company. While there, he decided that he liked one of his vendors, David Consulting Group, so much that he would buy the company; and last year, he decided it was time to change the name of the company to reflect his passion. In 2016, the David Consulting Group became DCG Software Value (now part of the Premios Group, following a merger with the Spitfire Group). Mike is a chartered engineer (CEng), a member of the Institution of Engineering and Technology (IET) in the United Kingdom, and a member of the Institute of Electrical and Electronic Engineers (IEE) in the United States. He is a Scaled Agile Framework SAFe program consultant and certified Scrum master.

With their much-loved, high-achieving kids all grown up and pursuing their independent lives, Mike lives with his high school sweetheart, Jane, outside Philadelphia, in southern Colorado, and on the coast of northern England as time, work, and whim permit.

Acronyms

ADD	(software) asset due diligence
AHR	AgilityHealth Radar
AIM	(software) asset integration management
AMA	(software) asset maturity analysis
ARM	(software) asset risk management
ART	Agile Release Train
BAC	budget at completion
CapEx	capital expenses
CDO	chief digital officer
CEO	chief executive officer
CFO	chief financial officer
CIO	chief information officer
CISO	chief information security officer
CMMI	Capability Maturity Model Integration
CMO	chief marketing officer
CMS	content management system
CoD	cost of delay
COTS	commercial off-the-shelf
CRM	customer relationship management
CTO	chief technology officer
DAD	disciplined Agile delivery
DSDM	dynamic systems development method
ERP	enterprise resource planning
EV	earned value
EVM	earned value management
FAA	Federal Aviation Administration
FASAB	Financial Accounting Standards Advisory Board
FDA	Food and Drug Administration
GASB	Governmental Accounting Standards Board
HR	human resources
ISBSG	International Software Benchmarking Standards Group
IT	information technology

LeSS	large-scale Scrum
MVP	minimum viable product
OBM	Office of Budget and Management (Ohio)
OpEx	operating expenses
PMBOK	Project Management Book of Knowledge
PMI	Project Management Institute
PMO	project management office
PPE	property, plant, and equipment
ROE	return on equity
ROI	return on investment
RUP	rational unified process
SAFe	Scaled Agile Framework
SFFAS	Statement of Federal Financial Accounting Standards
SMAC	social (media), mobile, analytics, and cloud
SVMO	software value management office
TSP	team software process
VMO	value management office
VSE	value stream engineer
VVF	value visualization framework
WBS	work breakdown structure
WIP	work in progress
WSJF	weighted shortest job first
XP	Extreme Programming

Chapter 1

Why Software Value?

The head of a large software development group in a major international corporation asked me, "How do I answer the questions from my peers in the business units about how much value I have delivered for them lately?"

If there were a single, largest driver behind the writing of this book, it would be this real-life question. It's a simple question, but the answer is multifaceted and, hence, complicated. Perhaps that is why so few organizations even attempt to track software value? In this chapter, I will define what I mean by the term *business value of software* (I will use this term and the term *software value* interchangeably), and I will demonstrate how businesses are suffering through their inadequate management of their software value assets and flows.

Why Not Information Technology Value More Generally?

Most people working in large corporations probably think that their software is just a standard part of the services that their information technology (IT) department provides to facilitate the organizations' operations. Traditionally, IT departments have been cost centers in the enterprise, sometimes treated as pure overhead, but more often funded in part or wholly by *charge backs* from the business units. People in business units looking at this arrangement can be excused for focusing on the *business value* of IT. Indeed, we wrote a book with that title (Harris et al. 2008), which contained a series of questions that the business should address to the chief information officer (CIO) to ensure that the business value of IT is maximized. A fair criticism of (or compliment for) that book was that there was a disproportionate focus on software. I am unapologetic because, in my opinion, software represents the best and biggest way to increase value from today's IT, as hardware becomes more and more commoditized. In their book, *The Real Business of IT*, Hunter and Westerman (2009) reported on a survey of 153 senior executives conducted by the Massachusetts Institute of Technology's (MIT) Center for Information Systems Research (CISR), "of the eighteen common IT and non-IT tasks, only four – application development; business process redesign and organizational change; need identification; and IT oversight – have a statistically significant correlation to the business value provided by IT."

This book is a double acknowledgment that we did not focus enough on the business value of software in the last book and that the thinking about and tools available for software value have moved on.

Of course, the rest of IT has moved on too since we wrote the last book. The latest *digitization* wave (I am old enough to remember several of these) is based upon the collective challenges presented to IT departments by social media, mobile smartphones, business analytics (sometimes called "big data"), and *cloud* hosting of applications and data. Collectively, these driving forces are sometimes referred to as *SMAC*. Leaving aside analytics for a moment, the real industry challenge is that these trends represent significant changes for the IT departments that previously had direct control (and often ownership) of the computing hardware that staff and customers are using. Sort of. Some perspectives on this follow:

■ The movement to cloud computing—essentially, renting the hardware that the software runs on—is not revolutionary because mainframe computers worked, and still work, that way. The key change here is the continuing movement from centralized hardware to decentralized hardware.

■ Social media is equally driven by this hardware decentralization because the real-time, personal nature of the interactions is encouraged by the ready, real-time availability of the communication medium, seemingly no matter where you are or what you are doing!

■ Mobile computing, in its basic form, covers most of the world through the wide availability of phones. Sophisticated mobile computing through smartphones covers most of the rich and corporate world. The rapid proliferation of mobile phones and then smartphones around the world is the embodiment of the decentralization of processing power that has driven attention on the opportunities (many) and threats (some) of the latest wave of digitization.

Returning to analytics, I consider the growth of analytics to be an effect rather than a cause of the decentralization of hardware. The way that people interact with their retail, banking, and other business environments has changed due to hardware decentralization. Organizations faced with interacting less with their customers in traditional environments (e.g., stores and bank branches) needed to understand how to best fulfill, make money from (or spend less on), and predict the future of these new interactions. The way that organizations have addressed these needs has matured over time according to priority. First, transactions needed to be fulfilled. Second, transactions needed to be economically viable. Finally, analysis (analytics) of transactions were needed in attempting to predict and optimize the future. Fortunately, the software and data needed to drive the transactions with the decentralized hardware were exactly what was needed to enable the analytics to try to predict future trends. Of course, collecting the data brings its own challenges, as personal privacy becomes an issue. I will consider the value of the data associated with the software in Chapter 4.

The impact of the continuing decentralization of hardware will not end with this current wave of digitization. The SMAC acronym does not take account of the *Internet of things*, essentially the decentralization and proliferation of Internet-capable monitoring and control capabilities to everything that is economically worth measuring in our environments, from the refrigerator door to the water flowing out of the shower.

While the preceding perspectives illustrate how our perception of IT value is changing due to hardware decentralization, there is a small counterflow that is worth noting. While cloud computing enables the distribution of processing hardware to be closer to the markets where it is needed, some software that had previously been distributed to personal computers (PCs) is being consolidated into *software-as-a-service* (SaaS), products of which the most often quoted example is the *customer relationship management* (CRM) service provided by Salesforce.com. Another more consumer-oriented example is the delivery of video on demand through Netflix. However, this software consolidation may be the exception that proves the point because I assert that SaaS implementations tend to make the software more pervasive as it usually becomes more accessible (no distribution of disks and complicated installation) at a lower cost.

My point here is that if the typical organization's IT department is about delivering hardware, software, and the connections between the two, then, while it has been said before but has never completely come about, I would argue that one side effect of SMAC is the increasing commoditization of the hardware in the hands of an organization's staff and customers. The response from organizations has been to manage this loss of control of the hardware through more and different software.

Hence, I argue that the business value of software has increased and has become relatively more important in the IT sphere than when we wrote our last book. In arguing this point, I recognize that the distinction between hardware, software, and *systems* is becoming smaller every year. I could have used systems throughout this book in place of software, but I felt that this would be too much of a distraction. If you prefer to read software as systems throughout the book, please be my guest.

Regrettably, the measurement of software value in organizations is sporadic and weak. As we will see in the rest of this book, there is a lot of opportunity to improve, more than enough to justify the focus of this book on software value.

Who Should Care about the Business Value of Software?

The easy answer is everyone. But let's dig a little deeper. In this book, I will argue for two different perspectives of the business value of software: maximizing software asset value and maximizing the flow of software value.

Software asset value must get the attention of the upper echelons of the organization, starting with the chief executive officer (CEO) and the chief financial officer (CFO) but also including the heads of business units and, much more so than it does today, the board!

But who should care about maximizing the flow of software value? It would seem obvious that "all the above" should care because if there is no flow of new software value into the software asset pool then surely the value of the software asset pool must simply decline over time. Currently, there are few organizations whose board, senior management, and business unit heads are sending strong signals to the IT department to maximize the flow of software value. Perhaps they assume there is no need because, again, "isn't it obvious?" Unfortunately, over many years, other signals from senior management have been so strong that business value is not the first thing that many development teams and development managers think about. Today's priorities are more likely to be

- Deadlines (often unrealistically imposed)
- Cost
- Staff utilization

Reinertsen (2009) has shown that product development, focusing on these priorities, especially in a localized way as is typical, does not maximize the flow of software value. Instead, the value (or relative value) of software programs and projects or epics and stories needs to be made explicit from top to bottom of the organization so that everyone who can influence the flow of software value is explicitly aware of the impact that their day-to-day, tactical decisions will have on the flow of software value. This, then, is a better definition of why "everyone" should care about the business value of software.

Before I leave this section, I should return to an assertion I made previously but did not justify. I claimed that, "the value of the software asset pool must simply decline over time." Here, I am not talking about the amortization of the capitalized cost of the software on the balance sheet—although that is certainly a consideration. Instead, I am asserting that the value of the current software to the business, the business value, will inevitably decline over time as the business environment changes. This is based on the assertion that software is most valuable to the business when it is *fit for purpose*. A static piece of software that is not evolving as the business environment evolves becomes less fit for purpose and therefore has less business value (see Figure 1.1).

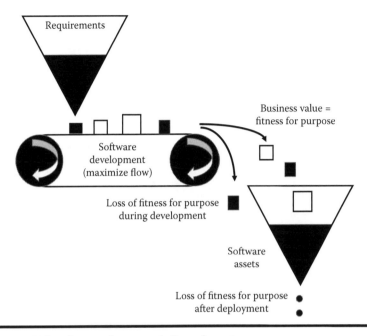

Figure 1.1 Value flow and accumulation of assets.

Interestingly, this leads to another conclusion: Not all new software added to the organization's software asset pool necessarily increases business value (see Figure 1.1). For example, there is no added value if the new software is not used (e.g., an ATM feature that cardholders never choose) or if the business environment has changed since the new software was requested and the new software is no longer relevant (e.g., a new, first-to-market insurance policy for which competitors have brought out a much better solution since the new software was requested). Hence, the value of a new piece of software cannot be assumed to be the value it was assigned when the business case for development was approved. Organizational process is needed to monitor, analyze, and manage the business value of the organization's software asset pool. I will suggest several such processes in this book.

What Is the Business Value of Software?

If we imagine an organization without software (yes, those things did exist), then the introduction of the first piece of software had a good chance of adding value to the business by increasing revenue or saving costs sufficient to cover the expense of buying or building the software. In short, the new piece of software had a good chance of increasing profits. Increased profits as a direct result of the introduction of a new piece of software is certainly the simplest form of the business value of software.

Impact of Perspective on Business Value

We need to acknowledge that software is viewed through different lenses at different times by different people. These lenses influence the definition of value, so it is worthwhile trying to identify some of the major ones, understanding that many organizations may contain all elements of a single lens. In Figure 1.2, I have illustrated the three main lenses that impact the business value of software perspectives:

- Profit lens: For-profit or not-for-profit organization. Typically, a government agency takes a not-for-profit view of the business value of software, but that distinction is blurred if governments drive their departments to take more commercial perspectives on their operations, often with a view to privatization. The business value of a particular piece of software can change significantly across this spectrum (e.g., the accounting needs of the organization are very different from one end of the spectrum to the other).
- End-client lens: In-house or external clients or both. This lens covers the different perspectives of organizations developing products or services for sale (e.g., Intuit's QuickBooks software developed to be sold versus an internally developed stock control system). A new piece of software designed to deliver a new online insurance product will almost certainly include functionality for in-house staff and external clients. Calculation of the business value of an additional feature to be thrown in immediately before launch will need to carefully consider the cost–benefit equation experienced by each group of users.
- Build-buy lens: Internally developed software or *commercial off-the-shelf* (COTS) software. I include outsourced software development in internally developed software because the organization is funding the development directly. There are nuances to this assumption because, typically, the value

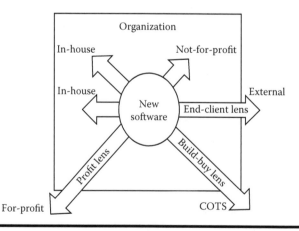

Figure 1.2 Business value perspective lenses.

proposition includes a profit for the outsourced development company; but my assumption is that this is just a variation of more expensive or less expensive resources. I assume that there are two dimensions to the introduction of COTS software: First, it is just as important to consider the business value of purchased software as software developed in-house; and second, it is a rare organization indeed that does not tinker with COTS software through configuration and customization to try to improve the business value (at least from a short-term perspective).

In this book, I will tend to focus on businesses seeking to make money through the sales of products and services other than software, even though these products and services will often use software for some part of their product or service delivery if only because, "What is money other than some numbers in some software somewhere?" In the context of the lenses, this means I will generally have in mind a for-profit, in-house build set of lenses. That said, I will consider the other lens' perspectives when the differences are significant.

Software Value Sidestep

Today, it is still possible for organizations to experience the simple instance of the first business value of software described previously, but such a scenario is rare. There are several reasons why the simple introduction of a new piece of software does not necessarily lead to a direct increase in profits. For example,

- The new software is a modification to existing software.
- The new software is not used.
- The new software fixes a defect: At face value, the removal of a defect should lead to higher value, but in most instances it represents the reinstatement of value that was expected in the software before the defect was fixed. Also, from a value perspective, the temporary loss of customer satisfaction could be more negative than the defect fix is positive.
- The new software makes customers happier.
- The new software makes staff happier.

For examples such as those listed previously, it is often a challenge to find a direct link between the new or modified software and an increase in business profits because the cause and effect has so many intermediaries. In the face of this challenge, our software industry demurs and defaults to rarely measuring the business value of software projects, carelessly tracking the cost of software projects, and almost never learning from the retrospective comparison of the two. However, while typical of the industry today as we shall see later in this chapter, this is just fuzzy thinking—let's call it the "software value sidestep"—that became acceptable under one set of historical conditions and remained an unquestioned habit when those conditions changed. The software value sidestep tends to occur when software can be developed or acquired so easily or cheaply that it is not worth incurring the expense of developing and sustaining a value model for the life of the software, from concept through cash to end of life. Put simply, using a modern consumer as an example, there is no point doing a business case and calculating total life cost for the $5 game app that I want to add to my smartphone. Naturally, there is a point in doing a business case to develop that app in the first place, unless, as is sometimes the case these days, the app was initially developed for fun or voluntarily to provide a useful service.

For much of the short history of software, this logic applied to software acquisition and development for organizations under the following conditions:

■ Hardware was expensive and not changed very often.
■ Software was easy to change especially if the changes were small; if the small, cheap software changes obviously improved end-user experiences then why not do them?

The problem with the software value sidestep was, and is, that small simple changes to a given piece of software increase its size and complexity incrementally to the point where even small changes become harder and more costly. The software ossifies. Indeed, despite the best efforts of software developers and new methodologies, most useful software reaches an age where the cost-benefit of small changes flips negative. It becomes harder and harder to justify the increased cost of a change based on the incremental business value that it delivers.

Software Value Life Cycle

So how has this habitual software value sidestep persisted for so long? The answer is that the leading edge of software development has kept pace with the continuous improvement and relative reduction in the cost of hardware. As new hardware platforms have been introduced—think mainframes to PCs to smartphones—new software has been developed for the new platforms. The new software for the new platforms has started small, with obvious impact on business profits. Small changes to new software are easy and cheap. Over time, as the complexity of the code in a given application has increased incrementally, small changes become more expensive. The pattern then repeats itself. We can think of this as the *software value life cycle*, illustrated in Figure 1.3.

So ingrained has the software value sidestep become that many businesses welcome the arrival of the newest hardware platform as a way to get out from under their ossified, "legacy" software, which mainly runs on the old platform. The change to some new software on the new hardware platform is experienced as more "flexible" (small software changes made easily and cheaply) than the old software on the old platform. This additional flexibility can represent genuine business value.

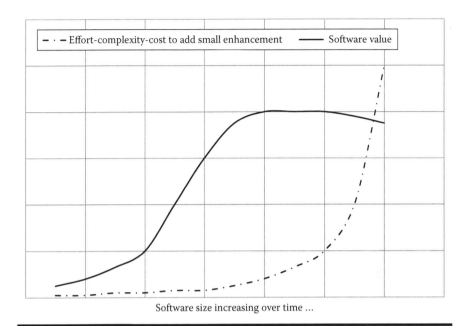

Software size increasing over time ...

Figure 1.3   Software value life cycle.

In explaining the software value life cycle, we must be careful not to dismiss the business perspective as a misunderstanding of challenges in continuing to deliver value from the old software. It may be true that businesses don't understand why small changes cost more and take longer on the old software, but they don't (and shouldn't) care. From a business perspective, the new software required by the new hardware is more valuable to them because it is more flexible. Even if it doesn't have all the (customized) functionality of the old. There are strong echoes here of *The Innovator's Dilemma*, first described by Clayton M. Christensen in 1997 (Christensen 1997). Briefly, Christensen made the case that new versions of established products tend to gravitate over time toward serving the top-end customers who demand the most functionality from the product. This leaves the established products exposed to competition from new, cheaper products (possibly but not necessarily based on new technology) that don't have the breadth of capabilities of the established product but meet the limited needs of a significant portion of the established product's customer base. Losing customers in this way undermines the business proposition of the established product because the payments of the many are used to fund the needs of the top-tier few. This is exactly how the value of long-lived software is undermined when small changes become more complex and more expensive.

As we can see in Figure 1.3, the business value of software over its lifetime is an S-curve. Our use of this shape of a curve is derived from the classic product life cycle models. Does this imply that I believe that software is a product like any other? Yes, in that the ways its users interact with it are subject to the same influences (e.g., *The Innovator's Dilemma* [Christensen 1997] and *Crossing the Chasm* [Moore 2014]) as "normal" products. And, no, in that software is almost unique in its human-created complexity and the fact that most of that complexity is invisible to the user. The S-curve works for our argument because software development is similar to product development, but software is different from most products.

What Role Does Time Play in the Business Value of Software?

Given our software life cycle view of software value, timing is clearly relevant to value over the life of the software. But is there a shorter time frame that is important? I believe that there are several other characteristics of software that make its value time dependent.

First, there is the rapid change of the overall technology environment. It is very hard to see what new technology innovations will be successfully rolled out beyond a 2–3-year horizon.

Second, the rate of business change, whether dependent or independent of underlying technology change, impacts business processes as new ideas generate new competition. New business processes demand new software to support them. Again, the rate of significant change in this area is probably once every 2–3 years. Finally, our experience tells us that, outside of government, if a software change takes longer than a year to implement (some of the enterprise resource planning [ERP] implementations took 3–7 years) or 2 years to pay back, then the business loses interest (partly due to the first two reasons stated), and the software project fails.

It is important not to confuse the value contribution of the incremental change that we are discussing in this section with the cumulative value of the software building up through many such changes in the early life of the software. That said, 2 years is a good constraint for expecting to see business value from an incremental change in software.

A More Sophisticated Definition of the Business Value of Software

We have seen that the drivers from new software to business value can be indirect, or even indistinct. We can conclude that the business value of software is non-linear over time, can tend toward an upper limit and probably decline in value toward the end of its life. We must also account for disruptive competition, sometimes having a gradual influence, such as the emergence and expansion of smartphone use, or sometimes quite sudden, as was the case for Blackberry® when the Apple iPhone® was released.

Instead of the definition proposed earlier in this chapter,

> *Software has business value if profits increase as a direct result of the introduction of a new piece of software.*

I propose a more sophisticated definition of the business value of software:

The business value of software is proportional to the customers' willingness and desire to use the software in such a way that the organization can benefit from that use by generating revenue, reducing cost, or meeting some other goal more effectively.

What Do We Mean by Software Value as an Asset and Software Value as a Flow?

As I have described earlier in this chapter, software in an organization has a software value life cycle. In our definition of the business value of software, I have described the accumulations of the asset value of software through the incremental flow of changes to the software. To think of this another way, consider the asset value of the software as being proportional to the number of independent features in the software that are economically useful to the user. Their economic utility can be notionally summed to give the total economic value of the software.

Consider a comparison to paper money (real, tangible stuff not "money as software"). A single feature in the software is comparable to a single paper bill such as $1 (or a note such as £5). Just like paper money ($10, £5), software features can have different amounts of economic utility. A flow of paper notes into, say, a bank, accumulates asset value. Similarly, a flow of software features through the delivery of epics and stories in the Agile software development world or projects in the Waterfall development world accumulates software value.

Just as I have described for accumulated software, the value of paper money accumulated in a bank is subject to change based on external, environmental factors, such as competition and the views of its users.

It is not too much of a stretch to expect organizations to pay as much attention to managing their software assets to sustain and increase their value (software maintenance) and, separately, maximize the flow of new value to the asset (software development), as they would to sustaining the value of and growing their pile of paper money in the bank. Why don't they?

Current Approach to Managing the Business Value of Software as an Asset

Most organizations have two perspectives on the asset value of their software: financial and software maintenance. Some have added or are adding a third perspective: portfolio management. We will cover each of these in more detail in Chapters 4 and 5, but here is an overview.

Financial Perspective

From a financial perspective, software purchased outright, whether purchased from a vendor or developed in-house, tends to be mainly treated as a financial capital asset to be accrued and depreciated on the organization's balance sheet according to the appropriate accounting rules. In addition, much of the software used today is not purchased outright but licensed annually or even monthly (e.g., SaaS). The costs of such software are treated as expenses to be deducted annually from profits. Indeed, the different financial treatments can influence an organization's desire to "own" or "rent" its software depending on profits and the health or otherwise of the balance sheet and taxes. CFOs of organizations may feel that they need read no further than this point because software value is there in the accounts, fair and square. Please read on because I submit that this accounting only captures the cost of the software, not its value.

Software Maintenance Perspective

From a software maintenance perspective, more software means more that can go wrong and more to fix. The fact that bigger software is almost always more complex software means that, unaddressed, the maintenance cost could increase exponentially. Here again, the value perspective is all about more or less cost, although it must be said that users can detect poor software very easily, and so there is always a reputational consideration when funding software maintenance (discussed in Chapter 4).

Fortunately, best practices of software development and testing can detect defects early in newly written software, and the often automated repetition of test scripts for previously developed software on the integrated combination of new and old software (regression testing) can minimize the number of defects that enter the software asset and become visible to the users. Unfortunately, some defects inevitably get through, and some of these can be hard to detect in a reasonable amount of testing time. Even more unfortunately, many software development groups choose not to, or cannot get financial support to, exercise best practices, which makes the situation worse.

The undiscovered defects, together with the tendency of the incremental addition of software to be suboptimal from an efficiency perspective, lead to the situation where *problem code* in the software asset builds up over time. Quite separately from the financial analogy that I used earlier in the chapter, this problem code is known as technical debt (discussed further in Chapter 4). Although the name *technical debt* is not derived from our analogy, it can be thought of as bad or forged bills/notes in our pile of paper money. The solution for technical debt is the same as for the bad paper money: manual or automated inspection of the whole in an attempt to weed out the bad—which may not be easily distinguishable.

As I have described it, the software maintenance perspective is essentially a negative value component. That's because the more software maintenance a company has to do, the less value its software has, since the cost of the maintenance must be subtracted from the net value of the software—negative value. But is this a linear relationship? Is it reasonable to expect maintenance-free software or should we set an expectation of a "reasonable" amount of maintenance? Taking this view, I could argue that less than the reasonable amount of software maintenance for a particular piece of software or a software application is a positive value. That sounds a bit contrived, but it is a consideration that we are accustomed to when we buy new cars—the cost of maintaining imported cars is often higher than home-built ones because of the additional cost of importing spare parts. Also, many of us are familiar with the vague point at which the cost of maintaining an old car exceeds the likely extra payments for a newer one—the "reasonable maintenance cost point."

Portfolio Management Perspective

From a portfolio management perspective, an organization has a collection of software applications, a portfolio, which individually and often collectively has value. What do I mean by applications having collective value? An example may be useful. Our company pays for three SaaS applications (among others) that each have an individual value to the company:

- Salesforce.com: A well-known CRM application that we use to keep a master record of all the customers and prospects that we interact with for sales and marketing.
- MailChimp: An independent application that we use for managing, distributing, and tracking marketing messages to, and interactions with, our community of contacts.
- DiscoverOrg: A market research database service that we use to identify potential new contacts in existing or new target companies.

These applications are integrated in such a way that we can search DiscoverOrg from within Salesforce and pull in prospect information. We can then combine the new information with extracts from our existing information in Salesforce to generate lists targeted to receive specific marketing messages (including information such as research papers) that we believe might interest them. MailChimp uses these lists to send out e-mails that contain various useful (or not) links. Every such e-mail includes an "unsubscribe" link. If an e-mail recipient is interested in the content or links in the e-mail, or unsubscribes, MailChimp captures that interest (or lack thereof) and records it against the contacts record in Salesforce.com. Subsequent e-mail lists take account of the current interests (or lack thereof) of each participant.

In assessing the value of these three applications to our company from a portfolio perspective, there is a good case for concluding that the sum of the whole exceeds the sum of the parts. Another, perhaps more familiar, example is the Microsoft

Office suite. If you use a word processor and a spreadsheet, there is a clear combinational advantage of being able to copy and paste information from one to the other.

The portfolio management perspective is the one from which future investment decisions should be made. For example, given, say, three strategic initiatives by the CEO and a budget of $x, which applications in the portfolio should have money spent on them in what proportions to maximize the value added in the directions specified by the strategic initiatives? Unfortunately, in many organizations, the combination of software maintenance and tactical changes to the software applications can mean that the $x set aside for strategic initiatives is not even the majority of the overall software spend. Clearly, this is a value issue that most CIOs would want to address before their CEO addresses it for them by getting a new CIO!

Another key area where value is an important consideration for the portfolio manager is in mergers and acquisitions (M&A). By way of example, let's assume that the two parties to an M&A transaction are in the same or similar business, and their portfolio of applications is significantly similar in functionality. The two parties may be very different in terms of whether their applications are in-house applications, COTS applications from different vendors, or COTS applications from the same vendor with different customizations. The task of the M&A due diligence team and then, if the due diligence team recommends the transaction, the integration team, is to assess and implement the combination of applications in the merged portfolio that will deliver the best value to the combined future entity. We have seen instances where that means abandoning both parties' applications in a particular functional area and replacing them with something newer, cheaper (certainly if integration costs are lowered), and easier to maintain—Christensen's (1997) Innovator's Dilemma at work for good! I will look into this topic in more detail in Chapter 11.

Current Approach to Maximizing the Flow of Software Business Value

In short, the current approach to maximizing the flow of software business value is not to even think about it. This is why I am so passionate about getting the message out and sharing simple steps to start thinking about the flow of software value.

There are two main methodologies for developing software that are prevalent today: Waterfall and Agile. I do not intend to explain these methodologies in this book when so much has been written on them, and many readers are familiar with the different approaches. However, readers in need of a simple introduction or reminder might consider reading the Appendix before proceeding.

From a flow of software value perspective, the Waterfall methodology was designed to try to optimize the amount of software that could be developed in large projects by large teams. The large teams are organized functionally by role (business analysts, designers/architects, coders, testers) to allow projects to be staffed to almost any required size to cope with the volume of requirements pushed through. In practice, the actual number of individuals assigned to any given role is always constrained by the availability of suitably qualified individuals in the organization and, ultimately, the budget. The assignment of individuals to projects in Waterfall has led to various suboptimal practices:

- It has been shown that assigning scarce, or indeed any, individuals to multiple projects concurrently decreases their productivity on all projects.
- Focusing on local optimizations, such as maximizing the productivity of developers at the expense of other roles in the software development life cycle, causes bottlenecks that are often hidden in work-in-progress queues. End-to-end productivity always suffers.

If we think of Waterfall, broadly, as the application of early mass manufacturing principles to software development, then perhaps it is not surprising that some of the benefits of role separation—perhaps even deskilling—that worked so well in manufacturing, present challenges in software development. In manufacturing, it is practical to increase value by controlling the variability of the inputs (fewer types of output from any given production line, tight control over the materials coming into the line) and the variability of the processes (small tasks, trained specialist operators, or, later, robots). Clearly, in product development, of which software development is a special subset, it is possible to control the processes but not the inputs. Every input to a software development process is different because it is a new feature to be added to an existing or new application.

The comparison of Waterfall to early manufacturing extends to the nature of the work flow. In both cases, work is "pushed" into the process with the goal of maximizing the flow by ensuring there is always work queued up at the front of the process and, hopefully, every stage within the process. Reinertsen (2009) and others have shown that these queues of *work in progress* (WIP) are actually costly and detrimental to maximizing the flow of work. Worse, for value maximization to occur, the inputs (projects) pushed into the input end of Waterfall must be prioritized for business value. But then we must hope that the business value prioritization stays the same throughout the time that the projects stay in Waterfall because, as with cars on the old production lines, it is very hard and costly to change the prioritization order of projects once started.

Unfortunately, as the Waterfall methodology was adopted more and more widely as a way to maximize the amount of work (not value!) that could be extracted in a controlled manner from large software development teams, the time taken to develop a particular set of projects as a release (e.g., 6 months) increased as more development led to bigger applications with more complexity. The reaction of the business to this increase in the duration of the end-to-end Waterfall cycle was to look ahead to see what projects they might need in the future release with a time frame of, say, 9 months instead of 6 months. They would then try to push 9 months' worth of projects into a Waterfall project release cycle designed for 6 months. The results were growing business dissatisfaction with missed (artificially imposed) deadlines, budget overruns (as extra resources were thrown in), and reduced scope (as software development teams concluded they could get fired for missing deadlines or budget targets but survive a reduced-scope release).

Clearly, if Waterfall was ever about maximizing business value then, in many organizations using Waterfall over time, business value became a long-forgotten priority.

By way of reaction to the frustrations with Waterfall, in the early twenty-first century, a software development counterculture, Agile, emerged from several different sources, which collectively found voice in 2001 in the "Manifesto for Agile Software Development" (Beck et al. 2001) created by 17 software gurus. It is worth quoting in full (see Figure 1.4).

The use of the term *counterculture* is not an exaggeration. Agile appealed to a wide range of software developers and testers who were feeling the weight and, some might say, futility of the Waterfall methodology. Agile was seen as a way to reduce the developer burn-out that was affecting many organizations.

Essentially, the priorities emphasized in the Agile Manifesto (Figure 1.4), were a reaction to the chief criticisms of Waterfall: it was taking too long to deliver value to the customers who couldn't adequately specify their needs up-front and changed their minds during the process because their needs had changed due to a business environment change (changed requirements) or a positive reaction to the delivered software driving new ideas (emergent requirements). A culture of disappointment led to the growth of a contract (internal and external) and project management oversight mentality that just added to the project overhead and further delayed

We are uncovering better ways of developing software by doing it and helping others do it. Through this work we have come to value:

Individuals and interactions over processes and tools
Working software over comprehensive documentation
Customer collaboration over contract negotiation
Responding to change over following a plan

That is, while there is value in the items on the right, we value the items on the left more.

Kent Beck	James Grenning	Robert C. Martin
Mike Beedle	Jim Highsmith	Steve Mellor
Arie van Bennekum	Andrew Hunt	Ken Schwaber
Alistair Cockburn	Ron Jeffries	Jeff Sutherland
Ward Cunningham	Jon Kern	Dave Thomas
Martin Fowler	Brian Marick	

Figure 1.4   Manifesto for Agile software development.

the projects. Instead, Agile applies lean software engineering principles advocated by the Poppendiecks (Poppendieck and Poppendieck 2006) and others, to deliver working software in small incremental chunks to benefit from regular frequent customer feedback. In this way, Agile maximizes the fitness for purpose of the software by prioritizing customer satisfaction over everything else. The result is that small increments of value are delivered to the customer frequently and regularly. The contrast with Waterfall is clear in Figure 1.5.

In some instances of Agile methodologies, such as the Scrum implementation of Agile created by Schwaber and Beedle (2001), lean software engineering principles have been adopted implicitly. For example, it is known from lean manufacturing that small batch sizes maximize flow. In Scrum, software development is carried out by small teams (5–9 people) working to produce working software deliverables in short "sprints" of 2–4 weeks. The combination of small teams and short durations creates "small batches." Per Reinertsen (2009), small batches help to reduce queue sizes—a challenge with Waterfall value flow. The Scrum teams work on requirements expressed as stories (small) and epics (large), which are gathered in "backlogs" waiting to be "pulled" into active development by the teams. Like Waterfall, these backlogs should be, and often are, prioritized by business value. Unlike Waterfall, these backlogs can change continuously both in terms of content and priority—the only rule constraining continuous change is that the content and priorities of a sprint cannot be changed once the sprint has started. Business value can be associated with stories during the process of prioritizing backlogs and/or the process of pulling stories from backlogs for particular sprints. This is mostly only

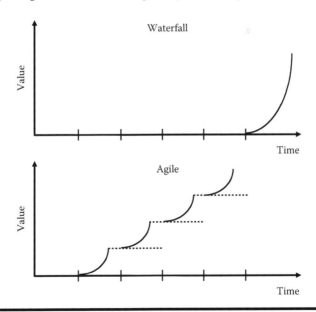

Figure 1.5   Value flow Waterfall versus Agile.

done by mature Scrum teams. However, Scrum is largely a team-level methodology, and the assignment and monitoring of business value delivered is, at best, a team-level process if, indeed, there is any assignment at all. Scrum is far and away the most prevalent instantiation of Agile principles in organizations today, and there are anecdotal reports that more than half of the organizations in the United States that do software development are now using Scrum. Of course, this does not mean that they are all using Scrum for everything. Given that Scrum is focused at the team level, there are a number of frameworks being defined (e.g., SAFe® and LeSS), which seek to address the challenge of many small Scrum teams working together on the same product or program. As these Agile scaling frameworks are adopted, maximizing the flow of software value becomes a challenge again. This book seeks to address that challenge.

What Is Lost When Software Value Is Invisible?

To summarize this chapter, let's consider why today's organizations are losing out by not building a systematic and pragmatic approach to software value into their management practices.

We have seen that the definition of software value is fuzzy. I have argued that it is the accumulation of fit-for-purpose software as assets sustained by the maximization of the flow of new software that sustains, enhances, or replaces the fitness for purpose of the existing software assets.

The business value of software does not attract as much attention in organizations at all levels as I believe that it should. I have shown that if attention is not paid, the business value of software assets naturally declines. Similarly, tactical decisions for the development of new software will not tend to maximize software value flow unless this is made an explicit goal of the organization.

The next chapter is a summary of the key areas of software value that the C-suite must address.

Chapter 2

Six Things the C-Suite Should Know about Software Value

"Even when executives understand explicitly that IT creates value, they need to be shown that their IT organization is creating specific value for the business where it counts most" (Hunter and Westerman 2009).

There is a lot of valuable information about the business value of software in this book, but we all know that an executive summary is beneficial, so that is the purpose of this chapter—to boil the message down to six key points for the C-suite. Thinking of it another way, the aim of this chapter is to identify those levers (see Figure 2.1) that the C-suite should be pulling to maximize the flow of business value from their software or keep their trains on the right tracks! Most of these levers represent actions to be taken that will directly or indirectly change the behavior of the organization and particularly the information technology (IT) department.

I present these six points in a slightly unusual way. I look at the most important software value characteristics that particular roles in the C-suite should care about from their own, unique perspectives.

Does that mean that the holder of each role can ignore their colleagues' perspectives? Of course not. This chapter is an executive summary for all. Does this mean that a particular role always has the same perspective? Again, no.

In Figure 2.2, we look at how the perspectives of the different roles change as the three lenses we defined in Chapter 1 (profit, end-client, and build-buy) are applied to this question.

Figure 2.1 Levers.

At the end of this chapter, I provide an explanation of some of the terms used in Figure 2.2. But for our main summary in this chapter, as in the rest of the book, we assume our lenses are set to: for-profit, external end-client, and develop in-house. To the extent that there is overlap between the primary interests of different roles, we have chosen secondary interests in some cases.

		The profit lens:		The end-client lens		The build-buy lens	
		For-profit	Not-for-profit	In-house	External	Develop In-house	Buy COTS
CEO		Higher profits	Higher discretionary spend	Cost reduction	Engagement	Intellectual property	Time to market
Board		Higher profits	Process efficiency	Cost reduction	Brand	Intellectual property	Reduced risk
CFO		OpEx v CapEx	Value for money	Cost reduction	Profit margin	OpEx v CapEx	Predictable cost
CMO		Customer satisfaction	Brand	Right tools	Brand	Fitness for purpose	Time to market
CDO		Better services	Process efficiency	Process efficiency	Engagement	Ability to transform	Technology leapfrog
CIO		All the above + technology leadership	All the above + repeatable processes	All the above + repeatable processes	All the above + customer satisfaction	All the above + focused offerings	All the above + functional utility

Figure 2.2 Roles, lenses, and value.

Chief Executive Officer

As part of the chief executive officer's (CEO) overall responsibilities, they naturally have perspectives on all the other roles I cover in the chapter, but I will concentrate on the CEO's focus on growth, sometimes delegated to business unit heads.

The one thing that the CEO should know about software value is, "How can our software contribute to higher profits?"

Stating the obvious, there are two ways that software can contribute to higher profits: increasing sales and lowering costs. The for-profit organization should use its software investments to pursue both of these contributions simultaneously, but this is often not the case. In many organizations, the acquisition and development of software is viewed and treated as a simple cost of doing business. In such cases, the levers available to meet the CEO's "higher profits" goal are artificially constrained to a lever for lowering the cost of acquiring and developing software. Consideration of the business value of software in use, being acquired, and being developed is all too rare. This can lead to poor tactical decision-making day to day. It can also lead to unnecessarily narrowly focused strategic decision-making as opportunities are missed to improve the organization by increasing the business value of the organization's software.

Figure 2.3 illustrates the levers available to the CEO to increase profits by focusing on software value instead of just concentrating on software costs or, indeed, being unaware of the business value of software altogether.

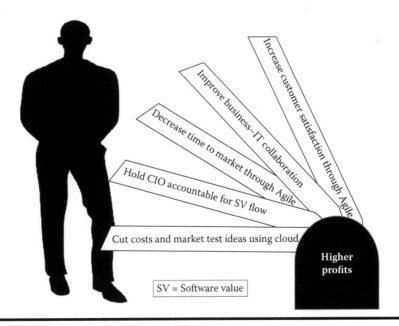

Figure 2.3   Software value levels for the CEO to improve profits.

The Board

Naturally, like the CEO, the board should be focused on value to shareholders and, first and foremost, that means higher profits. However, the board also needs to take a longer-term view, so the one thing that the board should know about software value is, "How can our software contribute to increased intellectual property?"

Software that has value to the business may be intellectual property in its own right or it may be the embodiment of intellectual property that has business value. For example, let's say an insurance company has come up with a clever algorithm for assessing the insurance needs of a new client based on just four pieces of information about the prospective client. The algorithm in its broadest sense is essentially a business secret with or without the software implementation, but it would be hard to envisage it operationally other than as a piece of software.

While it's fair to note that some of the rules around actually patenting software "inventions" are somewhat in flux with growing resistance against software patent claims such as Amazon's 1-Click patent,* trade secrets embodied in software will always be valuable intellectual property.

The board also needs to be aware of the true status of apparent software assets on the balance sheet that may or may not be masquerading as software-based intellectual property. I'm referring here to the long-established treatment of some of the costs of

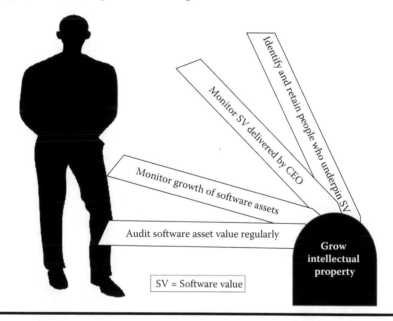

Figure 2.4 Software value levers for the board to grow intellectual property.

---

* Worstall, T. 2011. Amazon loses 1-click patent. *Forbes Business.* http://www.forbes.com/sites/timworstall/2011/07/07/amazon-loses-1-click-patent/#57141933788e

software development as capital expenditures rather than operational expenditures. I explain this more in the upcoming chief financial officer (CFO) section. For now, the board should take care to distinguish between those software assets that have arrived on the balance sheet as a result of the accounting treatment of some software development costs and those software assets that truly represent some form of intellectual property to the company. My guidance would be for the board to consider the value of each software asset based on whether someone else would buy it and how much they would pay. It is reasonable to expect that some of the "accounting standards" capitalized asset value could pass this test, but I would be surprised if it all did.

Figure 2.4 illustrates the levers available to the board to enhance intellectual property by focusing on software value.

Chief Financial Officer

The one thing that the CFO should know about software value is, "How will our software impact our balance sheet?"

In our previous discussion of the board's focus on intellectual property, we have already referenced what should be the primary value focus for the CFO—the business value of the software assets on the balance sheet.

A summary chapter such as this is not the place to dive into the details of the accounting standards for capitalizing some of the costs of software development. I cover this in slightly more detail in Chapter 4. Broadly, some of the costs of software development must be expensed in the year in which they are incurred—these are called operational expenses, often shortened to *OpEx*. These costs have a direct negative effect on the organization's profit or loss in that year. From a CFO's perspective in any given year, the business value of the software in the company as represented on the balance sheet will decrease if OpEx associated with software is high because profits and cash in the bank will be reduced. However, if some of the costs of software development can be "capitalized," then those costs will move onto the balance sheet as an "asset" to be amortized over time—usually 3–5 years for software. This part of the annual software development cost is capital expenditure or *CapEx*. Capitalization has the effect of increasing "natural" profit in the first year that it is introduced, but reducing "natural" profit in subsequent years as the capitalized amounts are amortized (charged back). I look at the "trap" this can cause in Chapter 4.

How do we decide which software can be capitalized and which cannot? Naturally, there is some "devil in the detail" and expert advice should always be sought, especially from the organization's auditors. That said, the general principle to apply is that the proof of concept of an "idea" to be implemented in software cannot be capitalized, the implementation of the idea can be capitalized. The "maintenance" of the implemented idea must be expensed in the year that it occurs. In the context of the classic Waterfall methodology for software development (described in the Appendix for those unfamiliar with the term), this general principle is, perhaps not surprisingly, easy to apply, as I have shown in Figure 2.5.

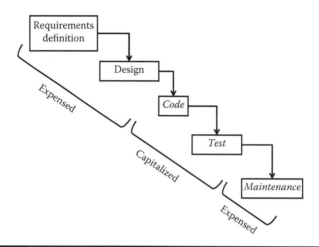

Figure 2.5 Waterfall methodology—Capitalized costs.

Requirements definition and design are generally considered to be about fleshing out the idea so these must be operational expenses. Coding and testing are certainly implementations of the idea and can be capitalized. Maintenance is an operational expense. For cost allocation purposes, the CFO simply has to put in place a way to capture the time spent on each activity. In some cases, it is necessary and appropriate to have software development staff record their time by task on an

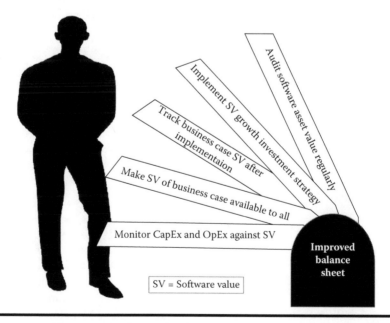

Figure 2.6 Software value levers for the CFO to improve the balance sheet.

hourly basis. Often though, it is broadly sufficient to apportion the project cost by head count numbers associated with each activity.

For the Agile methodology (described in the Appendix for those unfamiliar with the term), the separation of CapEx and OpEx activities is not so clear. More on this in Chapter 4.

The real challenge for the CFO in managing balance sheet value is the avoidance of surprises. This means that the CFO must develop an understanding of software development plans to comprehend the future impact on the balance sheet and on profits This requires CFOs to be more involved in software development planning several years ahead than, perhaps, their natural inclination would dictate.

Figure 2.6 illustrates the levers available to the CFO to enhance the balance sheet by focusing on software value.

Chief Marketing Officer

For the chief marketing officer (CMO), software development is not usually about efficiency. When discussing software value, the CMO should focus on, "How can our software increase customer satisfaction?"

In an ideal world, every piece of software would be built first time to meet the customers' needs, leaving them at least satisfied if not delighted. If not the first time, then surely it should be easy enough to get to delighted in a couple of iterations? Some readers will be smiling ruefully here—if only it were so easy. There are three main reasons why customer satisfaction tends to be a direction in which we aim rather than a destination at which we arrive:

1. It is very hard to perfectly transfer the customer's idea of what they want into the minds of all the people who must be involved in the implementation. Clearly, the bigger the idea, the larger the number of people needed to implement the idea, the harder the perfect transfer becomes.
2. Software is complex and opaque, which makes it hard to write flawless code even if we perfectly understand the idea. For example, the following simple piece of code has two possible paths:

   If (target persons' eyes are blue) then (choose blue shirt) else (choose other shirt)

Actually, to constrain this simple code to two paths, we have to specify what color the other shirt should be. Will it be different for other eye colors (e.g., brown eyes = brown shirt)? How many colors of eyes do we have to consider? Hazel? Grey? How many colors of shirts do we have?

3. The original idea often changes when the customer sees the software implementation for either or both of two reasons:

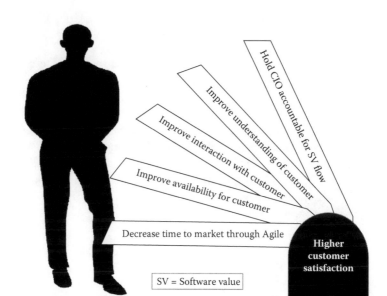

Figure 2.7   Software value levers for the CMO to improve customer satisfaction.

  a. The target environment has changed since the idea was described to the implementation team (the longer it takes to implement the idea, the more likely this will happen).
  b. The customer loves the implementation and now wishes they had known the software could do that because they would have changed the idea—often called emergent requirements.

For our purposes here, I will oversimplify the role of the CMO into two functions that are critical for enhancing the business value of the software built by an organization: Working out what will delight the customer (and what will not) and finding out if the customer is delighted (or why not). It is implied but worth stating explicitly that the CMO must share and explain this with the chief information officer (CIO) and the software development teams. This reminds me of a question that I am often asked: Should product management be part of marketing, or the business, or IT? My answer is always, "all the above!"

Figure 2.7 illustrates the levers available to the CMO to enhance customer satisfaction by focusing on software value.

Chief Digital Officer

Like the CMO, the chief digital officer (CDO) is typically less focused on the dollars and therefore should be asking, "How can our software enable better services?" when it comes to software value.

A follow-up question should be, "and what do we mean by 'better' services?" This requires an understanding of customer satisfaction that should have the CDO talking frequently with the CMO. However, while the customer perspective should be the most important, "better" does not need to be limited to the customer view. The CDO should take a "lean" view of the organization and strive for the removal of waste (all processes that do not add value are defined as waste) and continuous improvement. These activities may result in services that are better for the organization because they achieve the same level of customer delight with fewer resources deployed.

What is a CDO? At the time of writing, this is a relatively new title in the C-suite that is not yet omnipresent. In most organizations that have the role, the need for a CDO is driven by the desire to take advantage of the business opportunities offered by the new capabilities unlocked by new technologies that have become mainstream very quickly. These new technologies are often grouped together under the acronym, *SMAC*: social media, mobile, analytics, and cloud. The implementation of the new capabilities enabled by one or more of these technologies has become known as digitization of the organization or digital transformation. Hence, the "D" in CDO. Arguably, and some organizations do argue this, there should be no need for a CDO because the functions of a CDO—leading the charge to provide better services through the use of the new capabilities—should fall under the existing responsibilities of the CMO and CIO. The counter argument and justification for a CDO is that the CIO is too busy managing the mundane positive and negative impacts of the new technologies on business-as-usual operations, and

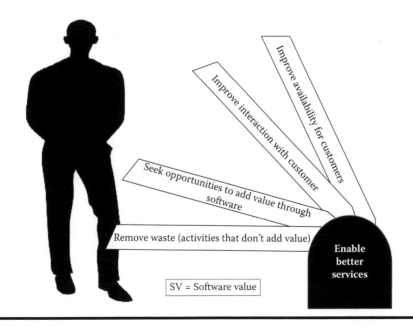

Figure 2.8   Software value levers for the CDO to enable better services.

the CMO doesn't understand the new technologies well enough to be able to lead the charge to take advantage of them. If it seems too harsh to imply that CIOs are struggling to come to terms with the new technologies, just ask a CIO about how they are managing employees who want to use their own devices for work, or how they are dealing with the tensions between the economic benefits and security implications of public versus private cloud.

Whether the role is separated and populated or not in a specific organization, the functions of a CDO still must be covered by someone in most organizations. I assert that an effective CDO must be the champion for increasing the business value of software in the organization through enhanced services.

Figure 2.8 illustrates the levers available to the CDO to provide better services by focusing on software value.

Chief Information Officer

Why leave the chief information officer (CIO) to last? All the other C-suite roles we have listed are the CIO's customers—even if the CIO has direct responsibilities to external customers. For the purposes of this chapter, the CIO covers several roles, which may be separated in some organizations: chief data officer (not to be confused with CDO), chief information security officer (CISO), and chief technology officer (CTO).

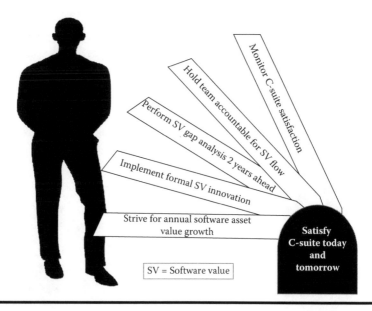

Figure 2.9 Software value levers for the CIO today and tomorrow.

The one thing that the CIO should know about software value is, "How can our software satisfy the needs of all my colleagues in the C-suite (and the board) today and tomorrow?"

Of all the members of the C-suite, the CIO must take the most responsibility for looking ahead at how technology will change and how best to position the organization to deal with the opportunities and threats that the technology change poses. In Figure 2.2 we have called this *technology leadership*. Technology leadership means that the CIO must take responsibility for achieving the organization's strategic goals through the best use of current and future technology. It does not mean that the CIO must ensure that the organization is always on the leading (some would say "bleeding") edge of the technology evolution.

Figure 2.9 illustrates the levers available to the CIO to meet the goals of the other members of the C-suite, and ensure that the software portfolio will be ready for their needs in 2 years by planning for the software that will likely be most valuable to the C-suite in 2 years.

Lenses

The meaning of the terms used in Figure 2.2 merit a little more explanation of their use in this context:

- *Ability to transform* is a capability that might be delivered by a particular piece of software or the implementation of a particular software architecture that enables new ways of delivering services. A good example of this was the introduction of the *software-as-a-service* (SaaS) application, Salesforce.com. Salesforce.com has become many other things over time; but when it was originally introduced, it had high value because it transformed the way organizations managed their clients and prospects.
- *Better services* are services that improve customer satisfaction and/or reduce the resources needed to deliver the services at the same level of customer satisfaction.
- *Brand* is that collection of tangible and intangible perceptions of the organization that cause customers and staff to feel more or less good about the organization or a subset of its products or services.
- *Cost reduction* is the desire to get the same software value in the current time period as was delivered in previous periods, but at a lower cost. While software developers might find this frustrating, it is a reasonable goal for the organization.
- *Customer satisfaction* is the customer's perception of how well their needs and desires are being met. While it is possible to achieve high customer satisfaction for a short time with an inadequate product or service, such a situation is unsustainable in the medium term because it eats away at the prior *customer satisfaction capital* built up by the organization through previous good performance. Once this customer satisfaction capital is lost, it is very hard to replace.

- *Engagement* is the degree to which users of the software interact with the software and the organization. A highly engaged user is more likely to derive more value from their use of the software, making the software more valuable in aggregate.

- *Fitness for purpose* is the degree to which software meets a user's needs. It does not include the user's desires! Typically, the stronger the connection from the customer/user through marketing to the development team, the better the fitness for purpose because any necessary adjustments can be identified and implemented quickly.

- *Focused offerings* are possible when the software developers are working closely with the customer and the marketing team. Focused offerings are an extension of fitness for purpose through which the software developers can identify and offer a capability for which the customers have not thought (or dared) to ask.

- *Functional utility* is the delivery of software value in a standard package that is typically used by similar functional units across the industry. Typically, this would be an area of the organization that is not a competitive differentiator. For example, buying a standard accounting package for the CFO usually makes much more sense than developing something in-house.

- *Higher profits* is fairly obvious in a for-profit company, but it can also be taken to mean higher discretionary spend in a not-for-profit organization. For example, while MasterCard is now a for-profit corporation, I worked there in the not-for-profit days. In those days, a good year of low costs and high income relative to budget meant that we could invest in "nice to have" projects at the end of the year in addition to the "need to have" projects in the budget. As senior managers, we all had a list of "nice to have" projects up our sleeves waiting for word to come down that we were ahead of the zero-profit budget for the year.

- *Intellectual property* is an asset (software in our context) that has saleable value outside of the organization.

- *OpEx versus CapEx* is finding the right balance for the cost of software development between expensing costs in the year they are incurred and capitalizing the costs for amortization over future years. The cost does not go away, it just gets delayed.

- *Predictable cost* is sometimes more valuable for planning purposes than unpredictable cost, which could turn out to be more or less from period to period. In the context of commercial off-the-shelf (COTS), there is also an aspect of shared cost to this predictable cost concept. The cost of the COTS software is shared across many customers of the COTS vendor. This tends to reduce the cost to an individual organization as well as make the cost more predictable.

- *Process efficiency* encompasses the lean concept of the removal of waste in the form of processes or process steps that do not add value to the end result.

- *Profit margin* is the difference between revenue (or income) and costs (or expenditures). Sometimes, the actual values of revenue and costs are not as important as sustaining the difference between them.

- *Reduced risk*, in this context, refers to the transfer of risk for the software development process from the organization to the COTS vendor. Of course, there is also a transfer of asset ownership.
- *Repeatable processes* are important to ensure predictable outcomes from the software development process. There is a need for realism when deciding whether having the software development process in-house, outsourced, or under the control of a COTS vendor is more likely to result in repeatable processes. In most scenarios, from a personal perspective in the United States, I would always prefer to have the software development processes in-house for maximum control and flexibility (not the same as maximum economic efficiency).
- *Right tools* refers to an organization's great ability to fine tune their software to the needs of their users and their users' clients if software is built in-house. In this case, the user is the marketing department.
- *Technology leadership* means that the CIO must take the responsibility for achieving the organization's strategic goals through the best use of current and future technology.
- *Technology leapfrog* refers to the ability to jump from the current generation of technology used in the organization to the leading-edge technology in the industry by using the expertise of an external vendor rather than attempting to train or recruit internal staff. Sometimes, it will be necessary to leapfrog several generations of technology.
- *Time to market* is sometimes called "concept to cash" in commercial organizations or "concept to value" in non-profits. Simply, it refers to the average time taken to move a piece of functionality from idea through software development to actual use by the end user.
- *Value for money* can take many forms depending on the way that value is defined (the subject of this book!). The concept is usually best understood in comparative terms (i.e., option A offers better value for money than option B). This opens the way for evaluating relative value rather than absolute value.

Summary

Six things the C-suite should know about software value:

1. How can our software contribute to higher profits?
2. How can our software contribute to increased intellectual property?
3. How will our software impact our balance sheet?
4. How can our software increase customer satisfaction?
5. How can our software enable better services?
6. How can our software satisfy the needs of all my colleagues in the C-suite (and the board) today and tomorrow?

Chapter 3

Make the Business Value of Software Visible

Why Visible?

Most of us are familiar with the expression, "A picture is worth a thousand words." Most of us can accept that expression as intuitively true, even though it is hard to explain (see Figure 3.1).

In this chapter particularly, and in the book more generally, I have tried to justify my assertion about the importance of making value visible by making my key points visually.

We must be careful that our visualization of the key points does not trivialize the importance of those points in the context of value visualization for software. There are three important ways in which visualization adds value, as shown in Figure 3.2: Learning about the problem status, learning about the process status, and learning about the solution status.

gigglebites

Figure 3.1   A thousand words.

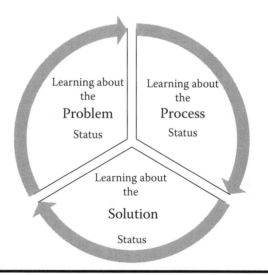

Figure 3.2   Three main value visualizations for software value.

Why Learning?

Clearly, these three visualization drivers have much in common. They are all about learning. In their book, *Implementing Lean Software Development* (Poppendieck and Poppendieck 2007), Mary and Tom Poppendieck devote a chapter to knowledge and their justification is worth quoting at some length:

> Centuries ago, the critical constraining resource was land. Those who controlled the land controlled everything. At some point, the constraint became skills, and guilds and merchants created more wealth than did landowners. Later, the industrial revolution moved the constraint to capital, and power became financially driven. Today, the constraint is knowledge: technical knowledge, management knowledge, process knowledge, and market knowledge. Much of this knowledge is expressed as software.

Learning is the process of attaining knowledge. Prior to researching this book, I would have intuitively accepted the Confucian philosophy spelled out in Figure 3.3, which ranks visual learning as being more effective than being told how to do something, with the tactile experience of actually doing something ranking highest of all.

Confucius, 450 BC,

"TELL ME AND I WILL FORGET. SHOW ME AND I MAY REMEMBER. INVOLVE ME AND I WILL UNDERSTAND."

Figure 3.3　Confucius.

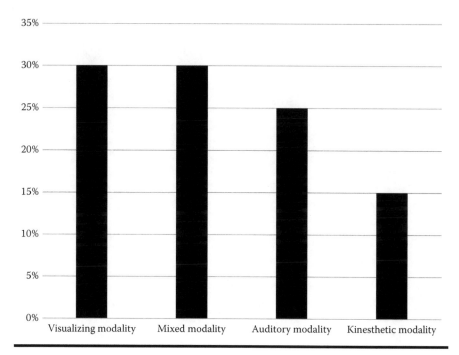

Figure 3.4   Learning modalities.

Walter Burke Barbe and colleagues* proposed four primary learning modalities through which people prefer to learn with the relative frequencies among the population shown in Figure 3.4. While there are some differing opinions on the research, learning through visual presentation of knowledge is likely to be more successful with most of the population than other approaches.

Why Status?

Learning is also the process of updating knowledge. In a changing environment, the value of knowledge decreases over time—put simply, knowledge becomes out of date. Hence, it is important that we learn by updating our knowledge regularly. Learning the status of the problem, process, or solution implies that all of these things can change and that we need to learn the current status.

I mentioned previously the importance of updating our knowledge of status regularly. What frequency of status updates constitutes regularly enough?

In the software development world, we have referenced two main methodologies for development: Waterfall and Agile (see Appendix for more details). One of

---

* See http://www.ascd.org/ASCD/pdf/journals/ed_lead/el_198102_barbe.pdf

the key differences between the two methodologies is that Agile assumes change will happen and is structured to allow for change, somewhat at the expense of knowing the certainty of the outcome. The Waterfall methodology is predicated on being able to fix requirements soon after the start of a project. Change in Waterfall generates disruption and is either managed away or incorporated at high cost, somewhat at the expense of customer satisfaction.

Considering our three potential status updates (problem, process, and solution), Waterfall assumes that the problem is stable (no changes), and so the solution is stable, leaving a need only to learn about process status, which means progress against the fixed plan. In an ideal world, this would be sufficient and the regularity of status updates would be related to the average size of the tasks in the plan. Hence, for Waterfall, it makes sense to have a status update cadence that is not so frequent that it generates data that cannot be used for decisions, and not so infrequent that it does not detect significant changes in the progress of work. For example, if the average task size is 3 weeks (or 3 days or 3 months) then the status update cadence should be weekly (or daily or monthly). Unfortunately, the ideal, change-free environment upon which the Waterfall methodology depends for its effectiveness is rare. In practice, change to the solution status is caused by change in the problem status, which is typically raised by the client who demands changes in the solution. These demands cause changes in the solution status or changes in the process status, such as a 3-week task actually taking 5 weeks and disrupting the plan.

Agile is designed to deal with change, so what constitutes a regular enough status update for Agile? There are many different techniques that have been pulled or pushed under the Agile umbrella, but only two of these really rise to the level of methodologies at the team level: Scrum and Kanban (see Appendix for a brief overview). Scrum comes with a cadence called an iteration or sprint, which is usually 2 weeks but can be 3 or 4 weeks. The Scrum methodology requires that each team commits to pull a set of work from a backlog for one iteration at a time, and their assigned work cannot be changed by anyone external to the team during that time. Hence, for people outside a team, an appropriate frequency of update for Scrum is the duration of an iteration. However, people inside a team need to update each other much more frequently, ideally, continuously in the same room. In practice, the Scrum methodology requires a short update once every day, at which completed work is reported and charted in a burndown chart (see Figure 3.5) against the work expected to have been completed by that day.

Like Scrum, Kanban is a pull methodology. Workers at the end of the development process pull work forward from their predecessors when they have capacity. Similarly, their predecessors pull work from their predecessors when they have capacity. In Kanban, it is important to understand the *flow* of work and so, not unlike Waterfall, the appropriate frequency of status updates is based on the average time that each work item should spend at a workstation. Checking status more

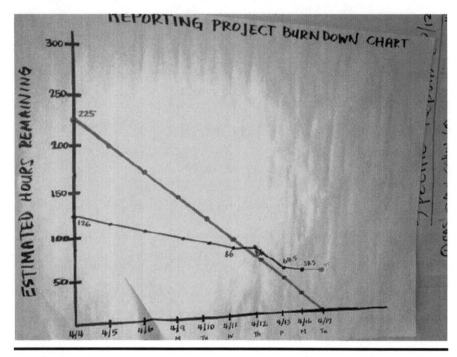

Figure 3.5 Burndown chart.

frequently than this average time will simply detect that a work item has not moved (when it was not expected to). Hence, it makes sense to update visual status (check what has moved) at about, or slightly longer than, the average time that a work item should spend at a workstation. Later in this chapter, we will consider the value of cumulative flow diagrams in Kanban processes for using visualization to predict developing issues.

Figure 3.6 summarizes the suggested frequency of visual status updates for different methodologies.

Methodology	Frequency of visual status update
Waterfall	1/3 of average task durations
Agile – Scrum – outside team	One iteration (sprint) duration
Agile – Scrum – inside team	Daily
Kanban	Average work item duration per workstation

Figure 3.6 Suggested frequency of visual status updates for different methodologies.

How Visible? Information Radiators

I really like the term *information radiators*. For those of us who grew up in the United Kingdom, heating in many homes across the country meant water-filled radiators—the water being heated by a central boiler or furnace and distributed through copper pipes to one or more of these steel radiators in each room that were the main, if not the only, source of heat in the room (see Figure 3.7). Unlike the central air that I am now very familiar with through living in the United States for many years, water-filled radiators were perfectly useful for safely drying clothes, towels, wet homework (don't ask), or anything else that needed drying.

So if, for me, the term *radiators* conjures up the dissemination of warmth and a little bit of moisture, how do information radiators help make the value of software visible?

An information radiator is a large, highly visible display used by software development teams to track progress. The term was first coined by Alistair Cockburn (2004) in his book *Crystal Clear: A Human-Powered Methodology for Small Teams*, as follows:

> An information radiator is a display posted in a place where people can see it as they work or walk by. It shows readers information they care about without having to ask anyone a question. This means more communication with fewer interruptions.

Figure 3.7 Typical central heating radiator.

According to the website of Atlassian,* a provider of software development tools, a good information radiator

- Is large and easily visible to the casual, interested observer
- Is understood at a glance
- Changes periodically, so that it is worth visiting
- Is easily kept up-to-date

Ideally, software development teams are co-located, and managers walk around so information radiators are on paper, posted in the team room or in the hallway. A typical example of an information radiator made up of notes on a board is shown in Figure 3.8. The burndown chart of Figure 3.5 is another good example of an information radiator.

Todd Little of Landmark Graphics made the interesting observation that information radiators generally serve to inform people outside the project team. The people on the project team generally know the information posted, because of their close communications with each other. It is the people outside the team who want or need to know that information in order to make their own decisions, and otherwise would interrupt the team to get that information, or would simply guess at it (often incorrectly).

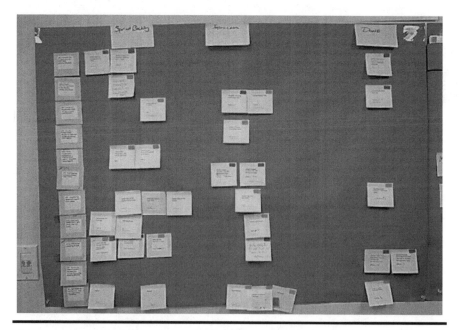

Figure 3.8 Visual plan.

---

* See https://www.atlassian.com/landing/wallboards/information-radiators/

Unfortunately, in many cases, either development teams, or management, or both are not co-located, and so information radiators need to be on a web page that people refer to frequently. There are a few challenges with online information radiators:

■ They tend not to be continuously visible—most developers will not tend to waste valuable screen space on continuous display of an information radiator irrespective of the number of screens they have available.
■ They tend to be too small—we have all experienced the challenge of getting a big picture onto a small screen.
■ An information radiator needs to be visible without significant effort on the part of the viewer.

Information radiators can be used on any project, large or small. A small team can use them very conveniently to maintain and, most importantly, share information that they otherwise would have to maintain on the computer (which is both slower to create/update and less visible). Information radiators are typically used to show status information, but they can also be used to convey designs (see Figure 3.9) and assumptions.

Intensive use of information radiators conveys two messages in addition to the information itself:

■ The team has nothing to hide from its visitors (customers, stakeholders, etc.).
■ The team has nothing to hide from itself—it acknowledges and confronts problems.

Figure 3.9   Solution design.

The main benefit of the practice is therefore to promote responsibility among the team members. A secondary benefit is that information radiators tend to provoke conversation when outsiders visit, which can yield useful ideas.

While information radiators are powerful and recommended, we need to be careful that the information we are looking at is the most important information for us to look at right now. Reinertsen (2009) states this succinctly:

> The current orthodoxy uses observation, a powerful tool, but it ignores the bias inherent in all methods based on observation. When we focus on observable phenomena, we can be biased by the fact that some characteristics are more observable than others. This increased visibility biases our findings.

A good example of this phenomenon can be seen in Figure 3.5, the example of a burndown chart. I have included this particular example because it is from a real team. You will notice that the units on the vertical axis are hours remaining. This is an input metric reflecting effort to be put into the work not an output reflecting value produced. It is an example of using an easily observable metric rather than a more difficult to observe but more valuable metric. Far better would be to measure the burndown of value to be delivered or, better still, a burnup chart of value delivered. Such value charts are all too rare, and we will come back to this point later in the book. The most common reasonably good practice in use today is to count stories or tasks (subsets of stories with estimated duration of 8–16 hours of effort) on the vertical axis of the burndown charts. These are certainly compromises because they assume that all stories or tasks have equal value but they are better than using hours of effort.

Value of Problem Status Visualization

One lesson that we have learned from about 50 years of software development is that initial customer requirements change. The fact that we seem to continue to have to relearn this lesson in major projects today is a topic for a different book. Customer requirements usually change for three main reasons:

- The customer didn't understand their requirements fully when they specified them.
- The customer's environment has changed since they specified their requirements.
- On seeing the solution or a prototype of the solution, the customer realizes that the software solution is capable of offering more opportunities or solving more problems than they were aware of when they specified their requirements.

It is quite normal for all three of these types of changes to occur on the same project. Hence, if we accept that the customers' requirements are likely to change, then the status of the problem will change, even if we limit the problem status to just two states: stable and under review. In practice, it is much more valuable to have the customer prioritize the different requirements that characterize the problem into a list (or backlog) with the most valuable requirements (or epics—large stories) at the top of the list. With this type of problem status visualization, requirements that are under review might be given a lower priority on the backlog, although this isn't an option if they have already been pulled into development.

Value of Process Status Visualization

The goal of software development should be to maximize the flow of value through software development. Unfortunately, the indicators of value flow in software development are obscured from view. The true manifestation of software development progress is hidden in files on servers that hold the latest versions of chunks of code that are passing through various stages of coding and testing before being integrated into larger chunks of code in larger files on other servers. To ensure that this is happening optimally, it is important to turn an otherwise hidden transformation into visible artifacts.

One of the limitations of Waterfall is that plans are created in the form of *work breakdown structures* (WBS) or Gantt charts, and then reality is tracked by making, often continuous, adjustments to these plans, such that, in some environments, the perception can grow that the plans are never accurate because they are never completely up-to-date. In contrast, in Agile, there is much less emphasis on creating plans (although plans such as backlogs and solution architecture are still important) and more emphasis on tracking the status of work in progress (sometimes called work in process—both use the same acronym, WIP).

Figure 3.10 shows a typical electronics assembly line. Figure 3.11 shows a typical software development work environment (well, it's a training class really, but the environment is close enough to make my point).

In Figure 3.10, there is a clear indication of WIP in the system from the trays on the shelf above the heads of the people working. A quick look along the line will show anyone who cares to look, whether manager or worker, if there are any obvious bottlenecks in the form of work stacking up leading into (or out of) one person. In contrast, there is no way to tell how much work is in progress in the software development environment in Figure 3.11. WIP in a software development office is invisible and so queues and bottlenecks are invisible.

In seeking to maximize the flow of value through the product development process, Reinertsen (2009) defines a principle of visual WIP (labeled W23 in his book):

Figure 3.10 Manufacturing workstations.

Figure 3.11 Software development workstations.

Make work in progress continuously visible.

Inventory in product development is information, and information is usually invisible. To manage this information effectively, we must make it visible. We can do this by using physical artifacts as tokens to represent this invisible inventory.

Figure 3.8 shows an example of a real Kanban board being used as an information radiator in a software development project. Note that while the Kanban board is being used, the team is using the Scrum methodology not the Kanban methodology. Each separate card represents a separate story being worked on by a team in a sprint. In this simple case, the Kanban board has just three columns:

■ Sprint backlog: The stories that the team has committed to complete in the sprint but not yet started.
■ In process: Stories that are being worked on.
■ Done: Those stories that have been completed or, more precisely, those stories that have met the team's definition of done.

Note that a glance at the Kanban board of Figure 3.8 tells us quickly about the amount of WIP, but it does not really help us to identify potential bottlenecks. More columns would help us to do that, and I might advise this team to break out the "in process" column into analysis, coding, and testing, understanding that sometimes these particular steps might be done concurrently for the same story. Also, the Kanban board does not tell us how well we are progressing in time. The team will have a sense of how well the sprint is progressing toward completing all the committed work because they will be aware of the clock ticking on the current sprint. An outside stakeholder would probably need to refer to the burndown chart to get a picture of the progress of the sprint in time.

In seeking to minimize the cycle time of value through the product development process, Reinertsen (2009) defines a principle of visible congestion (labeled F3 in his book):

Use forecasts of expected flow time to make congestion visible.

We cannot control congestion if we do not know it is there. Since only 2 percent of product developers measure queues, most developers are only vaguely aware of congestion in their processes. We can rarely see queues when we walk through the engineering department because…product development inventory is information, which is inherently invisible. We need to make high occupancy conditions visible.

To help us maximize value flow through software development, we can use some charts that give us a measure of predictive capability that allows us to act before constraints on value flow become too serious. The first chart I will look at is the cumulative flowchart. Figure 3.12 shows an example of an idealized cumulative flowchart for a software development project.

Figure 3.12 is based on a Kanban board in the form shown in Figure 3.13. Each card on the board represents a story to be developed. Note, that some columns on the Kanban board are marked with "maximum work in progress" (Max. WIP) limits. Driving down into the theory of WIP limits is not really relevant to this chapter on visualization, but, in brief, WIP limits drive the desirable behavior of limiting queue sizes in the process to maximize flow (and value flow!). I have included WIP limits here to illustrate how much easier it is to monitor this desirable behavior when the tracking mechanism—the Kanban board—is a visual representation.

There are seven columns on this Kanban board:

1. Backlog: A prioritized set of stories waiting to be developed. While they are in the backlog, they are available to be changed or groomed (a process of refinement that usually involves adding some detail for the benefit of the team).
2. Ready: The team decides which stories to pull from the backlog column when they are sufficiently specified to be developed. In Agile, the ready column is often equivalent to the sprint backlog.
3. Analysis: The team, or one or more members of the team, decides which stories to pull from the ready column into the analysis—in progress column for analysis or detailed design. Once the analysis is complete, the story is moved into the analysis—done column.
4. Coding: The team, or one or more members of the team, decides which stories to pull from the analysis—done column into the coding—in progress column for coding. Once the coding is complete, the story is moved into the coding—done column.
5. Test: The team, or one or more members of the team, decides which stories to pull from the coding—done column into the test column for coding. Once the testing is complete, the story is moved into the ready to deploy column.
6. Ready to deploy: Typically, though not necessarily, deployment occurs on a regular cycle, such as once per day or once per week. Hence, stories wait in the ready to deploy column for the next deployment exercise.
7. Deployed: Once a particular deployment exercise is complete, the story is moved into the deployed column.

The idealized cumulative flowchart in Figure 3.12 shows five plots. For a given sample time (e.g., week 9), the five points are calculated as follows (see also the illustration in Figure 3.13):

■ Ready: A count of all the stories in the ready column and all the columns to the right of the ready column. In other words, this is a count of all the stories that the team has worked on, is working on, and has committed to work on.
■ Analyzed: A count of all those stories for which analysis has been completed (i.e., a count of all the stories in the analysis—done sub-column and all the columns to the right of that column).
■ Developed: A count of all those stories for which coding has been completed (i.e., a count of all the stories in the coding—done sub-column and all the columns to the right of that column).

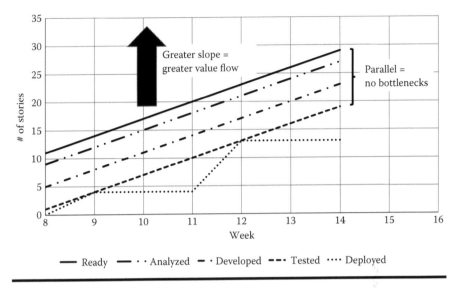

Figure 3.12   Idealized cumulative flowchart.

Backlog	Ready max. WIP = 4	Analysis max. WIP = 2		Coding max. WIP = 4		Test max. WIP = 3	Ready to deploy	Deployed
		In progress	Done	In progress	Done			

Count of stories in all above cells = "Ready" count = 15
"Analyzed" count = 12
"Developed" count = 9
"Tested" count = 4
"Deployed" = 3

Figure 3.13   Kanban board for software development.

■ Tested: A count of all those stories for which testing has been completed (i.e., a count of all the stories in the ready to deploy column and all the columns to the right of that column).

■ Deployed: A count of all those stories that have been deployed.

Figure 3.12 shows an idealized cumulative flowchart to make two important points. First, in an ideal world, all of the plotted lines in a cumulative flowchart will be parallel. This shows that there are no bottlenecks or queues between process steps. Second, the plotted lines should be as steep as possible. Steeper lines imply more stories flowing through the team in a given time period (which we will assume, for now, means more value flow).

Note that the vertical axis of this cumulative flowchart in Figure 3.12 has units of numbers of stories. From a value flow maximization perspective, it would be better to see value units on the vertical axis, and we will return to this point together with the ways to measure value and prioritize value flow in a later chapter. Counting stories is much more common and sufficient for my explanation in this chapter.

As in the idealized Figure 3.12, Figure 3.14 shows the cumulative effect of several states of the Kanban board over a number of weeks (shown on the horizontal axis, which could easily be days or even hours).

The difference between the two charts is that Figure 3.14 is a real scenario, and you will quickly see that the plotted lines are no longer parallel. What does this tell us?

Immediately upon glancing at Figure 3.14, we can see that the end-to-end process is not optimized for throughput. As the plotted lines get further apart, this tells us that queues are developing at certain points in the process. In fact, the real data is highlighting a real problem with the testing process that is causing a queue of WIP to build up in testing. The key point here is that the visualization of the process flow enables the human brain and eye to do something that they are very good at doing quickly—perhaps better than a computer—detecting patterns and trends. Looking again at Figure 3.14, by Week 14 we can clearly see that the plotted lines are not parallel. How early is it possible to detect that this particular pattern or trend might be emerging? Week 11? Week 10? This is an example of what I like

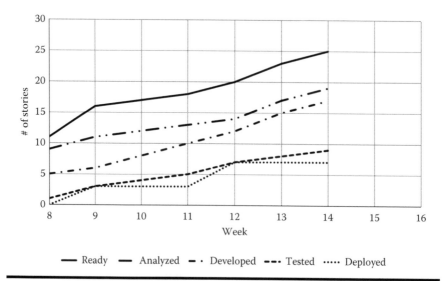

Figure 3.14   Real cumulative flowchart.

to call a "predictive metric." Even if there is doubt about our ability to detect this trend as early as Week 10, detecting at Week 14 is still better than we would do if we limited ourselves to only counting the output from the process. Counting only the output from the process would eventually allow the measurer to detect a drop in the output per week, but it would be later than the cumulative flowchart permits. The output count would offer no clue as to where in the process the problem might have occurred.

Cumulative flow metrics are not the only predictive metrics available to us. Figure 3.15 is a cumulative frequency chart on which are plotted the number of stories that have a particular *lead time* or *cycle time*, which we will define here as the number of days between a story leaving the backlog to enter the ready column and the same story entering the deployed column (see Figure 3.13). To understand how the chart is generated, let's assume that our first story takes 42 days to transition to the development process. This first story would be plotted as 1 occurrence after 42 days. If the next story takes 28 days, then we would plot a 1 against 28 days, and so on.

The chart in Figure 3.15 represents the distribution of lead times of over 200 stories, and we can see a pattern emerging that tells us that the lead times are not randomly distributed around a mean (i.e., this is not a normal distribution). Instead, we have a skewed distribution with lead times of around 42 days being much more likely than longer lead times. From this chart, we may be able to predict the time it takes to get stories deployed. However, the visualization also allows us to

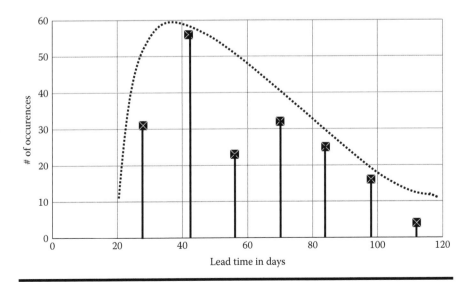

Figure 3.15   Lead time frequency distribution.

quickly see a couple of other important characteristics of our development process for this example:

- We have a discrete set of possible lead times (i.e., 28, 42, 56, etc., days). This tells us that there are probably fixed dates in the development process for moving stories from backlog to ready (at a sprint planning meeting perhaps?) and fixed dates for deploying completed stories.
- There is a wide spread of lead times for this example (i.e., 28–112 days). There are a number of possible explanations for this, which we can group under two categories: input variance and process variance. Either of these could be systemic or random. An example of input variance might be a wide variation in the size of stories. This is generally undesirable because flow is maximized by smaller batches of work. This could be random in that a few of the over 200 stories in our example just could not be broken down into smaller chunks—a perfectly reasonable explanation in software development where our inputs are not controllable as they are in manufacturing. Alternatively, the wide variation in story size could be systemic in that the team is not putting enough effort into reducing stories to their smallest reasonable size.

So, if Figure 3.15 tells us that we may have a problem, how do we know if that problem is getting better or worse? We can certainly track the incoming data and try to guess. A better way is to create the chart shown in Figure 3.16, where each incoming story lead time is plotted individually as it comes in. We can see on Figure 3.16 that while there is some variation around the trend, the trend is that lead times are increasing. Again, this is not desirable and warrants further investigation.

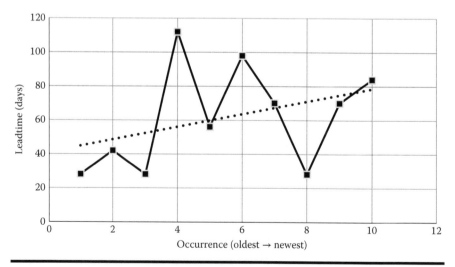

Figure 3.16 Individual lead time tracking chart.

Value of Solution Status Visualization

One of the key types of solution status visualization is the solution architecture. This is important because the high-level solution architecture can be available quite early in the development process. The solution architecture needs to be presented in such a way that the customer can understand it and provide early feedback. Figure 3.9 shows an example of the solution architecture being presented in two different ways. Note that in addition to the structures presented by the way the cards are arranged, there is more visual data in the dots on the cards, which are color coded, in this case to provide grouping information based on system groups. Sometimes, different color cards are used.

As the problem status changes, the solution status may or may not change depending on whether the change in the problem status has high- or low-level impacts.

In addition to providing value to the customer, the solution architecture is an important information radiator for the development teams because it provides context for their development decisions and guidance on their dependencies and the interfaces that they need to develop internally or with other teams.

Summary

In this book about the business value of software, I have dedicated this chapter to the importance of making software value visible because I believe that visibility is key to creating shared understanding about business value across an organization. Ideally, visibility is conveyed by physical, readily accessible charts. If this is not possible, then electronic substitutes can fill the need if everyone forms the habit of looking at them.

Visibility requires that complex data is simplified for presentation, and I have tried to include a lot of pictures in this chapter to help make my point. That said, every picture needs context. I was reminded of this while reading Gertrude Bell's descriptions of her travel in Syria in the early twentieth century in her book *The Desert and the Sown* (Bell 2016). She comments on the importance of taking nothing for granted:

> one of the great difficulties in searching for antiquities is that people in out-of-the-way places do not recognise a sculpture when they see it. You are not surprised that they should fail to tell the difference between an inscription and the natural cracks and weather markings of the stone; but it takes you aback when you ask whether there are stones with portraits of men and animals upon them, and your interlocutor replies: 'Wāllah! We do not know what the picture of a man is like.' Moreover, if you show him a bit of a relief with figures well carved upon it, as often as not he will have no idea what the carving represents.

From a business value perspective, we have looked at the importance of visualizing the status of the problem, the process, and the solution. Visualization is a simple way of representing small and large changes to the big picture, letting the viewer determine significance. I have demonstrated, with examples, that visualization of metrics can leverage the pattern- and trend-predicting capabilities of the human brain to get ahead of future events by designing predictive metrics.

Chapter 4

Forms of Software Value

In this chapter, we consider some of the most important forms that the business value of software can take, both financial and non-financial. Understanding the nature of the business value is important for deciding on, measuring, and communicating the best metrics to drive desired behaviors.

It is worth remembering here that, ultimately, our target audience in a commercial business for delivering business value from software is the shareholders: those people and organizations who have given the organization money and expect a return on their investment. Of course, in non-commercial organizations, we tend to call the people and organizations that provide the funds *stakeholders* or *sponsors* or *donors*, but these terms have broader and narrower meanings depending on context. The term *shareholders* is appropriate for commercial organizations and, though never used, it is also a good description of the role in not-for-profit organizations that we need to focus on when considering our priorities for delivering software value. For example, a charity does not normally have shareholders, but its sponsors and donors are supplying the funds that enable the charity to function and should have a reasonable expectation of business value from any software used.

Having brought shareholders into our considerations, for the sake of brevity, I must limit the scope of my coverage to shareholder value as it relates to software. In this chapter, I will consider the impact of the presence of shareholders on the behavior of the managers of the organization. There is a whole world of valuation of businesses that concerns shareholders of public companies listed on the world's stock exchanges. While these company valuations are important and sometimes, for some companies, impacted by software values (e.g., Microsoft), the valuation of companies usually involves many other factors, and I refer interested readers to other books for that coverage. A good starting point would be *The Quest for Value* by G. Bennett Stewart, III (1999).

The example of a charity is useful for considering the role of trustees. In business, and sometimes in a non-profit, the role of oversight of the management team on behalf of the shareholders (funds providers) is usually embodied in a board of trustees. The charity's trustees and the company's board hold the management team and, by extension the employees, accountable for the delivery of value in return for the money invested. Part, often a small part, of the value is related to the software used in the organization.

But how does software deliver value? This chapter will tackle this question; but before we do, we need to consider one other role in our value flow, the customer (or charity beneficiary). Who is the customer in the software business value chain? Well, without customers for, or users of, the software, the software has no value. In Chapter 1, we defined the business value of software as follows:

> The business value of software is proportional to the customer's willingness and desire to use the software in such a way that the organization can benefit from that use by generating revenue, reducing cost, or meeting some other goal more effectively.

An example of "meeting some other goal more effectively" might be, say, if the American Diabetes Association wanted to communicate some important facts about the disease on its website. This could be very valuable for early diagnosis or preventing the disease and, even if the financial benefits of these published facts would not benefit the organization, its donors (shareholders) would generally consider they were getting value for the funds provided, and the customers (users) of the software would generally agree.

The use of the word "generally" in this example was intentional. What if website tracking showed that no customers ever read the web page with these facts on it? Would the donors still consider they were getting value for their money? What if there were a mistake in one of the facts that could be hazardous to the customers reading it? The customers would consider the page's value significantly reduced, and the donors would be right to start worrying about lawsuits.

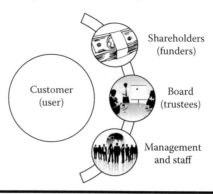

Figure 4.1   Parties to software business value.

It is important to continuously measure value in all its forms.

The parties to assessing and improving the business value of software are summarized in Figure 4.1. It is important to remember that an individual party can have multiple roles in the software value chain. For example, a member of the staff at a bank can also be, and probably is, a customer (e.g., online banking), a user of the software internally (e.g., teller), and a shareholder.

Financial Forms of Software Business Value

Ask a chief financial officer (CFO) about the value of an organization and they will start with the financial statement for the organization. For those of you with limited experience of financial statements, here is a simple definition from Chad Simmons (2002):

> A financial statement uses numbers to describe the business capital structure. The financial statement has two basic parts: the balance sheet, which includes a list of business assets and liabilities (essence of the capital structure) and the operating statement (often called the profit and loss statement or just P&L), which is a record of business revenue, expenses and earnings.

Figure 4.2 summarizes where you might see software value and costs popping up on a financial statement. We will now look at why software appears in all these different places.

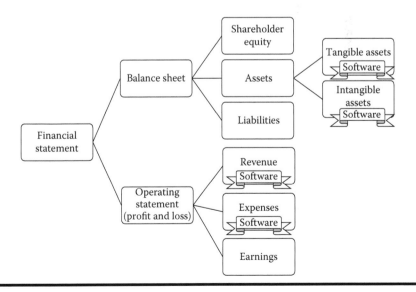

Figure 4.2 Software on a financial statement.

Software as an Asset or an Expense

From the financial perspective, software is only an asset if it appears on balance sheets. There are two types of assets on balance sheets: tangible and intangible assets. Tangible assets, as you might guess, are only things that you can touch and feel like property or tools or machines—usually termed *property, plant, and equipment* (PPE). An intangible asset is something of value that does not have physical form. Traditionally, intangible assets are NOT included as part of the assets used to value the business. Per Simmons (2002), "banks do not accept intangible assets as collateral for financing."

So, is software a tangible or intangible asset?

The short answer is that software is an intangible asset, but there are exceptions. Chizoba Morah, responding to this question on Investopedia,* provides a more definitive response to the treatment of *internal use software* (as opposed to "software to be sold, leased, or marketed"):

> Under most circumstances, computer software is classified as an intangible asset because of its non-physical nature. However, accounting rules state that there are certain exceptions that permit the classification of computer software as Property Plant and Equipment (PPE).
>
> Some of the statements that have rules concerning the classification of software include:
>
> - Financial Accounting Standards Advisory Board (FASAB) Statement of Federal Financial Accounting Standards (SFFAS) No. 10, "Accounting for Internal Use Software."
> - Governmental Accounting Standards Board (GASB) Statement No. 42, "Accounting of Costs of Computer Software Developed or Obtained for Internal Use."
>
> There are two general rules that are applied to determine whether or not software must be capitalized as PPE or expensed. If software meets the criteria of property, plant and equipment, meaning it will be used in providing goods and services, then it can be classified as PPE. For example, a computer company would capitalize computer software as PPE because it is used in a major part of the company's operations that is intended to provide profits. However, software that provides a means for a warehouse to efficiently perform inventory management duties would not be incorporated as PPE.
>
> The second capitalization criterion is based on cost. If an individual copy of the software package costs more than $100,000 it is classified in the PPE category. The software would then be amortized, like other

---

* See http://www.investopedia.com/ask/answers/09/computer-software-intangible-asset.asp

assets, over its useful life. However, as a general rule, if two software copies are purchased for $150,000 they are accounted for as intangible assets.

If the two preceding conditions are not met, then the software, whether purchased or created internally would be considered an intangible asset. The basic nature of the business and the stage of software development also play a significant role in the classification decision.

These exceptions are important and worth discussing further because if software is only an intangible asset on the balance sheet, then it doesn't add to the value of the business, so how can it have business value from a financial perspective? SFFAS 10 provides accounting standards for internal use software for the U.S. federal government. Hence, from one perspective, it is not universally applicable. However, as a simply stated, concise representation of a set of rules that are acceptable to the U.S. government, this document is well worth reading. Note that the statement "establishes accounting standards for the *cost* of software developed or obtained for internal use." Cost not value. However, because the rules cover the capitalization of some of the cost, they turn that part of the cost into value on the balance sheet.

The following extracts from SFFAS 10 are my selections of the most important points to help the reader understand the coverage of the statement and other aspects of this chapter and book:

SFFAS 10 Definition of Internal Use Software

1. Commercial off-the-shelf (COTS) software: COTS software refers to software that is purchased from a vendor and is ready for use with little or no changes.
2. Developed software

    a. Internally developed software refers to software that employees of the entity are actively developing, including new software and existing or purchased software that are being modified with or without a contractor's assistance.

    b. Contractor-developed software refers to software that a federal entity is paying a contractor to design, program, install, and implement, including new software and the modification of existing or purchased software.

SFFAS 10 Software Development Phases

Software's life cycle phases include planning, development, and operations. SFFAS 10 provides a framework for identifying software

Preliminary design phase	Software development phase	Post-implementation/ operational phase
Conceptual formation of alternatives	Design of chosen path, including software configuration and software interfaces	Data conversion Application maintenance
Evaluation and testing of alternatives	Coding	
Determination of existence of new technology	Installation to hardware	
Final selection of alternatives	Testing, including parallel processing phase	

Figure 4.3   SSAFS 10 software development phases.

development phases and processes to help isolate the capitalization period for internal use software that the federal entity is developing. Figure 4.3 illustrates the various software phases and related processes. The steps within each phase of internal use software development may not follow the exact order shown. This standard should be applied on the basis of the nature of the cost incurred, not the exact sequence of the work within each phase.

From a Waterfall perspective, the software development phases in Figure 4.3 are debatable around the edges, but basically clear. However, from an Agile perspective, the definitions are much more fuzzy. I have provided some definitions of Waterfall and Agile in the Appendix and if you are unfamiliar with the differences, you should refer to the Appendix now. Part of the philosophy of Agile software development, and particularly, its most common manifestation, Scrum, is that a team takes fairly high level but small chunks of work and is free to perform the detailed design, coding, and testing all within a short 2–4-week period from which the end result is working software. In some instances, this could include some or all of the activities in all three columns of Figure 4.3. The challenge is to find a way to separate out the time (and money) spent on capitalizable activities versus uncapitalizable activities without imposing a burdensome and bureaucratic time and activity recording regime that would be contradictory to the philosophy of Agile. We will return to this later in the chapter.

SFFAS 10 Recognition, Measurement, and Disclosure

- Software used as general PPE: Entities should capitalize the cost of software when such software meets the criteria for general PPE. General PPE is any property, plant, and equipment used in providing goods and services.
- Capitalizable Cost

- For internally developed software, capitalized cost should include the full cost (direct and indirect cost) incurred during the software development stage. Such cost should be limited to cost incurred after

  • Management authorizes and commits to a computer software project and believes that it is more likely than not that the project will be completed and the software will be used to perform the intended function with an estimated service life of 2 years or more.

  • The completion of conceptual formulation, design, and testing of possible software project alternatives (the preliminary design stage).

- Such costs include those for new software (e.g., salaries of programmers, systems analysts, project managers, and administrative personnel; associated employee benefits; outside consultants' fees; rent; and supplies) and documentation manuals.

- For COTS software, capitalized cost should include the amount paid to the vendor for the software. For contractor-developed software, capitalized cost should include the amount paid to a contractor to design, program, install, and implement the software. Material internal cost incurred by the federal entity to implement the COTS or contractor-developed software and otherwise make it ready for use should be capitalized.

■ Data Conversion Cost: All data conversion costs incurred for internally developed, contractor-developed, or COTS software should be expensed as incurred, including the cost to develop or obtain software that allows for access or conversion of existing data to the new software. Such cost may include the purging or cleansing of existing data, reconciliation or balancing of data, and the creation of new/additional data.

■ Cutoff for Capitalization: Costs incurred after final acceptance testing has been successfully completed should be expensed. Where the software is to be installed at multiple sites, capitalization should cease at each site after testing is complete at that site.

■ Capitalization Thresholds: Each federal entity should establish its own threshold as well as guidance on applying the threshold to bulk purchases of software programs (e.g., spreadsheets and word-processing programs) and to modules or components of a total software system.

■ Enhancements:

- The acquisition cost of enhancements to existing internal use software (and modules thereof) should be capitalized when it is more likely than not that they will result in significant additional capabilities.
- Enhancements normally require new software specifications and may require a change of all or part of the existing software specifications as well. The cost of minor enhancements resulting from ongoing systems maintenance should be expensed in the period incurred. [Note that this definition presents challenges for Agile development because it suggests a test for the size of enhancements that can be capitalized—the need for a new specification of the enhancement and, possibly, a change to the specification of the existing software—which does not have real meaning in the Agile world where the main specification of the software is the code itself.].

■ Amortization: Software that is capitalized pursuant to this standard should be amortized in a systematic and rational manner over the estimated useful life of the software. The estimated useful life used for amortization should be consistent with that used for planning the software's acquisition.

GASB Statement 42

While SFFAS 10 is largely about how to treat the transformation of the cost of internal software into value as an asset on the balance sheet, the GASB Statement 42 is about when it might be necessary to reduce the value of technology assets on the books due to the impairment of its value through significant and unexpected decline of its *service utility*. It is useful to quote the following example directly from GASB Statement 42:

> Technological development and obsolescence usually result in a reduction in demand for the affected capital asset. The capital asset has not experienced a decline in its physical ability to provide service; however, the product or service produced by the capital asset is no longer demanded because some other capital asset provides a better product or service or something has made the product or service undesirable. For example, many applications that once could run on only large, expensive mainframe computers have been adapted to run on small, inexpensive servers or personal computers. If a government had acquired a mainframe several years ago with the expectation that most applications of the government would run on the mainframe for another seven years before new technology would make it feasible to use less-expensive hardware, but found that the pace of development of servers and personal computers was so rapid that half of the applications had been moved to

servers and personal computers in two years with no alternative uses for the mainframe, impairment would be indicated. The mainframe can still physically process applications as rapidly as it could initially and can continue to do so for its estimated useful life. However, because of the advancement in technology for servers and personal computers, the demand for the services of the mainframe has greatly decreased.

There is a tension here in two different perspectives of software value in the accounting standards. SFFAS 10 uses software cost (after application of all the capitalization rules) to put an asset value on the balance sheet. Software lifetime is then used to systematically reduce the value of the software asset through amortization. However, GASB Statement 42 then turns to an assessment of the software's service utility to decide if its value should be reduced faster than amortization would imply. It seems to me that service utility should have been used to set the business value of the software in the first place, not least because the ability to capitalize the cost of software development and turn it into an asset on the balance sheet can act as a disincentive for some business executives to keep software development costs under control. That said, the amortization of software development costs has a self-regulating nature in that higher spend on software development this year results in higher amortization charges in the next, say 5 years, which puts downward pressure on the amount of money available to be spent in those years, assuming the budget stays broadly the same. I will discuss this later in this chapter.

How to Capitalize Agile?

We have already noted that for the Agile methodology, the separation of capitalizable and non-capitalizable activities in the day-to-day operations of Scrum teams is not so clear. There are two main capitalization challenges faced by the CFOs of organizations using Agile software development: the incremental nature of the deliverables and the small teams operating without the clear functional (requirements, design, code, test) separation of the activities of team members required for compliance with the guidelines.

The incremental nature of the deliverables means that most deliverables fall below the thresholds for "projects worth capitalizing" that organizations have inherited from their prior, and perhaps continuing, use of Waterfall. The nature of Waterfall (and one of its major limitations, of course) is that it works most efficiently when lots of deliverables are aggregated together. Hence, thresholds for the costs of projects that are worth capitalizing under the Waterfall methodology tend to be five figures or more. Given that deliverables in Agile are typically working software based on 2–4 weeks of efforts by a team of roughly five to nine people, there is clearly a need for some rules around how deliverables in Agile should be aggregated before the capitalization threshold test is applied.

The challenge of separating out the effort of the team is easy to define—there is a need to record how much time each team member works on capitalizable (C) and non-capitalizable (NC) activities—but is not easy to solve in a practical way. In a typical 2 week Scrum sprint, an individual might work 80 hours and carry out requirements elicitation (NC), design (NC), coding (C), testing (C), and maintenance/refactoring (NC) activities on, say, five stories (deliverables). Naturally, it will be hard to completely separate the activities, so let's assume, as best our individual can remember and record on a daily basis, that 1.5–2 hours are spent on NC tasks and 6–6.5 hours on C tasks (yes, I'm simplifying, I know that nobody is 100 percent efficient) each day. The uncertainly in the numbers for just one individual is about 6 percent, which seems reasonable except, of course, when we consider a 6 percent minimum uncertainty in the potentially millions of dollars to be capitalized across a large organization. Also, if it takes the individual 15 minutes per day to record their time to this level of accuracy, there is an immediate loss of available capacity of about 3 percent.

Unfortunately, to date, the solutions to these capitalization challenges have largely been locally restricted to conversations between organizations, their accountants, and their auditors. Having participated in many conversations around capitalization with accountants over the years, I do not envy either side when the time comes for the chief information officer (CIO) to explain Waterfall and Agile methodologies. Most organizations are using broad rules of thumb—often based on historic data from Waterfall, for example, "we used to capitalize 60 percent of our spend under Waterfall, so we will continue to do the same under Agile." I am not aware of any organizations that are requiring Agile developers to do the sort of time recording that would be necessary to produce auditable numbers. Most organizations are taking a conservative approach, but some may be sailing a little close to the wind.

The Dark Side of Software Capitalization and Amortization?

From a CFO's perspective, the ability to capitalize some software development costs increases the value of the software on the balance sheet in a nice persistent way and reduces expenses on the P&L. However, although the impact on profits is spread over the amortization lifetime, this effect is only purely beneficial for the first few years because amortization amounts aggregate over time, such that the cumulative impacts on profits end up being similar to expensing all the costs in the year they are incurred. Where the amortization costs are absorbed at the corporate level, the impact on local software development management is minimal, but where the amortization costs are, rightly, applied back to the local software development budgets, then the impact on the budget can lead to complex planning issues.

Let's walk through a real example (with some massaging of the numbers for simplicity sake) from my time at Sanchez Computer Associates, a developer of banking software products. Sanchez was a public company that was acquired by Fidelity Information Services in 2004. At the time of the acquisition, I was president of the banking division responsible for all of the product development, among other things. Some years earlier, at the insistence of our auditors, we had started capitalizing some of our software development costs where previously we had expensed

Row	Item	Year 0	Year 1	Year 2	Year 3	Year 4	Year 5	Year 6	Year 7	Year 8
1	% of annual software development spend capitalized	0%	60%	60%	60%	60%	60%	60%	60%	60%
2	% of annual software development budget expensed	100%	40%	40%	40%	40%	40%	40%	40%	40%
3	Actual software product development budget ($M)	25	25	25	25	25	25	25	25	25
4	Amortization cost charged to budget assuming 5 year software life @ 20% per year ($M)	0.0	0.0	7.0	12.6	17.1	20.7	23.5	18.8	16.5
5	Extra cash available for software development due to lower expenses (= row 3 * row 2) ($M)	0	10	10	10	10	10	10	10	10
6	Available software product development spend (= row 3 - row 4 + row 5) ($M)	25.0	35.0	28.0	22.4	17.9	14.3	11.5	16.2	18.5
7	Number of development staff fundable (= row 6/$100k)	250	350	280	224	179	143	115	162	185
8	Asset value on balance sheet (= last years asset value + % of soft dev spend this year)	0.0	21.0	37.8	51.2	62.0	70.6	77.5	87.2	98.3

Figure 4.4 Impact of a transition to software development capitalization.

everything up to that point. As owner of the software development budget, I saw and felt the impact on our capacity to deliver value as shown in Figure 4.4, which shows how the introduction of amortization affected the amount of money that I had to spend on software development in subsequent years.

For the purposes of Figure 4.4, I have simplified the numbers by assuming that my unadjusted budget each year stayed the same (at $25 million). Initially, it was great because I had more money to spend in Year 1 and Year 2, and so we brought in more developers. However, when the impact of doing that kicked in as higher amortization charges against my budget in future years, we were actually forced to reduce the number of developers below our original starting point. Or we would have if I hadn't spotted this impact ahead of time and fought for an increased budget (not shown in Figure 4.4). Figure 4.5 shows graphically the effects calculated in Figure 4.4.

Clearly, the capitalization of software development makes the planning of future budgets more complicated than simply expensing the costs. Of course, the impact of software value showing up on the balance sheet was huge, especially in the subsequent discussions about the value of the company during the merger. Figure 4.6 shows how the asset value on the balance sheet grew after we started to capitalize the software development.

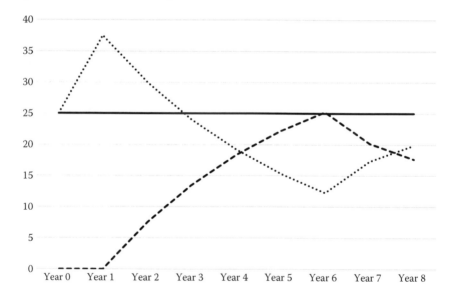

— Actual software product development budget ($M)
-- Amortization cost charged to budget assuming 5 year software life @20% per year ($M)
···· Available software product development spend (= row 3 - row 4 + row 5) ($M)

Figure 4.5 Impact of introduction of capitalization on software development capacity.

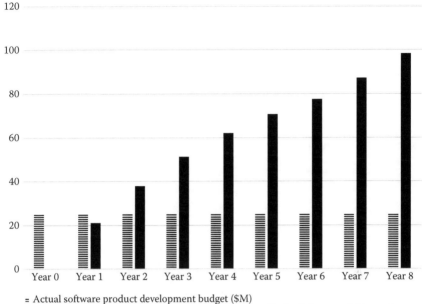

Figure 4.6   Asset value growth versus budget through capitalization and amortization from Year 1.

We have assumed in our example that the underlying budget for software development remained the same during the transition. Hopefully, you can see that if we were to introduce significant changes to that underlying budget during the period of our example, that could complicate the available funds in future years even further. This is what happens in companies whose transition to capitalized software development was made many years ago—complexity in forecasting capacity (and value?) comes from managing the future amortization costs that will hit the budget.

Another temptation from the dark side is the ability to add software value unrelated to cost to the balance sheet as "goodwill." According to Simmons (2002),

> Goodwill is created when business performance creates value that exceeds the fair market value of tangible assets.

Since the value of software is usually intangible (with an assumed fair market value of zero), then it is permissible to add a value to the balance sheet under the heading of goodwill that represents the difference between the capitalized cost of the software on the balance sheet and its fair market value. For example, let's imagine that a bank has developed software for sending statements by e-mail instead of by normal mail and that the cost of developing the software was $2 million. If the bank has 1 million customers who have agreed to use this software, and the bank avoids the cost of sending 12 statements per year worth, say, 47 cents per stamp, then the bank saves $5.64 million per year. Perhaps the true value of the software to the bank is somewhere between $2 million and $5.64 million. Perhaps this year, about $3 million of software value could be added as goodwill? Interestingly, with thanks to my colleague Harrison Zipkin for mentioning this to me, since 2001, it has not been mandatory to amortize goodwill provided that the assets that make up goodwill are marked up or down to true market value, ideally annually.

Software as Revenue

Our default business model in this book is the organization developing software for its own use, but when considering financial forms of software value, we cannot ignore those organizations that build software so they can sell it. The most obvious impact of the business value of software on the financial statement for these organizations is on the top line of the P&L as revenue, and on the bottom line of the P&L as profit!

The treatment of the investment costs of developing software products for sale is slightly different than those intended to be used internally. I am indebted to Eric Wilson at WithumSmith and Brown, PC* for his useful notes on the differences, which pivot around the point that the software project achieves "technological feasibility."

Wilson states:

> This [technological feasibility point] is important because the accounting standards state that all costs incurred on a software project prior to the establishment of technological feasibility are to be expensed as incurred. The standards also state that costs incurred subsequent to the establishment of technological feasibility may be capitalized. Capitalization of the costs should cease when the software is available for general release to customers. Any future costs relating to the software project should be expensed as incurred. What is technological feasibility? Technological feasibility is a term used to describe a certain point during a software project when the research and development phase has substantially been completed. The standards provide specific guidance as to when a project has achieved technological feasibility.

Specifically, for a computer software product, technological feasibility is established when

---

* See https://www.withum.com/wp-content/uploads/2014/05/How-Tech-Companies-Deal-With-Software-Development-Costs.pdf

1. The product design and the detail program design have been completed, and the entity has established that the necessary skills, hardware, and software technology are available to the company to produce the product.
2. The completeness of the detail program design and its consistency with the product design have been confirmed by documenting and tracing the detail program design to product specifications.
3. The detail program design has been reviewed for high-risk development issues (e.g., novel, unique, unproven functions and features or technological innovations), and any uncertainties related to identified high-risk development issues have been resolved through coding and testing.

Per Wilson, a detail program design is defined by the standards as follows:

> The detail design of a computer software product that takes product function, feature, and technical requirements to their most detailed, logical form and is ready for coding.

As with software for internal use, there is some leeway here for interpretation, and I recommend discussing any new assumptions with your accountants and auditors before assuming that they will be acceptable. Just as Agile throws up some new challenges for the capitalization of internal use software, the application of lean and Agile principles for software development presents some new challenges when the software is for sale. For example, in lean, the concept of building a "minimum viable product" (MVP) first is now widespread in software product development, thanks in part to the success of Eric Ries' book, *The Lean Startup* (Ries 2011). However, this raises questions on whether the point of technological feasibility and the completion of the MVP are the same—resulting in more discussions with the auditors.

Revenue Recognition

When I was working at Sanchez Computer Associates, we sold licenses to banks to install and use our software on their premises. We helped them to install it, interface it to their existing systems, set up all the data, train their staff, and hold their hands when it went live. The price of a deal was usually millions of dollars, but we were not allowed to recognize this revenue in our books all at once because there are rules relating to the nature of the additional services provided and the relative completion of the overall project that set out an acceptable revenue recognition timetable for each deal.

As a public company that was continuously growing its software product offerings, we were using current profits to fund new product development to win bigger deals, and I chafed at the revenue recognition rules that effectively slowed down the rate at which I could get my hands on the next slice of money to fund the next development.

Portfolio Management

The practice and process of portfolio management for software is about actively planning and managing the software applications that make up the organizations portfolio to ensure that the necessary functionality is available at the lowest cost and, sometimes, that new investments are optimized in the interests of sustaining and growing the business value of the software in the organization—In short, managing investment-funded activities to optimize the impact of those activities on the financial forms of value described previously. I will spend more time on this topic in Chapter 5.

Non-Financial Forms of Software Value

By adding this section to this chapter, I am acknowledging that not everything is about money and that there are forms of value that are easily recognizable to most people as value, which are nonetheless hard to translate precisely into dollars. In my lifetime, and with apologies to younger readers, the software that brought us live images of the first man to step on the moon had a monetary value, but I very much doubt that any number written down anywhere truly captures the value of that moment to the members of the human race watching it. Each generation has its moment.

Of course, there are many people who work hard to put monetary value on all sorts of things. Here are just two examples of software-related value that can be specifically defined in monetary terms, but whose value at any given time depends on more than just the software associated with them.

Software Reputation

Can something as intangible and techy as software truly have a reputation? Certainly. And the value of the software depends on its reputation. In the past, probably until the late 1990s, it was possible for functionally valuable software to survive in the market or in an organization even if there were known issues with its quality. Indeed, I recall new releases of some major, widely used software packages coming with lists of known bugs. It was much more important to grab market share or get the software into the hands of the company's users quickly than to fix every last defect. Today, it's hard for software to survive a reputation for poor quality even if it is functionally excellent. There are simply too many competitors out there and the users today have grown up accustomed to complex software that just works.

Hence, just one poor quality software release can seriously dent an organization's reputation, which can have a disproportionate impact on the organization's value compared with the value of the release. One big example that comes to mind is Microsoft's release of Windows Vista. Microsoft lost a lot of goodwill from its corporate customers with that one and, perhaps, just opened the door a little wider for Apple to get more devices into corporate offices than they had had for years.

Technical Debt

Although the name implies a financial form of value, and I would argue that it should appear on the financial statement as a liability along with the other company debts, technical debt is not a financial form of software value. Per Steve McConnell,*

> The term technical debt was coined by Ward Cunningham to describe the obligation that a software organization incurs when it chooses a design or construction approach that's expedient in the short term but that increases complexity and is more costly in the long term.

Technical debt is a negative form of software value in that it detracts from the business value of the software over time—think of it as the nasty stuff that accumulates over time on the walls of your blood vessels. You can get away with ignoring the build-up for a long time, but if it gets too bad then the first time you notice it can be very serious indeed. The best way to fix it is to take action continuously to ensure that it never gets too bad.

Technical debt is hard to quantify and so hard to monetize. There are various static code analyzer tools on the market today that are quite good at assessing the level of technical debt by comparing actual code against patterns of best practice. The results show those parts of the code that are not structured as well as they could be and hence represent technical debt. This is valuable although comparative measures for technical debt are fuzzy. Some tools try to take this further by estimating the amount of effort required to make the code conform to the best practice patterns, and some even estimate the cost of doing that, presumably based on some assumptions about developer costs and skills. In my opinion, these effort and cost estimates are, at best, a subjective guess made to look objective by being embedded in an algorithm, but the static code analysis tool vendors are continuously enhancing their products so we can hope for continuous improvement.

Data and Information

The world is awash with the data created by software. "Created by?" Yes. There was certainly data before software. For example, all the books written in the history of the world until probably about the 1960s were written without the assistance of software. My point though is that the amount of data created by software now dwarfs

---

* See http://www.construx.com/10x_Software_Development/Technical_Debt/

that created by any other source. Some of it is very easily monetized—indeed, money itself is mostly just bits and bytes these days. But much of the software-created data that exists today is barely monetized at all.

Recently, businesses have realized that there may be gold to be mined in all that data, and the practice of data analytics has grown up to look for business value in the data stored in the organization.

Although I acknowledge that some data analytics results are financial forms of business value, it seems to me that many of the results will be more like inferences or suggestions of ways to do things better that might make or save money. Just as data might be considered one step removed from software, then I suggest that the business value embedded in the data is one step removed from a financial form of business value. The best analogy I can think of is that a mountain full of bauxite (aluminum ore) is valuable but it does not really have financial form until it is dug out, smelted, and sold as aluminum. Nobody would deny the value of the mountain, and so I assert that data is a form of the business value of software. Of course, information is to data what aluminum is to bauxite.

Open Source

Open-source software comes in many legal forms from the "free to use and modify" to the "unusable for commercial gain (without the payment of license fees)." In the context of this chapter, open-source software has no financial value to the organization that uses it. This seems a stark statement—surely the organization would not use open-source software unless it had some value. True and we have it in this section for that reason. However, I suggest that open-source software can have no financial value because the organization does not own or even control the asset. Indeed, even though derivative works are possible for some forms of open-source software, I would argue that those derivative works should be treated very carefully from the perspective of financial valuation.

In some cases, the use of open-source software in corporate systems can be a liability if legal costs are incurred because a developer somewhere included the open-source software in their deliverables for a project without notifying the right people in the organization so that the appropriate licenses could be obtained.

Summary

In this chapter, we have looked at how software business value can take various forms in an organization. I have spent more time considering financial forms of value than non-financial forms of value because our focus is on business value. In the next chapter, we will discuss managing software value at the strategic level—essentially, portfolio management.

Chapter 5

Establishing Software Value Strategies

Establishing software value strategies involves a number of activities at the top of the organization to initiate the change to use business value as a metric for driving software development in the organization. In Chapter 4, I introduced the practice and process of software portfolio management as being about actively planning and managing the software applications that make up the organization's portfolio. The objective of this practice/process is to ensure that the necessary functionality is available at the lowest cost and, sometimes, that new investments are optimized in the interests of sustaining and growing the business value of the software in the organization. In short, software portfolio management means managing invest-ment-funded activities to optimize their financial impact on software value. In *Agile Software Requirements* (Leffingwell 2011), Dean Leffingwell (a founder of the Scaled Agile Framework® or SAFe®) quotes Mikko Parkolla's (2010) description of portfolio management:

> Portfolio management is a top-level authority that makes long-term investment decisions on strategic areas that affect the business perfor-mance of the company. The main responsibility of portfolio manage-ment is to set the investment levels between business areas, product lines, different products, and strategic portfolio investment themes; these are a collection of related strategic initiatives.

Leffingwell goes on to list three sets of activities that should be under the control or influence of the organization's software portfolio management team:

- Investment funding: Determining the allocation of the company's scarce research and development (R&D) resources to various products and services.
- Change management: Fact patterns change over time, and the business must react with new plans, budgets, and expectations.
- Governance and oversight: Assuring that the programs remain on track and that they follow the appropriate corporate rules, guidelines, and relevant standards.

As organizations start to establish software value strategies, introducing or refocusing a portfolio management team will be a big part of the change. However, to stand any chance of success using business value as the driver for the improvement of software development, the leaders of the organization must first instill a culture of lean software development. We will return to portfolio management later in this chapter.

Lean Software Development

The first step in establishing software value strategies is to learn about and commit to a philosophy of lean software development.

I do not intend to dive too deeply into the theory and history of lean manufacturing and the evolution of lean software engineering in this book. Interested readers should refer first to *Implementing Lean Software Development* by Mary and Tom Poppendieck (2006). Instead, I want to focus on some important ideas from lean, and lean software engineering in particular, that I consider to be important principles that an organization should adopt before it attempts to drive its software development around business value.

Removal of Waste

A key principle of lean is to remove from the process any activities that do not add value. "Activities that do not add value" is the definition of "waste" in lean. Of course, in the spirit of *kaizen*, or continuous improvement, the phrase "do not add value," is interpreted relatively as in "Activity A adds less value than Activity B—how can we make an improvement?"

From my perspective, value should always be read as business value first but not exclusively. From a technical perspective, I recognize that technical change is sometimes desirable and even necessary without any business value that is obvious today. There is a balance to be struck between a short-term view of value, such as might be driven by the quarterly reporting needs of a public company, and the long-term view of putting the organization in a place to deliver maximum business value in the future. Consider the utility value of getting a car serviced regularly. If the car is running perfectly then the investment of time and money to get it serviced regularly is hard to justify. You will probably notice little difference for a while, but eventually performance will start to suffer and possibly major things will start to go wrong requiring time off the road. The same can be said for investing in software applications and software development processes.

Pull Not Push

Historically, in software development, the business side of the organization has almost always created more ideas for work than the software development group can handle within the desired time or budget. This has led to competition between business heads to get their work prioritized by the software development teams ahead of their colleagues. Also, it led to a mentality that it was important to *push* as much work as possible into the software development group such that every available drop of capacity was utilized, even if this meant overloading and burning out development teams. This still happens today. In fact, as companies have outsourced their software development, it has evolved a new twist in some client–vendor relationships. In a client–vendor relationship, it is not possible to overload software development teams and expect the sort of large amounts of cost-free overtime that many expected from employees. Clients have developed control mechanisms to deal with this that can cause more problems than they solve. For example, I came across one large health-care client that had evolved a choke point just before development projects were released to the vendor. The health-care client decided that projects to be worked on by the vendor would need internal approval from an executive before being released to the vendor. The executive decided to perform this "gating" event every 30 days. In the light of other demands on the executive's time, this did not seem unreasonable, except that now the vendors face challenges of resource planning because they only have 30-days visibility of approved work about to be pushed to them. The client business teams are facing challenges because they have plenty of work to push, but are struggling to organize it in such a way that they can provide the vendors with forecasting greater than 30 days ahead of time.

In very small organizations, the (very small) software development team has always picked up and worked on software projects in the order they have been prioritized by their, usually co-located, business user(s). This very small process delivers value quickly and efficiently. In large organizations, work has tended to be organized into projects (based on various criteria) to which resources are assigned to maximize their utilization (on the assumption that utilization is a good proxy for productivity). However, flow theory based on ideas from lean manufacturing and telecoms routing (Reinertsen 2009) suggests that the strategy of bringing resources to projects and optimizing their utilization is a poorer (sometimes much poorer) strategy for delivering economic value than applying lean principles to the flow of work through small teams of expert resources. The lean answer is to establish appropriately sized teams for the desired work steps and the available budget, then let the teams *pull* work from a backlog of tasks that is ready to be worked on as and when they are ready to do the work. This approach, combined with work-in-process (WIP) limits at each step, avoids queues of WIP throughout the team. Queues represent waste because there is no value being added while work items are sitting in queues. These principles are fundamental elements of *Kanban* systems, which we will return to later in this chapter.

Importantly, *pull not push* requires a change in understanding at the strategic level. Executives must be persuaded, and accept, that in organizing software development under lean principles to maximize flow, they need to organize their desired deliverables into *portfolio backlogs* in which the desired deliverables are prioritized. The whole point of this book is that, I believe, all software development backlogs can and must be prioritized by business value.

We must acknowledge that this is a big cultural change because most executives' experiences (and possibly egos) tell them that the software development department is there to do what executives want, when they want it. The fact that executives pushing requirements (and delivery dates) onto software development results in projects that are short on scope, over budget, and late seems to manifest itself in many executives' experiences emotionally as disappointment and lack of trust in software development. All too often, the perceived best remedy for disappointment and mistrust is shouting even louder the next time. Now, we are asking these same executives with these same prior experiences to accept that the software development group will decide tasks they will pull from the portfolio backlog with no guarantees of delivery dates. Instead of perceived but unreal certainty, the executives get a promise of greater value flow, greater agility, and some acknowledged uncertainty (grounded in reality). I believe that the change is worthwhile and the benefits are real but I acknowledge that the cultural change is difficult and important. That's why I wrote this book.

Monitor and Control Variation in the Process but Not in the Inputs

There is a major difference between the development and application of lean principles in manufacturing and their application to software development. In manufacturing, it is practical and desirable to monitor and seek to minimize variance in the inputs and the process. In software development, the process can be monitored and, to some extent, controlled but the inputs are necessarily highly variable, and it is desirable to keep them that way to facilitate innovation.

Manufacturing takes a set of highly specified inputs and assembles them into the finished product. In the old days, such as at the Plessey Avionics and Communications factory in Ilford, England (where I was a "sandwich student"—similar to co-op programs in the United States—and my first job out of university was running a production line), manufacturers would inspect the incoming sub-assemblies for compliance with specification on a sample basis before attempting to assemble them. Today, lean manufacturing largely removes that non-value add step as waste and replaces it with contractually punishable higher expectations on deliveries from suppliers.

By contrast, in software development, we know that each set of requirements is going to be different and, indeed, it is the ability of software to do previously unthought-of things that enables the innovation by the business that drives business value. This has real implications for how lean software engineering is designed. Primarily, lean software engineering is designed to facilitate change, whether due to changes in the external environment or changes in understanding in the software development process, as the detail of the problem to be solved and the limitations or opportunities presented by the technology become clearer.

Reinertsen's Principles for Optimizing Value Flow through Product Development

In *The Principles of Product Development Flow*, Don Reinertsen (2009) defines the eight lean principles that he asserts are critically important to maximizing value flow as the following:

1. Economics
2. Queues
3. Variability
4. Batch size
5. WIP constraints
6. Cadence, synchronization, and flow control
7. Fast feedback
8. Decentralized control

I have touched on some of these principles already in this chapter and will do so elsewhere in the book, so I will not attempt to elaborate on them here. Instead, I suggest the following priorities for executives as they start to shift the organizational culture to lean software engineering at the strategic level:

■ Economic focus—This might seem obvious to a senior management team and they are likely to push back on the suggestion that they do not prioritize everything with an economic focus. Further, they might jump quickly from the term *economic focus* to the concept of business cases. Many of us have experience of business cases as *box checking* in the bureaucratic culture of some organizations. Such business cases do not add value and should be eradicated as waste from a lean perspective. The economic focus we want to engender in the executive team is that of maximizing the flow of value through software development. This means assigning relative business value to projects or epics at the strategic level. Executives must be aware that, as Reinertsen tells us, "If you only measure one thing then measure *cost of delay* (CoD)." CoD provides economic focus and is a useful default metric, which includes business value, timeliness constraints, and risk reduction or opportunity enhancement (I will come back to CoD later in this chapter). Where hard data is not available, CoD can be evaluated relatively across all available options. *Weighted shortest job first* (WSJF) is a more refined economic metric for prioritizing by business value that can still be easily and quickly assessed on a relative basis by a knowledgeable group of business and IT stakeholders (e.g., VVF example at end of this chapter).

■ Queue control—Queue control is simply the identification and removal of bottlenecks that are either systemic or temporary. As we discussed in Chapter 3, quick identification requires making the bottlenecks visible. This is as true for project ideas making their way from conception to the portfolio backlog (or not) as it is for stories being worked on by a team. The Kanban board approach can be used at the portfolio level.

■ Applying WIP constraints—By applying WIP limits to each stage of the processing of portfolio backlog candidates, we can help to minimize queues between process steps and improve focus on the projects under consideration. This also tends to speed up consideration of projects so that those that are not going to make the cut are removed quickly and don't clog up the works.

■ Reduced batch size—This is a key point for lean software engineering and software portfolio management. We cannot and do not want to reduce the variability in the content of the inputs, but we can and do want to reduce the variability in the size of the inputs. Specifically, we want to keep the inputs as small as possible. This is another potential area for culture clash as the lean transformation is introduced because there is clearly a tension between strategy at the executive level being all about deciding on the big things that need to get done, while Reinertsen is telling us to reduce batch size, which implies pushing small things through the portfolio backlog pipeline. I will offer a resolution to this apparent tension later in the chapter. For now, it is sufficient to imagine that a mix of sizes of objects going through any pipeline tends to cause blockages and backups. More efficient flow can be achieved when the pipeline is designed for and receives similarly sized objects, and smaller is always better.

■ Decentralized control—In a push culture for software development, there tends to be a real or implied message from the top down of, "this is what I want and this is when I want it." The most commonly used term to describe this type of culture is *command and control*. It's not necessarily a bad way to manage, it's just not appropriate for the lean-principled pull culture I am advocating. However, from a cultural transformation perspective, there is a real shift of perceived control from the top to the bottom. I say perceived control because in practice, even using traditional approaches, executives couldn't achieve anything without all of the people working for them. But now, we are asking the executives to put things in a prioritized backlog and allow the people below them (and the people below them, etc.) to decide what to pull from the backlog first. The executives and many of the line managers have reached their positions based on their competence in a command and control model. Many will adapt to the new model and some will not but, either way, it will not necessarily be a comfortable transition.

It is worth stating explicitly that while these are changes to enable lean software engineering, they are changes in culture that must be introduced and understood across the organization at the strategic level (i.e., the executive management team). I have mentioned elsewhere in the book, and particularly in Chapter 7, that lean principles can be deployed at the tactical, team level. While introducing lean-Agile at the team level is a good step forward, the transformational impact of lean-Agile becomes limited as it is rolled out to more teams in an organization if the whole organization is not operating on lean principles. If you try to push projects into a software development process that is optimized to pull them from a backlog then, at best, you get suboptimal performance and, at worst, chaos.

Kanban

Like many other terms in software engineering, the original precise meaning of the term has been used and abused in many different ways to the point where I could be having a discussion about Kanban with someone and we could be talking about two different things. I will attempt to clarify in the hope of not confusing you even further. Most people agree that the term *Kanban* comes from the lean manufacturing established at Toyota. Not everyone knows that a Kanban (most often translated as the *signal*) was the name of a card used to signify available capacity (or the need for more materials) at a workstation in a manufacturing flow. The appearance of a Kanban in the bottom of an empty bin at the input to a workstation called for or *pulled* more inputs from the preceding workstation. Of course, the preceding workstation could be an external supplier. This simple method went a long way in eliminating waste in the form of WIP queued up in front of workstations. This improved flow and reduced the *idle* inventory that sat around in queues, costing money. This system has also been characterized as *just-in-time* manufacturing and, as I recall, this is the name that I first heard it under—certainly in the United Kingdom.

As simple as the process seems, further rules are needed, and Toyota formulated the following six rules for the application of Kanban (Ohno 1988):

■ Later process picks up the number of items indicated by the Kanban at the earlier process.
■ Earlier process produces items in the quantity and sequence indicated by the Kanban.

- No items are made or transported without a Kanban.
- Always attach a Kanban to the goods.
- Defective products are not sent on to the subsequent process. The result is 100 percent defect-free goods.
- Reducing the number of Kanban increases the sensitivity.

It is important to note that the Kanban referred to by Toyota is clearly a card (although nowadays it is often an electronic communication or, at least, an electronically readable card). The Kanban contains information about the size of the next batch to be produced, which must be defect-free or it cannot be sent on. No items are made without a Kanban, which authorizes the production at each workstation.

It is reasonable to ask how on earth this card system can be applied to software engineering and, perhaps, easy to see how the abuse of the term has occurred. For example, if, as a software team or portfolio team, we put information cards on the wall, is that a Kanban system? Well, yes. The Kanban card is a signal card so any card that signifies information is arguably a Kanban. Another example might be, if we set up a series of steps (let's call them workstations) in a software development process, and set up some rules such that work can only flow by being pulled from the end of the flow as capacity becomes available, is that a Kanban process, even if we don't use cards? Well again, probably yes.

At the software team level, Kanban is generally considered to be a lean and/or Agile technique. Although, of course, the appropriateness of this depends on how the term is being used. Another confusing concept is that Kanban can be used in systems that look very much like Waterfall, as we will see. The main justification for treating Kanban as Agile, even when applied to a Waterfall process, is that Kanban applied to Waterfall forces small batches of work and avoids the picture of long *death march* projects that Waterfall conjures up (often unreasonably) in the minds of many. As an aside, death march projects often occur in organizations where the push toward software manufacturing in an environment akin to a production line has been taken too far for too long, with the result that the software development process has ossified. As soon as the *time to market* for the next piece of software to be developed starts to grow, business representatives lose sight of when their new software needs are likely to be delivered and start to speculate about what they might need delivered in many months. In this way, projects start to grow as they are padded with probable rather than actual needs. Of course, this exacerbates the problem as bigger projects tend to slow down flow. As time to market increases, so do the number of likely changes to the requirements and the added delays and wasted effort during software development. So, reducing batch sizes generates other positive, self-reinforcing side effects, and increasing batch sizes generates other negative self-reinforcing side effects.

The range of interpretation of the terms *Kanban*, *Kanban board*, and *Kanban system* in software development is large but, generally, the visual (physical or electronic) representation of a Kanban board looks something like that shown in Figure 5.1.* A picture of a more informal version of a Kanban board was included in Chapter 3, Figure 3.8.

In Figure 5.1, we can see a number of key features of a Kanban board:

- Process steps (e.g., analysis, development): The work to be done is broken down into a number of process steps. First sight of this sometimes generates a negative reaction in Scrum teams because they feel that they are being pushed back into a Waterfall model, but that is neither the intent nor the practical outcome. Once the team experiences the use of the Kanban board and sees that this is just a practical way of tracking stories during a sprint, most team members quickly get comfortable. It is important to note that my example process steps in Figure 5.1 are not intended to be prescriptive.
- Backlog: This is the prioritized queue of work for the team.
- Ready process step: In many teams, this is not an explicit step, but I like to include it in my model because it makes explicit the fact that there is probably work to be done on some or all of the backlog items before they are ready to be worked on by the team.
- Queues: While lean software engineering is about minimizing and removing queues, Reinertsen's advice on making queues visible is equally important.

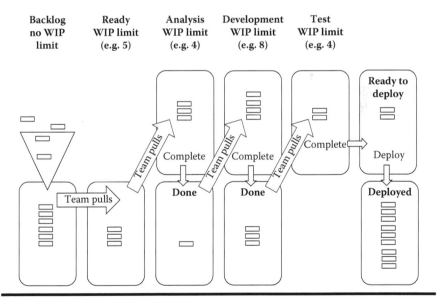

Figure 5.1 **Example Kanban board.**

---

* I have seen many versions of Kanban boards for software development, but I really like and have used with clients the game simulation for software development Kanban called "the get-kanban game," see https://getkanban.com/

Hence, in addition to the backlog and ready process step already discussed, we have three queues in Figure 5.1:
- Analysis "done" (awaiting development)
- Development "done" (awaiting test)
- Ready to deploy (awaiting deployment)

■ WIP limits: Four of the process steps have WIP limits. Note that the WIP limits include both the items that are actively being worked on and the items sitting in queues at that process step awaiting a pull from the next step in the process. Hence, for example in Figure 5.1, the analysis process step is at its WIP limit because it has three items being actively processed and one completed in its "done" queue. I am often asked about the "right" values for WIP limits when Kanban boards are processed and first set up. Of course, there is no right answer to this, but my usual advice is to start with and try to sustain single digit (i.e., less than 10) WIP limits. This forces minimal queues and a real focus on small batches. It is really important to measure the end-to-end throughput of the Kanban system and adjust the WIP limits carefully to maximize that throughput.

A Portfolio Management Kanban System

Figure 5.2 illustrates the sort of portfolio Kanban system that can be used at the portfolio level to prioritize new software development investment. It is important to emphasize here that the goal is prioritization of new software development projects (or epics) to maximize the flow of business value. This implies that we have a way to measure business value at this level. Later in this chapter, I describe a simple, default technique, WFJS, a method that can be used to measure business value. It also implies that some overarching strategic directions have been set for the organization, against which competing investments with similar value (to different business units?) can be prioritized. I will use SAFe® as an example of how this can be done later in this chapter.

The portfolio management system in Figure 5.2 is just one example and is not intended to be prescriptive. The process steps are as follows:

■ Ideas backlog: Any and all ideas from the business go into this backlog. At this point, the ideas are high level with limited descriptions and a simple value statement, because there is no point in wasting effort (good lean practice!) in preparing detailed descriptions or value statements if these ideas are never going to make it to the next step. There is no WIP limit because there is benefit in considering all ideas and let the best float to the top. In practice, weak ideas will *age out* of the ideas backlog as better ideas continue to be prioritized above them.

■ Ready for review: The key activity at this process step is for the portfolio management team to pull "the best" ideas from the ideas backlog for further

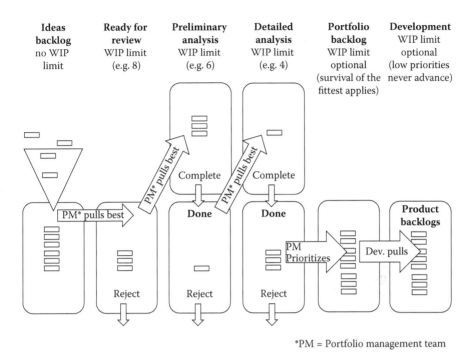

Ideas backlog	Ready for review	Preliminary analysis	Detailed analysis	Portfolio backlog	Development
no WIP limit	WIP limit (e.g. 8)	WIP limit (e.g. 6)	WIP limit (e.g. 4)	WIP limit optional (survival of the fittest applies)	WIP limit optional (low priorities never advance)

*PM = Portfolio management team

Figure 5.2 Portfolio Kanban board.

analysis. Some sort of simple algorithm is required for establishing "the best." Probably, it should include inspection of the ideas for certain minimum information, such as a business value statement, and then a ranking based on that business value statement and the current strategic priorities of the organization. Some interaction between the portfolio management team and the business will be required to develop and document a refined understanding of the idea. There is a WIP limit on this step because the organization has limited funds to invest in software development, the portfolio management team has limited capacity, and the WIP limit acts as a filter to accept the best ideas. I have heard it argued that funds are never limited to invest in new ideas that have a great return on investment. That is true, but at this point the portfolio management team has no idea if the idea in front of them is going to make money or waste money. Ideas that are processed in this step may be rejected, returned to the ideas backlog, or passed on for preliminary analysis.

■ Preliminary analysis: In preliminary analysis, it is necessary to make a first pass at measuring relative business value. Note that this is a prioritization process and so relative business value is more important than actual, specific business value. Further, it is unlikely that future business value flows can be predicted with any real accuracy so there is little point wasting effort to try. For relative business value at this point, I recommend using CoD and

WSJF—the relative values of these can be estimated by a workshop involving business, portfolio management, and software development representatives. More details are provided subsequently. The project with the highest relative WSJF should be done first. At this point, ideas become projects (or epics). Projects that are processed in this step may be rejected, returned to the ideas backlog, or passed on for detailed analysis.

■ Detailed analysis: At this stage, there is some certainty that the projects under consideration have real business value. Hence, it is appropriate for the portfolio management team to work with the business to develop a light-weight business case—a few pages of structured information—and with the software development group to build some high-level cost and duration estimates. Information from these documents should be used to refine the WSJF estimate. Projects that are processed in this step may be rejected, returned to the ideas backlog, or moved into the portfolio backlog according to their relative WSJF priority versus the items already in the portfolio backlog.

I mentioned earlier in this chapter that there is a tension between strategy at the executive level being all about deciding on the big things that need to get done, while Reinertsen is telling us to reduce batch size, which implies pushing small things through the portfolio backlog pipeline. Perhaps, it is clearer now that big ideas can certainly enter the ideas backlog, but their chances of progressing quickly and smoothly through the portfolio management Kanban system are limited by their size. Hence, savvy business heads will submit smaller ideas to the ideas backlog to increase their chances of getting investment quickly.

Cost of Delay and Weighted Shortest Job First

Before I consider CoD and WSJF, I must describe a technique for estimating that uses the shared expertise of a group of informed people to achieve a relative estimate. The technique is based on the Delphi method* developed by the Rand Corporation in the 1950s, which was simplified as *Planning Poker*† by Agile guru, Mike Cohn. The relative estimates for a set of items are considered by a group of informed people. First, the group agrees on which item has the smallest estimate. This is arbitrarily assigned a value of 1. Next, each individual considers another item from the set and privately evaluates its estimate relative to the smallest unitary item from a specified, limited set of numbers. Typically, a modified Fibonacci sequence is used, such as the Cohn scale popularized by Mike Cohn for use in *story points*. For portfolio management purposes, I recommend a simple set: 1, 2, 3, 5, 8, 13, 20. Having privately decided on an estimate for the item under consideration, all the estimating group share their estimates. The resulting reconciliation of

---

* See http://www.rand.org/topics/delphi-method.html
† See http://store.mountaingoatsoftware.com/pages/planning-poker-in-detail

individual estimates based on sharing individual knowledge and justifications is the true value of the process because all of the individual assumptions upon which the individual estimates were made are made explicit and accepted or rejected by the group. The process continues with consideration of the next item to be estimated. It should be noted that at this point I have not specified what attribute of the items the group is estimating nor what units they are using. The technique can be applied to any attribute and there are no units because the estimates are relative.

There are many stories about why modified Fibonacci number sets came to be used for estimation. My preferred version is that it is relatively easy to estimate when something is double the size of something else but much harder to distinguish if something is 17 or 18 times the size. Hence, it is fruitless to waste time and effort debating such small distinctions higher up the scale.

All projects, epics, stories, and tasks have a CoD. The CoD is the hourly, daily, or monthly cost associated with NOT starting the project. For our prioritization purposes, we are interested in the CoD if we start Project A while setting aside Project B (i.e., the CoD of Project B). Consider two software projects, A and B, to be carried out by the same team over 60 days and similar in every way except that Project A requires an external specialist in Oracle databases who can be hired at $100 per hour, and Project B requires an external specialist in Mumps databases who can be hired at $150 per hour. Both specialists are available and must be hired now. The team can only do one project at a time. Which should they do first? Well, they should do the project with the highest CoD first. If Project A is deferred, it has a CoD of 60 days * 8 hours * $100 = $48,000. If Project B is deferred, it has a CoD of 60 days * 8 hours * $150 = $72,000. Project B has the highest CoD so it should be started first.

For the CoD in this example, I was able to use explicit financial values. More often, this sort of explicit financial information is not available or is, at best, fuzzy. So how would this have looked from a Planning Poker perspective? Most likely, we would have been clear that Project A had a smaller cost of delay than Project B because Oracle databases are much more common than Mumps, and therefore, the supply of Oracle experts would probably be greater and their costs lower. We would assign Project A an estimated CoD of "1". The discussion around Project B would revolve around how much more expensive Mumps experts were than Oracle experts. Probably, we would have assigned an estimated CoD of "2" (although in similar circumstances I have seen groups reassign Project A an estimate of "2" so they can assign Project B an estimate of "3" because they don't believe B is twice the size of A!). The key lesson here is we are seeking to prioritize so the absolute dollars are not as important as their relative size in the set under consideration for prioritization.

In the previous example, I was careful to use the same duration for both projects (i.e., 60 days). What if the duration had been different? Let's say that Project A, the Oracle project, had a duration of just 10 days. The CoD for Project A would stay the same at $48,000 because Project B still has a duration of 60 days. However, the

CoD for Project B is now 10 days * 8 hours * $150 = $12,000. In this case, Project A has the highest CoD and should be started first. Clearly, duration has an impact on CoD and must be considered in prioritization decisions. Hence, we define a new metric, WSJF, where

$$\text{Weighted Shortest Job First} = \frac{\text{Cost of Delay}}{\text{Duration}}$$

Now, we prioritize those projects with the highest WSJF at the top. Typically, we do not use Planning Poker to estimate relative WSJF. Instead, we use Planning Poker to estimate a relative CoD and a relative duration for each project and then apply the formula for WSJF. In SAFe,* it is recommended to break down CoD into three constituent parts, which are estimated using Planning Poker and then summed to give the total relative CoD:

$$\text{Cost of Delay} = \text{User or Business Value} + \text{Time Criticality}$$

$$+ \text{Risk Reduction or Opportunity Enablement Value}$$

Since the same Cohn scale numbers are used, this might effectively weight CoD at three times more than duration in the WSJF formula but, in my experience, one of the three sub-components of CoD usually dominates in a given business case so the potential distortion is rarely realized in practice. When we use relative numbers to calculate WSJF, we can call the resulting WSJF result *value points*. We will look at a specific example of the application of WSJF when we discuss the *value visualization framework* in Chapter 7.

Connecting Up the Dots between Portfolio Management and Development Teams

This book and this chapter are intended to suggest techniques that can and should be applied to both the Waterfall and Agile methodologies. When we consider portfolio management and development strategy though, it is fair to say that portfolio management has not yet fully adapted to support lean and Agile development. The software development investment strategy and budgeting process that evolved for Waterfall was based on strategic decisions at the top of the organization being pushed down to the software development teams. Agile has had a positive, revolutionary effect on software development in the twenty-first century. While it may not be true that the majority of all software development is Agile yet, it is almost certainly true that the majority of software development organizations are using

---

* See http://www.scaledagileframework.com/wsjf/

Agile in some way. In many, if not most, cases, the introduction of Agile has been bottom-up with a few Scrum teams being started to test the ideas, sometimes without the knowledge of senior executives. This required small but significant local changes, such as organizing requirements in the form of backlogs and breaking down requirements into smaller chunks to be pulled into active development by teams.

At some point, as the number of Scrum teams pulling work off of backlogs grew across the organization, there was bound to be a clash between the pushing of strategic requirements from the top and the pulling of requirements from the bottom. This clash has come to be known as the problem of *scaling Agile*. Fortunately, several approaches to this problem have been proposed (e.g., the Scaled Agile Framework or SAFe*, Large-Scale Scrum or LeSS,† Disciplined Agile Delivery or DAD,‡ and Dynamic Systems Delivery Method or DSDM§). This book is not about the pros and cons of the different approaches to scaling Agile, but it is useful for us to examine more closely one of these approaches to see how the maximization of software business value is addressed. I have chosen to look more closely at SAFe mainly because I am more familiar with it, but also because it appears to tackle the business value issue explicitly.

Figure 5.3 shows version 4.0 of the four-level SAFe Big Picture—the version that was current at time of writing. There is also a three-level version, which simply excludes the *value stream* layer. As mentioned previously, all of these Agile scaling models continue to evolve so further iterations can be expected, but one of the current strengths of SAFe is that it is mature enough to have been implemented, and tested, by many organizations.

As we can see from Figure 5.3 (right-hand side), the four layers of the SAFe model are

- Portfolio
- Value stream
- Program
- Team

We will return to the program and team layers in later chapters and we will focus on the business value aspects of SAFe rather than attempt to make this a book about SAFe. Hence, for our purposes in this chapter we will concentrate on the top two layers and on the path for business value through the end-to-end system.

Our goal, after all, is to maximize the flow of business value end-to-end through the model, so it is appropriate to start with that. I have discussed a portfolio

---

* See http://scaledagileframework.com/

† See https://less.works/

‡ See http://www.disciplinedagiledelivery.com/

§ See https://www.dsdm.org

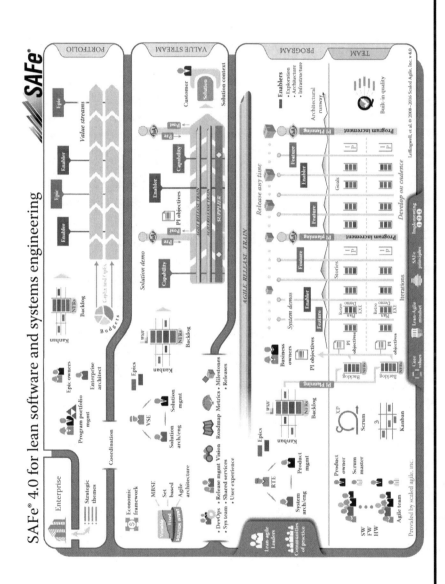

Figure 5.3 SAFe 4.0 big picture.

management Kanban system earlier in this chapter and the start of our end-to-end business flow in SAFe is just such a system in the portfolio level of SAFe (labeled Kanban and backlog in Figure 5.3).

For larger organizations, the highest level strategic portfolio management initiatives must be mapped onto the organizational structure at the next level down. In SAFe, this is called the *value stream layer*. The value stream layer is important for our understanding of how business value flows from end-to-end in large enterprises, so a little more explanation is provided later. For now though, it is sufficient to see that there is a value stream backlog, organized as a Kanban system in the value stream layer. Projects and epics are pulled from the portfolio backlog into the value stream backlog and decomposed into smaller units. Note that the WSJF values of the projects/epics continue to be reviewed and updated at this level.

The next layer below the value stream layer in the end-to-end business value flow (and also the layer below portfolio for smaller businesses or smaller SAFe implementations) is the program layer, which is also sometimes thought of as the product layer. Again, the flow of business value is via epics being pulled into a program backlog, where they may be decomposed into smaller units, organized in a Kanban system with WSJF reviewed and updated.

From the program backlog, in Agile software development groups, epics are decomposed into stories at the team level and pulled into the sprint or iteration backlogs of individual teams. This is a key step because at this point, teams control the prioritization of work flow. How the teams do the prioritization is important for the flow of business value and we devote a whole chapter to it (Chapter 7) later in the book.

We have reached the point where requirements are turned into working code, but we have not yet delivered any business value. In SAFe, integrated, working code is a deliverable of each 2-week iteration. The deliverables from these 2-week iterations are aggregated up and demonstrated as working code in *program increments*, which may contain four to six iterations. Developing and delivering working code in structured time boxes like this is called "Develop on Cadence" in SAFe. Still we have not delivered business value into the hands of the users and business. In SAFe, this last step is decoupled from the delivery of working code. A release management team prioritizes the working code that best suits the immediate needs of the business and releases it into production, usually with the assistance of a DevOps team, hence, "Release on Demand."

End-to-End Business Value

Finally, we have delivered business value and the end-to-end flow is complete. But let's return to the questions that opened this book: How do we know how much business value we have delivered? Does this represent the maximum that we could have delivered?

In SAFe, we have applied prioritization by WSJF at each level except the team level. We could have applied other business value metrics and prioritized using them but, by using WSJF, at least we can be sure that we have a basis of prioritization by economic value. To ensure that this is the maximum that we could have delivered, we need metrics—the WSJF values as value points are a good start—and monitoring. We also need a culture of lean thinking and continuous improvement.

Orphan Stories

The glue that holds together the prioritization process from the portfolio level down to the team level should be *explicit* business value. One of our clients coined the term *orphan stories* to describe what sometimes happens to them if connectivity between epics and stories is not maintained when requirements are decomposed as they transition from the portfolio level to the team level.

Let's use an example of a strategic initiative at the portfolio level to implement a new phone billing service. The lightweight business case for the new service estimates a profit increase of $60 million per year when the service is implemented. The project at the portfolio level has a high WSJF and the resulting 30 epics at the program level also have high WSJFs. The 30 epics are decomposed into 146 stories at the team level and spread across nine teams. Stories are pulled into the teams' sprints/iterations at the team level, and the stories that embody the obvious functionality in this key strategic initiative are built over the next 8 months. Finally, the working code is released to the business but it doesn't do what the business needs—only $40 million of the potential $60 million increased profit is realized in Year 1. Why? Because not all of the 146 stories have been implemented. Some are still left somewhere in the system because the teams were not aware of the importance of the stories to the overall business value and so did not prioritize their development—those stories have been "orphaned."

Our client had a modern tool for tracking stories, but the connectivity between the stories and the original strategic initiative was lost because the value information was not mapped down at each decomposition event BECAUSE IT WASN'T THOUGHT NECESSARY TO INFORM THE DEVELOPMENT TEAMS ABOUT BUSINESS VALUE!

SAFe Portfolio Layer and Software Value

In a pull organization, informed decisions about the prioritization of the items on the portfolio backlog are vital and add to the relevance and workload of traditional portfolio management teams. The activities associated with preparing items for the portfolio backlog justify the introduction of a software portfolio management team in those organizations that do not already have one. Hence, in SAFe, we see a program portfolio management team at the portfolio level.

I mentioned earlier in the chapter that the portfolio management team needs an algorithm for deciding which ideas might be best from the ideas backlog, which "should include…a ranking based on…the current strategic priorities of the organization." At the portfolio level, SAFe includes the concept of *strategic themes* derived from the enterprise goals to address this need.

In addition to driving prioritization decisions in the portfolio management Kanban system, strategic themes should also drive the prioritization of budget allocation at the portfolio level. For example, if a bank decides that it wants or needs to build its business banking capabilities as a priority, then that becomes a strategic theme. When the time comes to allocate annual budgets to software development value streams, it could be appropriate to allocate more of the budget to business banking (more software development teams) at the expense of, say, consumer banking (fewer software development teams).

SAFe Value Stream Layer and Software Value

The organizational structure in large enterprises most often consists of business units organized around functionality (e.g., human resources [HR], design, IT, manufacturing), or business units organized around products and services (e.g., Ford trucks division, Ford cars division), or business units organized around customers/geographies (e.g., consumer division, B2B division, North America, Europe). In many, if not most, large organizations, some combination of all of these is in place.

SAFe applies lean principles by seeking to orient and organize software development teams around the stream of business value *from concept to cash*. Clearly, this concept-to-cash model is most easily understood in the context of the *for-profit* end of our lens but restated as *concept to value*, it can work equally well for the *not-for-profits*. This means that sometimes value streams are defined by individual business units in large organizations if the business units are organized around products/services or customers. More often, SAFe value streams involve parts of several business units.

Once a value stream is defined, SAFe recommends the assignment of several functions and roles at the value stream level as can be seen in Figure 5.3. For our interests in maximizing the flow of business value, I have picked out a few key functions/roles:

- Economic framework: This is the embodiment of all the economic principles that we have discussed at the portfolio level starting with Reinertsen's number one priority, "take an economic view" and going right down to WSJF.
- VSE (value stream engineer): The name of this role derives from the use of a train analogy from the earliest days of SAFe and refers to the train driver rather than any particular engineering capability. The role is important though because the VSE is effectively the Scrum master of the value stream. It is the VSE's job to remove impediments that hinder the value stream's ability to deliver value.
- Customer: "Customers are the ultimate economic buyer of every solution."*

---

* See http://scaledagileframework.com/customer/

While the value stream level is only really relevant for large organizations with large, interdependent software development activities, it certainly helps to manage scale in such large organizations. The value stream concept is important for understanding how to organize multiple teams working on the same product or program. I will return to value streams in Chapter 6.

Summary

In this chapter, I have introduced some of the main challenges that organizations will face when applying executive-level, strategic decision-making to a business value-driven software development group. Primarily, this chapter has been about a new approach to portfolio management. Lean thinking and scaled Agile techniques, even if the predominant methodology is Waterfall, will help, and there are techniques that will help with prioritizing work by business value.

In the next chapter, I will dig deeper into the functions and roles that need to be in place to connect the dots between portfolio management and the teams.

Chapter 6

Business Value from Products and Programs

In Chapter 5, I discussed how to plan for and manage software value at the strategic, portfolio level. In this chapter, I will discuss how the sort of business value-driven approach at the portfolio level described in Chapter 5 is best handled at the product/program level and the implications of value-driven software development. However, as this is being written, most of the challenges in managing for maximum business value at the product/program level are not being driven by downward pressure from senior IT management, but by upward pressure from the Agile teams.

Product or Program?

Already in this chapter and earlier in the book, I have referred to products and programs interchangeably. To some readers, this may have seemed odd, perhaps even confusing, so it's time to clarify the similarities and differences between the terms in the sense that I use them in this book before we proceed further. I have consciously avoided use of the term *project* in this section because that term is so ill-defined and overused in our field that it would only add to the confusion. Readers should feel free to add their own interpretation of project to my definitions in this section. Also, in the interest of avoiding further confusion, I am not going to use the term *services* in this chapter. Instead, I am going to assume that products include services.

Similarities between Products and Programs

The main similarity between product and program (and my primary excuse for using them interchangeably at times) is that they both represent a level of logical aggregation and purpose above the day-to-day team level of software developers, designers, analysts, testers, and so on working to produce software.

Let's assume that a group of developers, testers, and so on can be identified as working full-time on a set of deliverables that are logically separable from the work that their colleagues are doing. Let's call this a team. In Scrum, such a team would be defined as usually having five to nine members, but that's not a hard and fast rule and it would certainly not apply to Waterfall teams.

Using this definition, if the deliverables of this initial team will be combined with the deliverables being worked on concurrently and, usually, sequentially by other similar teams, then our initial team is most likely part of a product or program that consists of many teams.

If our initial team has no dependencies on other teams and the code being worked on has no interfaces to code that other teams are working on, then our initial team is likely not part of a product or program in the sense that I am using in this book. Of course, there are plenty of exceptions that disprove the rule. For example, I know of one organization that uses Agile with a small development group of about 50 people organized into 6 scrum teams. This group cannot be aggregated tidily into a product or program group because, based on the way the organization defines its products and services, the 6 teams work on around 45 products.

How many teams is too many? Is there an upper limit to the size of a product or program?

In Waterfall organizations, in practice, there is no upper limit to the size of a product or program group. This is both a strength and weakness of Waterfall. As car manufacturers found out early in the twentieth century, if you decompose work into functional jobs, then the decomposition can continue to very small chunks of work and the work can be scaled effortlessly. Unfortunately, decomposing and scaling software development is not quite as easy as this, but there are some huge products and programs out there employing thousands of developers concurrently against plans called *work breakdown structures* (WBS). Such large groups require a strong, efficient, and effective project management infrastructure to succeed and often they fail—usually because of the exponential increase in communication difficulty and overhead as the team size grows.

Agile is in many ways a revolutionary movement against the massive development team working off of extensive WBS. And yet, even with the strongest Agile principles implemented, some organizations need to work on big projects that require a lot of staff. As I have mentioned in Chapter 5, there are a number of *framework* approaches (usually referred to as *scaling Agile*) that provide this aggregating management infrastructure for the Agile methodology.

We have seen Figure 6.1 before in Chapter 5. It shows one approach, the *Scaled Agile Framework* or SAFe. SAFe offers an interesting answer to how far teams can be aggregated into products or programs by introducing a new building block above the team level, which they call the *Agile Release Train* (ART). To avoid the

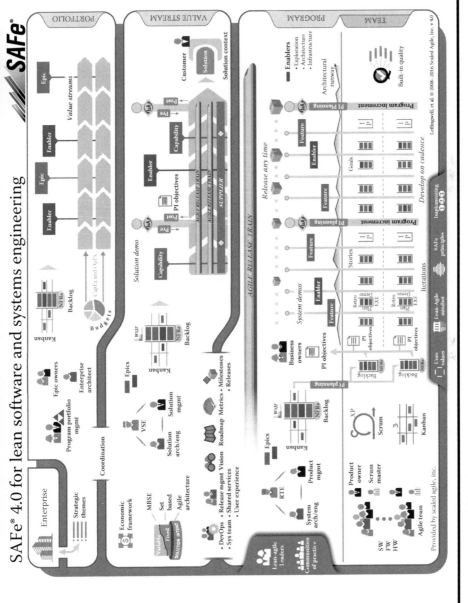

Figure 6.1   SAFe 4.0 big picture.

huge destructive communications overhead of larger teams, ARTs are constrained in size to 5–12 teams, which equates to roughly 50–125 team members (based on Dunbar's number*). This is thought to be the largest organizational size at which all group members can continue to communicate effectively without too much overhead. In SAFe, if products or programs require more than 125 people or 12 teams, then a second ART is started and so on. The upper constraint on size in SAFe is defined by all of the ARTs contained in a single *value stream*. We have considered the SAFe *value stream layer* in Chapter 5, and value streams are a critical concept in maximizing business value from software. I will return to them a little later in this chapter.

Differences between Products and Programs

In the context of this chapter, there are two major differences between products and programs:

- Longevity: Programs tend to be set in place to build a particular new system or large enhancement to an existing system, such that the program ceases when the system is built (although, of course, ongoing maintenance and future small enhancements can sometimes be included in an ongoing program). Products tend to have a longer life involving multiple upgrades, multiple versions, multiple platforms, and so on.
- Lens: Programs tend to be used to build software for in-house use whereas products tend to be built for sale.

For the purposes of this chapter, the similarities are more important than the differences.

Software Value for Product/Program with Enabling Portfolio Strategy

In Chapter 5, I discussed some of the ways to organize software portfolio management to maximize business value. I described the four layers of SAFe and the assumption that value streams sit within or below the portfolio level as a way of sub-dividing funding and work according to the priorities at the portfolio level. If an organization has a portfolio management practice, then that practice and its processes must be integrated with the value prioritization processes at lower levels. In this section, I will assume that there is a portfolio management system in place and that it includes, or can relatively easily be aligned with, the concept of value

---

* https://en.wikipedia.org/wiki/Dunbar%27s_number

streams. In the next section, I will look at how the product/program level might be organized in the absence of an enabling portfolio strategy.

As an aside, I have had two conversations with clients in the past month about how software development managers can interface their Agile planning for the coming year with the budget planning demands of the chief financial officer (CFO) and the portfolio management team. These two groups use different business languages and still think largely in terms of funding projects as in the old Waterfall days. Interestingly, both conversations opened with, "Is there a tool that will interface my Agile team plans with finance's budgeting systems?" In both cases, I recommended attempting to close the cultural gap between the top-down, command, and control portfolio management (*push*) and the bottom-up, lean-Agile *pull* development model BEFORE trying to introduce or modify a tool. The first step in this process is to introduce the concept of value streams.

Value Streams

Value stream is another one of those terms that has several meanings in software engineering and, hence, is almost useless as a core concept because it means different things to different people. However, it is so important to our desire to maximize the flow of business value through software development that I am going to stick with it and use the SAFe meaning of the term,*

> Value streams are the primary SAFe construct for understanding, orga-
> nizing, and delivering value. Each value stream is a long-lived series of
> steps that an enterprise uses to provide a continuous flow of value to a
> customer.

Note that we are referring to value streams generically here, not the specific instance of the SAFe value stream layer. Another term frequently used to help define a value stream is *concept to cash* (sometimes modified to *concept to value* for non-profits). Some examples are probably necessary before we go any further:

■ Let's first consider a product development company like Apple. The idea of concept to cash for, say, the first Apple iPhone is a relatively simple value stream where further enhancements and new versions of the iPhone are extending the life of the value stream. There were hardware teams and software teams working on this value stream and, if it had been organized under SAFe, probably several ARTs.

■ Taking the Apple example to a slightly more complicated place, the iPod was a breakthrough product, which depended on the availability of the iTunes music marketplace for its success. In retrospect, we can see that there are two

---

* http://scaledagileframework.com/value-streams/

value streams here, but initially they could have been part of the same value stream.

■ Banks offer some good examples of choice for value streams. Arguably, but not practically, a bank is one value stream providing banking services to its customers. In practice, we can see that different bank customers have different needs (corporate, small business, consumer, mortgages, credit cards, etc.). So, as far as software development goes, each of these different bank offerings is a good candidate to be a value stream in its own right. Equally, a smaller bank might just have two value streams, say, business and consumer.

■ For a bookseller like Barnes & Noble in the United States, with traditional stores, online sales, and an electronic reader, those three *channels* to the customer could be one value stream or three value streams.

■ For a not-for-profit like a government department, value streams are likely to align with departments (e.g., health, social security), but even within departments there might be enough work for separate value streams. For example, in social security, there might be a value stream related to providing services and a value stream related to providing payments. Payments could be split into pensions and welfare.

Perhaps you can see from these examples that a pattern is emerging. Separate value streams are possible, even desirable, when the customers' expectations for value are different. We must expect that different value streams will have different measures of business value from software. The corollary of this statement is that similar value streams are likely to, and should, have similar measures of business value. For example, Barnes & Noble's online book sales should have very similar measures of business value to Amazon's online book sales.

Value streams are an important link between portfolio management and the development teams, because looking from the developer's perspective up to the program management level, value streams should look like logical organizations of related work on related systems and applications. Looking from the top, portfolio-level down, value streams look like a logical breakdown of the organization's activities. Further, looking from the portfolio-level down, the size and funding of the value streams should reflect an appropriate distribution of the organization's investment monies according to the organization's current strategy.

Two important points about value streams fall out of these examples: First, to the point made in the SAFe definition, some value streams will be very long standing to the point of being, to all intents and purposes, permanent. (Will Amazon ever be out of the online books business?) Second, if we are funding long-standing value streams, then the construct for organizing software development work that we call "projects" becomes much less important as a funding mechanism. Instead, we fund the number of teams (and ARTs or their equivalent) within a value stream that are enabled by the strategy-defined proportion of total software development funds flowing to that value stream in a given period. The ARTs and teams pull work packages (projects, epics, or whatever) off of the value stream's prioritized work backlog (derived from the portfolio backlog) in business value order (and/or weighted shortest job first) to implement the organization's strategy with business value flow maximized.

Hence, value streams (and ARTs or similar structures) provide the connection between an organization's strategic priorities to deliver business value, the number of software development teams assigned to particular strategic investments, and the order in which the teams do the work.

Value streams have other side benefits. By being organized and funded around long-standing organizational value flows to the customer, teams assigned to value streams are likely to be longer-lived than teams assigned to projects with short-term funding. Hence, they are likely to develop knowledge about the value stream, including some business knowledge, and expertise around the systems, platforms, and code associated with that value stream. This will improve the team's productivity and increase the flow of business value per unit cost.

Some executives might be getting nervous at this point about value streams. Projects come and go, they can be funded and defunded or cancelled very easily—won't long-lived value streams start to look like fixed costs with no flexibility to meet changing needs? The short answer to this is that they shouldn't be allowed to. While some value streams may be long-lived, that does not mean that they should, or are likely to, have the same level of resources every year. For example, my Amazon online book sales value stream example might have 12 teams for 3 years, 2 teams for 6 months, and 10 teams for the next 6 months.

According to Weinberg (1992) and others, it is counter-productive to split people's time or move people around between too many different projects. The same applies to too much movement between unrelated value streams. It applies to a much lesser extent to movement between teams in the same value stream.

Value Stream Mapping and Analysis

In SAFe, value streams have a specific meaning and use, which is consistent with the way that value streams are defined more generally in lean software engineering (Poppendieck and Poppendieck 2007) as concept to cash value flows. However, in pursuing the lean goal of removal of waste (non-value add) activities, we can examine value streams in more detail by using value stream mapping and analysis. An example of a value stream map and analysis in shown in Figure 6.2.

Figure 6.2 shows a flow chart of the actual activities that might occur in developing a particular piece of software (Poppendieck and Poppendieck 2006). The flow chart has been annotated with the duration of each step, the value added during that step, and the cumulative duration of the project. For simplicity's sake here, we are assuming that the time reported when actual work was being done is the same as the value added. As

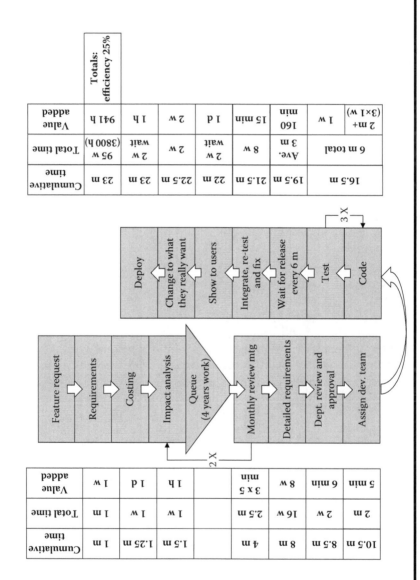

Cumulative time	Total time	Value added	Totals: efficiency 25%
16.5 m	6 m total	1 w	
19.5 m	Ave. 3 m	160 min	
21.5 m	8 w	15 min	
22 m	2 w wait	1 d	
22.5 m	2 w	2 w	
23 m	2 w wait	1 h	
23 m	95 w (3800 h)	941 h	

Deploy — Change to what they really want — Show to users — Integrate, re-test and fix — Wait for release every 6 m — Test — Code

3 X

Feature request — Requirements — Costing — Impact analysis — Queue (4 years work) — Monthly review mtg — Detailed requirements — Dept. review and approval — Assign dev. team

2 X

Cumulative time	10.5 m	8.5 m	8 m	4 m		1.5 m	1.5 m	1.25 m	1 m
Total time	2 m	2 m	16 w	2.5 m		1 w	1 w	1 w	1 m
Value added	5 min	6 min	8 w	3 x 5 min		1 h	1 d	1 w	

Figure 6.2   Value stream example.

we all know, that is not necessarily the case, but that is a matter for a different book. From our perspective of maximizing the business value of software, there are some key features of Figure 6.2 that should be noted:

■ The overall efficiency is about 25%. That is, 75% of the elapsed time did not include any value-add activities. This clearly represents an opportunity for improvement in time to market. That being said, this does not mean that resource utilization was necessarily low because we can assume that people were working on other things during the various times when this project was stalled. Indeed, it is likely that several of the delays were due to staff being utilized on other projects and not immediately available for this one. Examples are all over the flowchart from the 1 week of requirements work that took 1 month to complete through to the delay of 2 months to assign a development team. It is a fundamental tenet of lean that maximizing resource utilization does not maximize end-to-end efficiency of a process.
■ There is a queue before the management review step labeled with *4-years' work*. The 4 years' work is the size of the queue in terms of the sum of the efforts required for all of the projects in the queue divided by the capacity of the software development teams. For example, if there are 40 projects in the queue, each requiring 12 person months of effort, a total of 4800 person months, and the size of the development team is 10 people, then the length of the queue is 4800/10 = 48 months or 4 years. The implication is that, if nothing else enters the queue, then the last project will be completed in 4 years' time. However, if our example team in Figure 6.2 typically has a 25 percent efficiency then the time to market is more likely to be closer to 16 years (unless the inefficiency has been perfectly factored into the estimates)! In practice, of course, projects that have sat in the queue for more than three to four management reviews are never going to be developed and should be removed from the queue. Our example project in Figure 6.2 was assumed to get approved after only two passes of the management review.
■ The flow chart clearly reflects a Waterfall development model, and there are a couple of characteristics of our example that suggest our hypothetical company might want to consider Agile to improve the business value of their project! The time to market of 21 months is a good first sign that the users' needs might have changed considerably since the initial *feature request*. Indeed, if the *show to users* and *change to what they really wanted* steps truly only took 4 weeks of elapsed time, then this development team is either very diligent or very lucky or maybe both. In this context, notice that our example team waited for 3 months to get into the 6-monthly release before the project could be shown to the users. In an Agile world, the users input would be sought much earlier—certainly before the code was loaded into a release—and the users input could have been quickly accommodated. Much more frequent releases in Agile remove this period of time waiting for releases, but even in

Waterfall, a lean approach would move the user feedback into the release wait period and save some time after the release.

▪ Agile advocates may have glanced at Figure 6.2 and quickly concluded that, as a Waterfall flow chart, it does not apply to their world. However, if they are still reading, I would recommend a second look because most, if not all, of the activities in Figure 6.2 still have to occur in the Agile model—they are just greatly sped up. Herein lies a challenge. If all the activities cannot be sped up in your organization, then your ability to benefit from Agile will be constrained. For example, if your management still insists on a monthly review meeting and only processes a limited number of projects in the queue each month, then that inefficiency remains built into the process no matter how good the Scrum teams are. The same is true if approved projects still have to wait two months for a development team to be assigned.

Value stream mapping and analysis clearly has a place in improving the flow of business value from software development, whether an organization is using Agile or Waterfall. It is particularly useful in Agile organizations for detecting if the program and portfolio levels above the Agile teams are enabling or constraining the flow of business value.

Software Value for Product/Program without Enabling Portfolio Strategy

What part does software value play at the product or program tier of an organization if the organization's top-level strategy does not consider or measure software value? Frankly, of the two scenarios I consider in this chapter, this situation is currently the most likely to be found in most organizations carrying out software development.

The answer is different for Waterfall organizations and Agile organizations and very confusing for organizations that use both models (a large percentage of organizations at the time of writing this book). Before I consider these answers separately, I recommend the concept of value streams with value stream mapping and analysis that I covered earlier in the chapter for starting the process of thinking about value even when there is no downward pressure from executive management or a portfolio management team. Quite simply, a single product or program has a high probability of being a value stream in its own right so management at the product or program level does not need broader span of control than their own product or program to start to plan and act with a concept to cash value stream mentality.

Product/Program Value in Waterfall Organizations

Starting with the assumption that there is no requirement being imposed from the portfolio level to manage or measure software value, it is very unlikely that software value will ever be considered at the product/program level by the development team in a Waterfall organization. Remember that this is a command and control model in which the development teams are organized to best process the work that is pushed onto them. As such, the responsibility for any maximization of software value flow falls onto the product managers and program/project managers, and input from the business unit tends to be minimized (or even excluded).

Program/project managers have a limited set of goals, which contain implied but not explicit value delivery goals. In my experience, program/project managers live, and die, by delivering on budget, on time, on quality, and on scope. Usually, their priorities follow that order. Of course, achieving some of these goals for a program or project will deliver some business value, and achieving all of them will deliver more business value. However, in the absence of top-down pressure to measure business value, there is rarely any incentive for the program/project managers to assign different business value to different projects within the program or to different new features within the product.

This raises the question, especially from a lean software engineering perspective, about if and how program/project managers add value to the software development process. I believe that the most value added by program/project managers is in large projects, which require careful planning and monitoring due to the complexity of communications between the various parts of the project/program. However, these are precisely the sort of projects that fail most often. As I have stated before, such failure in large projects has led directly to the Agile movement and, consequently, more questions about the value of program/project management offices (PMOs). Agile is not right for all organizations or all products/programs, so how should PMOs adapt to add more value and, just as importantly, continue to have their voices heard on issues of communication and coordination (a weak link of most large Agile implementations)? Whether your organization uses Waterfall, Agile, or a combination of the two, I believe that program and project managers have a role to play in a new software value management office (see Chapter 9) working alongside the product managers and system architects.

Product managers have to be the champions of maximizing value flow through the Waterfall organization. It is the product manager's job to ensure that the work pushed to the development teams is prioritized such that the highest value work is done first. Product managers are also responsible for maintaining and communicating a product vision externally and internally of where the product is going (including end of life) and a product roadmap for getting there. These two documents are hugely important for driving tactical decision-making by the development teams. For example, in choosing how much time to spend on the implementation of a new feature, knowing how important that feature will be in the future system will inform the development teams' decisions on how robustly the feature needs to be built and tested, how much it is likely to need to be extended in the future and so on.

In my experience, most product managers recognize their role in prioritizing the most valuable features, but this is not an easy task in the face of conflicting business priorities. For example, in a software product company, there is often a conflict between the needs of existing customers and the needs of prospective customers who are considering buying the product. By definition, if the prospective customers were satisfied with the product "as is" then they would have bought it already. Instead, they are looking for those extra features that will make it easier for them to implement without too much business process re-engineering, or those extra features that will match competitors' capabilities and, consequently, make their product selection easier. For existing customers, such new features can be either irrelevant ("we are doing very nicely with the software as is, thank you") or desirable. Either way, the new features can be problematic if they result in increased license fees or new costs to change business processes. Most of the time, existing customers prefer stability over change and prefer improvements to existing features over the addition of new ones.

Hence, product managers must tread a careful path in planning the roadmap and the development work priorities. Unfortunately, very few product managers have or use value management tools like the value visualization framework described in Chapter 7 to help them make, communicate, and get consensus on their value prioritization decisions. To enable the implementation of the tools and processes necessary for product managers to do their jobs and work better with the program/project managers in a Waterfall organization, again, I recommend the creation of a software value management office.

Often, when we are looking at a program rather than a product, there is no clear product manager in place. In this case, the program manager or one of the program management team must explicitly take on the role of product manager to ensure that the program delivers or enhances a sustainable product. With the creation of a software value management office in a program, the role of product manager can be readily accommodated.

Product/Program Value in Agile Organizations

In Agile organizations, it is common that there is no requirement to manage or measure software value being imposed from the portfolio level. Historically, Agile found its way into organizations through the activities of a few curious people in entry-level positions of the organization doing some research online, maybe taking a class or two, and then finding a way to create a Scrum team for a small project. The first couple of Scrum teams often went unnoticed by the PMO, but not by the business people and/or product managers involved who were delighted to be involved in the early feedback process and even more delighted to see desirable results coming quickly and regularly. Developers enjoyed the relative freedom to be creative and even the accountability associated with delivering small chunks of work. They did not miss the death marches or mandatory "voluntary," unpaid overtime work often associated with Waterfall. At this small, informal level, Scrum was confined to the team level and did not seriously impinge on the product/program level.

While some early adopters saw the need for and implemented top-to-bottom processes to support an Agile development environment, most have tripped over the challenges of providing structure at the product/portfolio level by accident. Part of this challenge is that the number of scrum teams often grows organically with limited structure with, perhaps, a Scrum of Scrums structure or some form of planning and coordination assistance from the (Waterfall-oriented) PMO. As soon as the number of scrum teams working on a particular product or program grew above the three or four teams who could self-organize relatively easily, more structure was needed at the product/program level.

The bottom-up revolution of Agile in many cases created organizations with a strong left-sided *Agile Manifesto** culture (and some revolutionary individuals) at the team level that resists any and all attempts to introduce any type of structure around and above the teams that might threaten the Manifesto's declaration of valuing, "individuals and interactions over process and tools." While the Manifesto makes some strong statements about "value," the bottom-up evolution has left many teams inwardly focused when they think about value. Some, more mature Scrum teams have processes for deciding the business value of the stories they are working on (see Chapter 7), but the insularity of the teams usually means that these metrics are not shared outside the team, are not scalable, and are probably based purely on the product owner's assessment, which may or may not be in line with the product/program or portfolio manager's perspective.

To build a business value-based Agile development product or program, the product and/or program manager needs to work with the product owners to develop a product/program backlog prioritized by business value (perhaps using weighted shortest job first). Each epic or story should be assigned a business value with a consistent process across the product or program, such that product owners can work with teams to measure value delivered over time, even if such metrics are only relative. I discuss some ideas for implementing this at the team level in Chapter 7, but the initiative to coordinate and measure the process must come from the product/program level whenever there are enough (greater than five) teams to justify structure at this level.

Where there are large or multiple products and/or programs, I recommend coordinating the measurement process and analysis of results through a software value management office.

---

* http://www.agilemanifesto.org/. By "left-sided culture," I refer to the tendency of some people to interpret the manifesto's assertion, "that is, while there is value in the items on the right, we value the items on the left more," as meaning "the items on the left are good and the items on the right are bad." Not the original intention.

Organizations Using Agile and Waterfall

For organizations using both Agile and Waterfall without the imperative for value management at the product/program level coming from above, I recommend starting with a software value management office as described in Chapter 9. My justification is that understanding the different ways that value is delivered through the two processes is essential to establishing a means for prioritizing and coordinating work. Some years ago, as head of product management, I ran a project through which a new (to the organization) Agile team developed a new front-end for a legacy software product, which was to undergo three new feature releases during the initial duration of the Agile front-end project. The Agile team quite rightly decided that the early activities for them, which would add the most business value, would be to develop the interfaces to the legacy product under the new technology being used for the front-end. For the legacy team, this meant that they would also have to do work on the legacy product's application program interfaces (APIs) to enable connectivity to the new front-end. That work would require dropping some legacy product features from the next release that had already been promised to existing customers. We worked out a clever compromise, but only through a lot of coordination and the development of a context-specific value system for prioritizing the work of the two groups based on business value as defined (and defended) by my product management team.

Contributions to Maximizing Software Value at the Product/Program Level

While it is very beneficial to have a full organizational software value strategy with some elements (e.g., budgeting and accounting using value prioritization) being much better implemented at the portfolio level across the whole organization, it is important to recognize here that value management at the product/program level is both the most important level of value management and the only potentially self-sufficient level of value management.

If the portfolio-level assigns strategic business value to software development initiatives explicitly by using Kanban techniques to build portfolio backlogs, it can be very helpful in maximizing business value flow. However, it is not a necessary function for maximizing business value flow because strategic value decisions can be inferred from the budgets assigned to products or programs. In the absence of prioritization at the product/program level, either there will not be value metrics or mature teams may include value information in their tactical prioritization decisions. Such team-level prioritization may result in local optimization of business value flow but not the end-to-end maximization of business value we are seeking.

This, then, is the responsibility of the product/program level: to ensure end-to-end business value flow is maximized.

Summary

In this chapter, I have looked in more detail at the product or program level of aggregation of software development activity. I have considered the role of the product/program level as a channel for the implementation of strategic decisions when there is a process for top-level value management and when there is not. I have highlighted the important role of value streams in organizing product- and program-level work based on connectedness through a concept-to-cash model.

We have seen that value stream mapping and analysis can help to make software development activities leaner and perhaps even drive the transition from Waterfall to Agile. I have introduced the concept of a software value management office at the product/program level and some of the roles it can play—more of this in Chapter 9. Finally, I have stressed the importance of the product/program level in maximizing end-to-end value flow.

In the next chapter, I will consider how value management impacts the teams and some of the techniques that can be used to communicate value between the product/program level and the teams.

Chapter 7

Establishing Software Value Tactics

In Chapter 5, I discussed how to plan for and manage software value at the strategic, portfolio level. In Chapter 6, I looked at the program or product level of organizing software development to maximize the *business value* of software. In this chapter, I will discuss how the business value-driven approach at the portfolio and product/program levels can and should positively impact the tactical decisions made by software development teams and individuals at the level where code is written, reviewed, and tested—the team level.

My premise in this chapter is that teams and individual members of teams will make better decisions if they are given a mission to maximize business value from software by increasing the flow of business value through software development. To do this, they need information about the business value of the various deliverables they have in front of them so that they can make the right tactical decisions to maximize business value flow and/or ask questions about the choices they face. It is important to note here that I am not advocating the replacement of one type of command and control (i.e., classic Waterfall) with another—always do the highest labeled business value task first. Instead, I am seeking to make the conversations about priorities between individuals, teams, and product or program managers revolve around, "How can we maximize business value flow?" Perhaps surprisingly, at the team level, the answer is to manage queues!

The Why and How of Queue Management for Software Development

We have discussed the use of backlogs at the portfolio and product/program levels of organizations and these are certainly queues to which good queue management principles should be applied. However, it is at the team level where tactical decisions are being made daily about which tasks should be worked on and which should sit idle. It is at the team level where management of queues is simply about making those tactical decisions in the best way possible for maximum business value flow.

In Chapter 3 of his book, Don Reinertsen (2009) provides an overview of queuing theory in the context of product development, which I would recommend to readers wishing to do a deeper dive, particularly into the mathematical justifications, which I have not included here.

While all of the principles espoused by Reinertsen are relevant to software development, the following six principles, summarized in Figure 7.1, represent a simplified, logical thought process for establishing a value management capability at the team level for managing queues:

1. Software development inventory is physically and financially invisible.
   a. Making value visible is a key driver for improving business value at the team level. I describe some ways to approach value visualization later in this chapter.

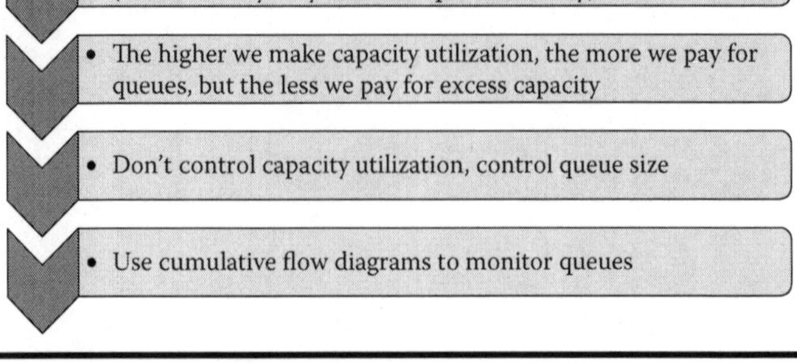

- Software development inventory is physically and financially invisible
- Queues are the root cause of the majority of economic waste in software development
- Increasing resource utilization increases queues exponentially (but variability only increases queues linearly)
- The higher we make capacity utilization, the more we pay for queues, but the less we pay for excess capacity
- Don't control capacity utilization, control queue size
- Use cumulative flow diagrams to monitor queues

Figure 7.1 Six principles of queue management.

2. Queues are the root cause of the majority of economic waste in software development.
   a. Queues create
      i. Longer cycle time—because tasks spend more time in queues (waste) and less time being worked on (value).
      ii. Increased risk—because the world changes as time passes so the longer a task sits around in queues, the more likely that its usefulness, as originally defined, will diminish.
      iii. More variability—when process flows are operated at or near capacity, more tasks are held in queues and the actual cycle time for any particular task becomes less predictable.
      iv. More overhead—because more tasks in process equals more tasks that have to be tracked and reported.
      v. Lower quality—because feedback from users is delayed, potentially to the point where the users can't remember why they asked for that feature in the first place. This is particularly true in Waterfall systems where delayed tasks can miss their scheduled release date.
      vi. Less motivation—development team members are not motivated to finish quickly or get creative about their solution when they know the task they are working on is just going to go into their colleague's (long) queue. Over time, they may question why they are working here at all. Unfortunately, it is often the best and quickest developers who experience queue delays most often and least sympathetically.
3. Increasing resource utilization increases queues exponentially (but variability only increases queues linearly).
   a. Reinertsen covers the mathematics behind this assertion, but the key point to understand is that managing queues is significantly more beneficial than trying to standardize tasks. Unlike in manufacturing, in software development it is both difficult and undesirable to manage variability. It is reassuring then that something we cannot control (i.e., variability) only has a linear impact on queue size, while something we can control (i.e., utilization) has a much more significant impact. Of course, it is unfortunate that many, if not most, organizations are managing utilization to maximize it at the expense of value flow!
4. Optimum queue size is an economic trade-off.
   a. Reinertsen (2009) expresses the, often hidden, trade-off concisely, "The higher we make capacity utilization, the more we pay for queues, but the less we pay for excess capacity."
   b. Queue cost is affected by the sequence in which we handle the jobs in the queue. In manufacturing, queues of a given production line are relatively homogeneous because the production line tends to be making the same

(or very similar) things at any given time. Hence, the order in which tasks are pulled from the queues does not matter. However, in software development, different tasks are likely to have very different characteristics in terms of business value, resource requirements, time to complete, dependencies to and from other tasks, and so on. Hence, in software development, different tasks in a queue have different costs of delay. Cost of delay (CoD) is a strong proxy for business value, and Reinertsen advocates strongly that,

"If you only quantify one thing, quantify cost of delay."

5. Don't control capacity utilization, control queue size.
   a. This is an important and radical message for teams and team leaders in software development because it is different from what most of them do today. Making queues and their impact visible is very important.
6. Use cumulative flow diagrams to monitor queues.
   a. Cumulative flow diagrams chart the flow of tasks through a process and can provide predictive information about the build-up of queues between the steps in the process. Cumulative flow diagrams were described with examples in Chapter 3.

Waterfall and Queue Management

As I have noted before in this book, Waterfall is primarily a command and control methodology for software development. Consequently, it might come as a surprise that there is any scope for decision-making at a tactical, team level. It might be more surprising that such tactical decisions can influence the flow of business value. However, within the broad constraints of the project plan and the work breakdown structure, it is at the team and individual levels where information about the flow of work is up-to-date and decisions are made by team leads and individuals on a daily basis to maximize resource utilization.

It is the pursuit of efficiency through maximizing resource utilization at the team level that has the biggest negative effect on the flow of business value in Waterfall software development teams. Put simply, the teams and individuals are pursuing the wrong goal. To understand how to better maximize business value flow, Waterfall managers need to be able to understand the impact of queues and visualize their value flows using tools such as the cumulative flowchart described in Chapter 3.

The breakdown of the software development process into separate functional steps in Waterfall often leads to (probably well-meaning) local optimization of the operations in one or more separate functions (e.g., design or testing), which causes queues of work-in-progress to build up between separate functions and, hence, suboptimal flow. The problem is made worse by the fact that the queues are not very visible. Even when there is some visibility in Waterfall, often the issues cannot be resolved at the team level because of the hierarchical structure of the Waterfall organization by function (e.g., the test team lead sees the problem, but the development team lead does not). It might require a conversation between the head of development and the head of test to resolve the problem.

While providing information about the relative business value of tasks in a Waterfall organization can help, it cannot fix these problems because a change of goal from maximizing utilization to maximizing business value is required. It is difficult to achieve this change of culture in a Waterfall organization where everything else stays the same.

One of the reasons organizations changing from Waterfall to Agile have experienced greater productivity is that Agile provides a tangible new process that people can focus on that can bring cultural change with it. Agile has an advantage over Waterfall in that it is easier for teams with the ability and authority to self-organize to respond positively to information about the relative business value of their tasks. However, in my opinion, Agile without the cultural change is not enough, and too often I have seen organizations implement the mechanics of Scrum without understanding the economic drivers. The result works mechanically in that tasks get accomplished, but the potential for business value maximization is not met.

The functionally hierarchical nature of Waterfall makes the team level something of an arbitrary construct because people are assigned to projects and tasks based on their availability and functional capability rather than being a member of a team that decides which tasks to take on next. Consequently, I believe that Kanban (see Appendix) is often a better first step for Waterfall organizations than Scrum because the process steps from Waterfall can stay in place and each functional team can pull work from the preceding team's queue without necessarily forming a strong cross-functional team relationship. The lean software engineering drivers are clearer, the queues are easier to make visible, and the cumulative flow diagrams are easy to generate. The Agile community has, somewhat debatably, adopted Kanban as its own, and so it is seen as an Agile practice, but I would suggest that it is really closer to Waterfall with a strong lean driver.

Agile and Queue Management

Most Agile practitioners are aware that Agile practices are built on the principles of lean, but few understand that the most common practices are designed to maximize flow by reducing batch sizes and minimizing queues. For example, the effect of the practices of small teams (7 ± 2) and short iterations/sprints (2 weeks) is to break the work up into small batches, which tends to reduce queues. It is this lack of understanding of why Agile practices work that can harm organizations that attempt to implement Agile practices in a customized way to minimize change from their status quo—the so-called Scrum-but implementations. For example, we have seen in this chapter that maximizing resource utilization increases queue size exponentially, which then reduces value flow. Unfortunately, many software development team leads and, indeed, even the most junior staff believe that if they are sitting idle for a short period of time then they are not being effective or contributing fully. This is an understandable mistake, which simply requires training to correct.

I mentioned earlier in this book that there are several different approaches to scaling Agile once the number of teams working on a single product or program grows to more than about five. However, at the team level, while there are endless variations on a theme, the vast majority of Agile teams use the Scrum methodology first established by Ken Schwaber and Mike Beedle in 2001 (Schwaber and Beedle 2001). For readers not familiar with Scrum, an overview of this methodology is included in the Appendix. Over the past 10 years, a few Agile teams have started to use the Kanban methodology borrowed from lean manufacturing and updated for software engineering. If there is a logical case for choosing between the adoption of Scrum or Kanban for a particular team, and often there is not, Kanban is most often chosen where there is a steady flow of small tasks with little effort needed by the team to prioritize or understand the tasks. A good example of where Kanban might be a good choice is where a software maintenance team has been set up to work through a backlog of defects or small, low priority enhancements in the software.

I have already discussed the relatively easy identification of queues in Kanban—between the functional steps—but where are the queues in Scrum? Figure 7.2 sets out the five main types of Scrum queue.

The most obvious queue in Scrum is the sprint backlog.* The sprint backlog is certainly a queue that needs to be managed, but it is a good example of how lean thinking and knowledge of the importance of queue management has influenced the design of Scrum because the sprint backlog is highly visible to the Scrum team and should be cleared at the end of every sprint. However, the sprint backlog in many (perhaps most) organizations is not a good queue from a business value perspective because when stories are pulled into the sprint backlog from the product/ program or portfolio backlogs, they are not prioritized from an economic, business value perspective. There is little or no consideration of CoD. Even when the product owner assigns (personal?) business value points to stories, as is the case in some mature Scrum teams (and I like this if nothing else is in place), this represents local optimization.

Sometimes the sprint backlog is not fully executed because of unexpected difficulties, bugs that emerge, or changes that the product owner or customer wants to make at the sprint review. This feedback can lead to the second type of queue—one that is not explicitly defined in Scrum and therefore not visible in many teams—the *rework queue.*

---

* I use the term "sprint" in this chapter rather than "iteration" because sprint is "what I grew up with." This is pure habit, not a judgment about which of the two terms is better.

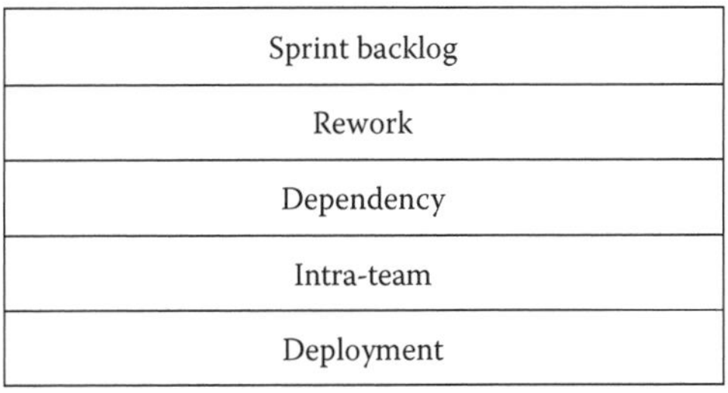

Sprint backlog
Rework
Dependency
Intra-team
Deployment

Figure 7.2 Scrum queues.

A third type of queue emerges when there are dependencies between Scrum teams or a dependency between Scrum and Waterfall teams. Perhaps some work can be done with interfaces stubbed out (not fully implemented) before the dependency is delivered, but often the task with the dependency is simply delayed until the dependency is available. Either way, work in progress starts to accumulate in the *dependency queue* until the dependency is delivered. There are always small *intra-team queues* that occur as tasks are passed around the team or delayed pending more information from another team member. Finally, there is a queue for the work that has been completed by the Scrum team but has not yet been deployed (or passed to another process such as integration testing).

With all queues, minimization starts with visualization. Generally, any visualization of queues in software development is a big step forward. The best visualization of queues includes information about business value at a granular, team, task level derived from the business value assignments made at the product/program and portfolio levels. The next section of this chapter on value visualization sets out some ideas for what this information might look like at the team level.

Value Visualization

The Problem

Generally, information technology (IT) management is not focused on value delivery. More often, they are focused on getting a few high-profile projects finished as quickly as possible. Then, because most of their budget consists of people costs (either directly or through outsourced vendors), they focus on maximizing resource utilization to minimize cost. As a consequence, IT often makes decisions for their software development projects based on

- Difficulty of the project
- How many and which resources are required
- Who shouts the loudest

Findings* from more than 1,500 software development projects analyzed by DCG Software Value (now part of the Premios Group) in 2013 and 2014 suggest that the median *cost* of a software development project for a Fortune 500 company ranges from $114,000 (offshore) to $164,000 (onshore). Without getting too statistical here, the use of the term median rather than average is important because the size and cost of projects is not a normal distribution (i.e., evenly distributed around the average). Perhaps unsurprisingly, there are many more small projects than medium-sized projects and more medium than large projects. It seems that few companies have this type of data about the size of their projects. We also found that very few of the companies surveyed knew the distribution of the *business value* of their projects so they could not communicate that information to the tactical decision-makers who are prioritizing software development resources to projects, even if they wanted to.

Why would this be so? Surely no project gets started if there is not an approved business case, right? Our experience and follow-up inquiries revealed that in most large corporations, large projects or programs usually require business cases, while most small projects don't have these requirements. Those large projects that have business cases are usually sub-divided into smaller projects. Breaking out the business value across these smaller projects is perceived to be too difficult or worthless (we will return to this challenge later).

Doesn't Agile software development solve this problem? Well, yes and no. Mature implementations of Agile prioritize product backlogs (lists of the next tasks or *stories* to work on) by business value. In some methodologies, such as the *Scaled Agile Framework* (SAFe), business representatives are encouraged to put numeric values on stories to allow for prioritization by value when tactical leaders and teams are making resource allocation decisions. However, there are three challenges even with Agile implementations:

1. There are too few Agile implementations that are mature enough to include value information.
2. Portfolio or product/program value information is not disseminated to the actual tactical decision-makers, so local product owners either make local value decisions or are simply not aware of the importance of prioritizing by business value (while the person in front of them is shouting loudly for their favorite project);
3. The information about value is not structured enough to be captured as an output metric or, even if structured, it is simply not captured. We have seen an example of this where the story management system in one corporation is perfectly capable of handling the necessary value tracking; but the teams are not held accountable for entering any data into the story management system after a particular story has been approved and funded.

---

* http://bit.ly/2qF4pua

What are the consequences of tactical decisions being made using criteria other than business value? It is not necessarily a disaster. If software development managers and teams are prioritizing based on, say, resource utilization, then resource utilization will be high, but value delivery almost certainly will not. If our goal is to maximize business value delivery or flow, then we must be able to measure value flow and identify ways to optimize it.

The solution to this problem is end-to-end *value visualization*.

Why Value Visualization?

All stakeholders and team members must know the business and economic value of the project and work toward the same goal of maximizing business value flow.

Specifically for software development, business units and IT must collaborate to define the value for each initiative, right down to the lowest level at which resourcing decisions are made. For example, in corporation X, there must be an approved business case for every project or program above a certain size, let's say $10 million. This business case will presumably include some metric such as *return on investment* (ROI). Let's assume that the project ROI can be banded as shown in Figure 7.3.

Now, let's say we have a $15 million project with a medium value ROI. For software development to start, we need to break the project up into, say, epics and stories. It probably does not make sense to do an individual business case for each epic and story, but we need to make sure that each epic and story is linked to the master project AND inherits the "T-shirt size" value label of the master project (i.e., in this case, "medium"). There should be no orphan stories (see Chapter 5).

Accountability is essential to monitor progress and assure successful attainment of the goal of maximizing business value flow. This requires slightly different metrics and, more importantly, the visualization of those metrics. A key example of the new type of metric is a cumulative flowchart, which shows the flow of stories through a software development team. Cumulative flowcharts and how to use them are covered in Chapter 3.

When we think about value visualization, it is important to remember that cost is not value any more than price is! So, why do the business units only talk

ROI	Value
Less than or equal to 5%	Rejected
6% –10%	*Low*, but worthwhile
11% – 20%	*Medium*
21% – 40%	*High*
Greater than 40%	*Very high*

Figure 7.3 Example mapping of ROI to value.

to IT about cost? If these organizations can share business value details for their initiatives, they will enable IT to become part of the ROI solution.

So, is there a comprehensive way for organizations to communicate business value information for software development projects? We should first acknowledge that even simple ways to communicate and visualize business value to the tactical decision-makers are better than none at all. I am quite happy to start with T-shirt sizes. But, we can do so much more if we use a concept such as the *value visualization framework* (VVF).

The Value Visualization Framework

VVF is a five-step process, summarized in Figure 7.4, which operates in parallel to the process that creates the business case for a project and then breaks the project down into epics and stories (or some level of tasks in a work breakdown structure).

Each epic and story should have the following information associated with it:

STEP 1: Define the units of value delivery (e.g., number of subscribers, hours saved in the process).
STEP 2: Define the value of the project in specific units (e.g., 17 new subscribers once deployed).
STEP 3: Define the size (e.g., 100 story points).
STEP 4: Define the CoD of the implementation challenge, including level of complexity, duration, and so on (e.g., $2000 penalty for a missed deadline).

Figure 7.4 Value visualization framework (VVF).

STEP 5: Quantify the economic value once deployed (e.g., $10, $15, and $20 per subscriber at weeks 9, 12, and 15 respectively)

VVF Step 4: Define the Cost of Delay

I have discussed CoD in earlier chapters. Defining the CoD is of fundamental importance to prioritizing work packets or projects or stories. Essentially, we should always prioritize projects with the highest CoD. However, identifying the CoD for a particular story is neither intuitively obvious nor easy. There are many possible approaches of which I give three examples here:

1st Approach: Explicit Cost

1. Penalty if completion date is missed (e.g., $2500 fine if not completed by Day 15)
2. Missed opportunity (e.g., the loss of an incentive—30 new subscribers will sign up if delivered by Day 17 or not!)

2nd Approach: Penalty Cost if Stories Are in Software Development Too Long

Figure 7.5 shows examples of ways to measure CoD for stories that spend too long in software development.

3rd Approach: Relative CoD of One Story against Another

This approach can allow CoD to be assigned by an informed, experienced, and representative (business and development) team with relatively little data. The process is similar to story estimation in Agile using planning poker. Usually, a limited set of numbers (e.g., Cohn scale for use in story points: 0, 0.5, 1, 2, 3, 5, 8, 13, 20, 40, 100, ?) are used, and participants must choose from this set to estimate relative CoD for each story against the other stories as in Figure 7.6.

	Example 1	Example 2	Example 3
	Count all stories with ID's S1–S14 that have not yet been deployed	Count all stories with "Day ready" < 10 that have not yet been deployed	Identify all stories with "Day ready" < 10 that have not yet been deployed. Sum the ages of these stories.
Number	6	8	36
Subscribers lost	60 (10 subscribers lost per delayed story)	–	72 (2 subscribers lost per day in process)
Total refunds	$350 ($35 per lost subscriber)	$400 ($50 per delayed story)	$1080 ($15 per subscriber-day)

Figure 7.5 Examples of costs of delay for excessive times in software development.

	Week 9	Week 12	Week 15
New subscribers this billing cycle	23	48	37
Total subscribers to date	23	71 (= 23 + 48)	108 (= 23 + 48 + 37)
Billing cycle revenue	$230 (= $10 *23)	$1065 (= $15 * 71)	$2160 (= $20 * 108)
Fines or payments	–	–	– $2500 (fine for missed regulatory deadline)
Billing cycle gross profit	$230	$1065	–$340 (= $2160 – $2500)
Cost of delay refund	–	–	–$400 (see Fig. 4, Example 2)
Total gross profit to date	$230	$1295 (= 230 + 1065)	$555 (=1295 – 340 – 400)

Figure 7.6 Example of quantifying the economic value of stories once deployed.

VVF Step 5: Quantifying the Economic Value of Stories Once Deployed

Delaying the assignment of actual market value to functionality until it is actually deployed allows fluctuations in value due to market forces or environment changes to be taken into account. The example in Figure 7.7 assumes that the value of subscribers increases as the subscriber base grows.

Hence, in week 9, each subscriber is worth $10. This goes up to $15 in week 12 and $20 in week 15. This is based on advertising revenue per subscriber increasing as the number of subscribers increases. Of course, the value could just as easily fall!

Resource Allocation at a Tactical Level

With the full VVF in place (even if only T-shirt sizes), teams and team leads with resources to deploy against incoming stories or tasks must prioritize based on

1. Business value
2. CoD
3. Resource availability

Story	Cost of Delay*
Story 1	5
Story 2	1
Story 3	8
Story 4	5

Figure 7.7 Relative CoD using a modified Fibonacci set of numbers.

Lenses on the VVF

Is the VVF useful in all software development scenarios? Let's consider the three lenses that I described in Chapter 1:

■ The Profit Lens: For-profit or not-for-profit organizations. Whether using relative business value or actual business value in the form of ROI or payback period, or some other financial metric, the VVF is clearly relevant to for-profit companies. For not-for-profit organizations, the ability to prioritize by relative business value avoids, or at least shortens, the long discussions about if and how the benefits delivered by not-for-profit organizations can be expressed in financial terms. Of course, the term business value is, in itself, a potential stumbling block for not-for-profits, but most are very much focused on delivering value whether they define it as *services value, member value,* or something similar. Indeed, one of our not-for-profit clients was delighted by our modification of the *concept-to-cash* model for value streams into a *concept to value* model. Having painted a positive picture for the use of VVF by not-for-profits, one word of caution is justified. Not-for-profits have to be just as disciplined as other organizations when it comes to the application of VVF. Most important, the units of value in step 1 must be clearly defined and measurable. For example, while the goal of a particular software project might be, "to improve the lives of children in care," the units of value should be defined as something more like, "the number of children in care whose lives have been demonstrably improved." I believe that this type of thinking about outcomes is consistent with the work of the Bill and Melinda Gates Foundation* and others.
■ The End-Client Lens: In-house or external clients or both. VVF should be easily applicable to in-house and external clients. Indeed, as I have noted before, many projects will include a mix of both. Some caution is needed in

---

* http://www.gatesfoundation.org/

choosing the units of value. For example, a new software feature might attract more loan applicants to a bank's website, but it might also speed up the time that the bank's employees take to process the loan. From a business value perspective, the units could be either number of new loan customers added or hours saved in employee processing time. My recommendation would be always to pick one (not more) unit and always to pick the unit that is more likely to change the bottom line of the business. In this example, I would choose the number of new loan customers added.

■ The Build-Buy Lens: Internally developed software or commercial off-the-shelf (COTS) software. For this lens, VVF is certainly important for internally developed software but it's applicability to COTS software is not obvious. Interestingly, the challenge is not so much whether VVF is useful for COTS purchases, but whether and how many COTS purchases add business value. Again, the thought process must start with the units of business value that must be defined, but we must remember that VVF helps us prioritize between projects. Examples are helpful here so let's start with an easy one—what are the units of business value in deciding between signing up for Salesforce.com and continuing to enhance the in-house *customer relationship management* (CRM) system? In this case, external customers are largely unaffected, so we are looking for units of in-house business value. These could be cost savings or opportunity enhancements. The costs for the COTS system should be some sort of fixed monthly fee based on the number of users, but also needs to include the short-term costs of changing systems. The costs for extending the in-house system will probably include the development and ongoing maintenance costs. Hence, my suggestion for the business value units for VVF would be cost savings per user per year. On the opportunity enhancement side, the units of business value are probably going to be related to the challenges the sales and marketing teams are facing with the current system. One example here might be that it is time-consuming for sales staff to target e-mails to new prospects on the existing system. The new COTS systems (Salesforce.com) is supposed to make this easier. Here the units of business value might be e-mails to prospects per sales person per month. Presumably, based on some analysis of pipeline conversion, a monetary value could be assigned to the extra e-mails that sales people are able to send out each month.

A VVF Example

Let's try applying some of these ideas to an example to which most of us can relate. I have run this exercise with different groups at different conferences and achieved broadly the same results. I fly American Airlines a lot, so I'm going to use a hypothetical example that came to me while I was stuck on a runway one day. American Airlines now provides paid Internet access on flights, so let's assume they want to

Step	VVF	Economist	Lumosity
1	Define units of value delivery	Number of subscribers added	Number of subscribers added
2	Define value of project in specified units	Small	Small
3	Define "size" of the project	1	5
4	Define the cost of delay	1	3
5	Quantify economic value once deployed	1	3

Figure 7.8 VVF example.

increase subscribers by adding valuable apps to be included in the Internet access price. We'll further assume that their team have identified two new potential applications and wish to use VVF to prioritize based on business value. The stories that describe the two fictional options are

- As an airline passenger, I want to be able to read the *Economist** magazine online to update my worldview.
- As an airline passenger, I want to be able to access Lumosity[†] to keep my brain active.

When presenting this example, I usually tabulate the VVF process for the group as shown in Figure 7.8 and take them through the steps. For VVF step 1, I stipulate the same units of value delivery: number of subscribers added. This sometimes provokes a discussion about whether the number of subscribers added is truly a reflection of the success or failure of these particular additions and it's a fair comment, which might demand a more sophisticated resolution in real life, but, for this example, we can extend our assumptions to say that an analysis of the number of subscribers added could be "scrubbed" to some degree to offset increases in passenger volumes, and so on.

For VVF step 2, I ask the group for T-shirt size estimates starting with the option they think is the smallest. In Figure 7.8, you can see that most groups believe that the business value of the *Economist* option in this context will be "small". Some groups suggest that the Lumosity option could be "medium," but most agree on "small". With two "smalls" for business value, we don't have a basis for prioritization yet.

---

* www.economist.com
[†] www.lumosity.com

For VVF step 3, I remind the group of the modified Fibonacci sequence that I want to use for relative estimating: 1, 2, 3, 5, 8, 13, 20. I then ask the group, which of the two options they think will be the "smallest" to implement. I explain that, as with story points, "smallest" in this context includes complexity, effort, dependencies, and anything else they can think of that might contribute to the "size" of the implementation. Invariably, the *Economist* option is chosen as the smallest, and so I arbitrarily assign it a size of 1. I then ask the group how much bigger they think the Lumosity option will be. Try it for yourself. Considerations that I have heard include the need to support interaction (as opposed to just displaying the *Economist*), the potential need for more frequent refreshes of the data depending on the nature of the games and so on. I have had groups argue for relative sizes of between 3 and 8. For our example, I have used a relative size of 5.

For VVF step 4, I ask the group which of the two options has the smallest CoD. This usually requires some explanation and examples of what we mean by CoD. My first clarification is a reminder that we measure CoD as a ratio such as dollars per day. Secondly, the delay part means that we are describing the cost we will incur if we don't do that option. For example, I might have sufficient staff for just one of two projects A and B except that I need to commit to hiring an additional analyst for project A at $60/hour and a consultant for the project B at $120/hour. Unfortunately, to be sure that I have both resources for the duration of both options, I have had to commit to hiring both resources from day 1 irrespective of which project I start first. At the end of the first project, I can release the specialist resource that is not needed for the second project. Clearly, it is more expensive to have the consultant sitting around doing nothing, so the highest CoD based on this set of data would be for project B.

Returning to the *Economist*/Lumosity prioritization, without any resource considerations, the CoD conversation in the groups I work with tends to revolve around the relative loss of revenue if the potentially more lucrative option is delayed. This can be somewhat subjective along the lines of, "I would definitely spend more for XXX," but this is where the group dynamic is helpful and if consensus is impossible, then a majority vote is sufficient. In our example, the *Economist* option is the smallest CoD and is scored "1" and the Lumosity option is scored "3."

In our example, VVF step 5 is not particularly useful because the purpose of step 5 is to measure the actual delivered value in order to build historic data of actual value versus the estimates. The goal of step 5 is to improve future estimates.

Prioritizing based on business value is not possible in this example, so we can go to CoD and prioritize the Lumosity option over the *Economist* option. But, we can go further and develop a better prioritizing metric using *weighted shortest job first* (WSJF) value points—described in Chapter 5. Using WSJF over CoD allows us to take into account the duration of the work, which likely influences business value flow because a longer duration project is susceptible to greater risk. We don't have "duration" in our example of Figure 7.8, but at the team level, size is a reasonable proxy for duration. Hence,

$$\text{Weighted Shortest Job First} \approx \frac{\text{Cost of Delay}}{\text{Size}}$$

For the *Economist* option, WSJF = 1/1 = 1 value point. For the Lumosity option, WSJF = 3/5 = 0.6 value points. This tells us that the *Economist* option should be done first because it has the higher WSJF. The rationale for this outcome is that getting some value in a short time economically outweighs the option of getting more value in a proportionally much longer time. Another way to think about this is that the net present value of the *Economist* option is greater.

Of course, I have "managed" the numbers in this example to provoke thought about how economic benefits over time can be assessed relatively to enable prioritization without the need for explicit business cases with detailed cash flows and ROIs.

Summary

This chapter makes the case that we can only get more value out of software development if we use business value as the most important consideration in prioritizing the flow of work through software development in particular and IT in general. Even though new methodologies such as Agile seek to bring value into the tactical decision-making of teams, we assert that very few businesses measure or track value with sufficient rigor. I accept that measuring and tracking value through software development is hard. I have offered a series of examples of how relative value can be measured and tracked. For prioritization to maximize the flow of business value, relative business value is all we need.

Value visualization means not just measuring and tracking value, but making value information visible to tactical decision-makers so they can use it to prioritize work flow and, hence, value flow. Capturing value data has a number of other benefits not least in aligning the business and IT.

Chapter 8

Metrics for Business Value in Software Development

In a book about the business value of software, it would be a surprise if I had reached this point without describing some of the most important ways to measure the business value of software. Rather than repeat those descriptions, but to serve the needs of readers searching for specific topics, I will start this chapter with a quick review of important metrics covered previously in this book:

- Cost of delay (CoD) and weighted shortest job first (WSJF): Prioritization metrics and techniques—see Chapter 7.
- Value visualization framework (VVF): Refer to Chapter 7, Figure 7.4, and associated text.
- Value visualization: Cumulative flowcharts, and so on—see Chapter 3.
- Different forms of software value, see Chapter 4 and Figure 4.2 for a summary
- Lean and waste: Refer to Chapter 6, Figure 6.2 and associated text

This chapter looks beyond the most important business value metrics already described to some other considerations for building a business value measurement system.

Value Metrics for Agile Governance

Agile implementations, particularly Scrum, are rich in simple, team-level metrics, such as story points, velocity, and burndown charts. Unfortunately, these team-specific metrics are not very useful for planning or monitoring across an entire software development organization. There is often a gap when attempting to measure an organization's efficiency, economy, and effectiveness.

Software value visibility metrics are a better choice for governing your Agile software development organization-wide. In this chapter, you will learn how to create top-down Agile metrics that are compatible with, and extend, traditional Waterfall metrics.

Traditional Waterfall Metrics

The following metric definitions are examples from a real Waterfall organization:

- *Delivered as promised*: Defined as the software delivered and must have the functionality promised in the requirements section of the project scope agreement—percentage of checklist completed.
- *Productivity*: Defined as the number of function points delivered, divided by the total number of work years of effort charged against the project from start to completion.
- *Timeliness*: Defined as a comparison of the agreed-upon baselined implementation date against the current implementation date of record.
- *Quality*: Defined as the number of defects delivered into production.
- *Accuracy of effort estimate*: Defined as a comparison of the originally agreed-upon baselined effort estimate against the current effort estimate.

Even though these metrics can be captured initially at the project level, they can be readily aggregated up to the program and organization level for governance purposes. As a result, project progress can be easily summarized. Without any significant understanding of software development methodologies, any executive would be able to read and understand trend lines for these metrics on a dashboard. The challenge is the absence of a *value-delivered* metric.

At least for the software development community, Agile offers better benefits than Waterfall on two main fronts: value delivery and customer satisfaction. As Agile practitioners and champions, we can smugly review the list of Waterfall metrics mentioned previously and observe that none of these metrics measure business value delivery or customer satisfaction directly. It is a fair observation. But, does Agile really do any better?

In comparison, let's look at how Agile teams measure value. As part of sprint or release planning processes, more mature Agile teams ask the product owner to assign relative value sizes to individual stories or epics at the team level. From a governance perspective, these value sizes do not aggregate well because the value sizes are relative, and each team has its own scale. Hence, rightly, few organizations even attempt to aggregate and track these team-level value metrics. Instead, new value metrics are required that can be aggregated.

The Metrics Challenge for Agile

For organizational governance purposes, we need Agile metrics that will match the Waterfall governance metrics, and we need scalable value metrics for Waterfall and Agile. For example, anyone familiar with the Scrum methodology will recognize that the conversion is not necessarily straightforward for all of the Waterfall metrics discussed previously. The Waterfall metrics focus on assumptions built into the Waterfall approach; for example, the timeliness metric assumes that it is difficult to predict when the functionality will be complete and operational. Agile, on the other hand, focuses on how much of the functionality is operational by a fixed date.

From my experience, Agile implementations tend to fall into the trap of trying to deliver to executives the same reports that Waterfall delivered. Figure 8.1 shows a set of the default reports from a popular Agile life cycle management tool. It is not

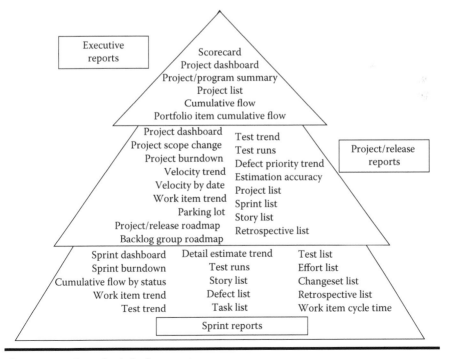

Figure 8.1   Sample default reports.

the only popular tool on the market, and I don't mean to imply that others don't have slightly better reports. My point here is that the reports listed at the executive, project, and sprint levels do not include any explicit references to value delivery or customer satisfaction.

There are reports that imply business value delivery just as there is some implied value, which may be business value for the Waterfall metrics (e.g., timeliness). For example, at the sprint-report level, work item cycle time is not a bad proxy for value delivery. On the assumption that work items are broadly similar in size, a trend to deliver them more quickly implies more value being delivered over some time period. There are two problems with this view of value delivery. First, work item cycle time is not visible in executive reports. Second, the assumption that all work items have the same business value is unlikely. Cumulative flow reports are available in both executive and sprint reporting. These reports are powerful tools for identifying bottlenecks that can be tackled to help maximize value flow. However, in the absence of metrics for value, they cannot explicitly report value flow.

Customer satisfaction is entirely absent from the executive, project/release, and sprint reports in Figure 8.1. Maybe that's understandable in a tool that is focused on Agile life cycle management, but shouldn't it be reflected in the dashboard at the executive level? Executives need to see summaries, in addition to aggregate and detailed information about customer satisfaction. To meet the needs of executives, many organizations have separate groups and tools to conduct customer satisfaction surveys. This is better than nothing, but too often there is no connection between these high-level surveys and the Agile teams who need fast, pertinent customer feedback to drive their product and process improvement.

Figure 8.2 shows my analysis of the set of metrics for Agile proposed by Rico, Sayani, and Sone in their otherwise excellent book, *The Business Value of Agile Software Methods* (Rico et al. 2009). The metrics proposed by Rico, Sayani, and Sone are interesting because they are grouped around the five principles of the *Agile Manifesto* (Beck et al. 2001). Despite the book's title and the ubiquity of the influence of the Agile Manifesto in today's software development, very few of the proposed metrics measure business value directly. Indeed, if anything, the traditional metrics do a better job than the proposed Agile metrics, many of which are highly subjective. Some of these subjective metrics are important for the long-term health of Agile teams, which will indirectly contribute to business value. There are ways to measure some of the subjective metrics, so we will return to this challenge later in this chapter under "Individuals and Interactions."

Some of the entries in Figure 8.2 require more explanation:

Metric	Measured in Waterfall*	Measured in Agile*	Business value metric?
Traditional			
• Software size	S	Y	Perhaps indirectly
• Software effort	Y	Y	No but drives cost
• Software cost	Y	Y	No but important for ROI
• Software productivity	S	R	No but drives cost
• Software complexity	R	Y	No but may detract from value
• Software quality/reliability	Y	Y	Yes
Customer collaboration			
• Interaction frequency	R	S	No
• Communication quality	N	R	No
• Relationship strength	R	S	No but helps maximize BV
• Customer trust	N	R	No but helps maximize BV
• Customer loyalty	N	R	No but helps maximize BV
• Customer satisfaction	S	Y	Yes
Individuals and interactions			
• Team competence	S	R	No
• Team motivation	R	R	No
• Team cooperation	R	R	No
• Team trust	R	R	No
• Team cohesion	R	R	No
• Team communications	S	S	No
Working software			
• Time-boxed iterations	N	Y	No
• Iteration size	N	Y	No
• Iteration frequency	N	Y	No
• Iteration number	N	Y	No
• Operational iterations	N	Y	No
• Validated iterations	N	Y	No
Responding to change			
• Process flexibility	N	R	Perhaps indirectly
• Technology flexibility	N	R	Yes
• Design flexibility	N	R	Perhaps indirectly
• Individual flexibility	N	R	Yes but indirectly
• Management flexibility	N	R	Yes but indirectly
• Organizational flexibility	N	R	Yes but indirectly

* Y = Yes. N = No. S = Sometimes. R = Rarely.

Figure 8.2   Waterfall versus Agile metrics and business value. (Adapted from Rico, D.F., Sayani, H.H., Sone, S.J. *The Business Value of Agile Software Methods.* **Ross Publishing, Fort Lauderdale, FL, 2009.)**

Software Size

Software size can be a business value metric if function points are used. Function point analysis* is an internationally standardized and repeatable process for measuring the functional size of a software requirement and design from a user perspective. It does not require the software code to be available. As such, it is a measurement of the size of the business requirement. This is a useful input to development estimation, but it can also be considered as an output metric of the amount of business requirement delivered. Function points can be measured for individual enhancement projects or for a whole application. In the latter case, function point analysis can identify functionality that has been added, changed, or removed, such that the total functional size of the application can be tracked over time.

Where such tracking over time is implemented, there is a good case for automated function point sizing based on static code analysis. Unfortunately, this is not useful for estimation of project development because it depends on the availability of the code.

Importantly, function points can be aggregated across many projects and applications because they are designed to be independent of technology. Hence, they are particularly useful at the product/program and portfolio levels of organizations.

Of course, the volume of business requirements delivered is not the same as the business value delivered because we cannot assume that all business requirements are of equal, or any, value. Also, function points are not perfect—by definition, they tend to do a poor job of predicting the effort involved in non-functional software development activities. For example, re-platforming an application from COBOL to Java without any changes to the functionality, would be a project with zero function points. I submit that for our purposes of measuring the business value, the fact that a re-platforming project yields zero function points is actually quite helpful because, in and of itself, it adds zero business value. The International Function Point Users Group (IFPUG) has recognized this occasional constraint on the use of function points and developed the Software Non-functional Assessment Process† (SNAP) to fill the gap.

In the absence of value metrics, function points are a good proxy for value delivered, so far as they offer a widely accepted, user-oriented metric of business requirements delivered. In Figure 8.2, I have indicated that this valuable metric is only sometimes measured in Waterfall, because the use of function points is far less widespread than their value and relatively low cost might suggest.

Unfortunately, despite the fact that function points are used by a number of large organizations (some of which are my clients) for Agile, they are viewed with hostility by many advocates of Agile. It is not entirely clear to me why this is the case. It is fair to assert that function points are not a useful metric for Scrum teams

---

* http://bit.ly/2oYpvao
† http://bit.ly/2qG7Wbr

because the expertise required to size-in function points consistently is not, and should not be, readily available to teams for sprint planning. But the size metric used by many Scrum teams, story points, is not very suitable for aggregation across teams, projects, and applications, because each story point–sizing activity is a quick assessment by one team of the relative size of the tasks in front of them today. Also, story points tend to be an informal blend, different for each team, of a team's assessment of software size, effort, and complexity. Hence, aggregated story points are not as good a metric for evaluating business value delivered as function points. That said, I would use them for value measurement if nothing else was available, with the caveat that something better should be implemented soon!

Software Productivity

I have already explained (Chapter 5 and elsewhere) that when productivity is defined in terms of its assumed proxy, resource utilization, then it is not a desirable primary goal for maximizing the flow of business value. However, if productivity is measured in its true sense—output/input—then it is useful. Some (but not enough) organizations have productivity metrics like "function points delivered per effort month" or "hours per function point" (an inverted productivity metric that is often easier to talk about). Given my previous comments, it can be seen that these could be indirect value metrics because they are closely related to return on investment (ROI), where the return is function points and the investment is in the funding for effort hours. Agile teams often measure their team *velocity* as the number of story points delivered per sprint/iteration. Superficially, this appears to be a reasonable equivalent of the function points per effort-month metric. However, while it is a useful metric for sprint planning, it is a poor productivity metric because the team has direct control over the output sizing mechanism—the story points. Teams with very different velocities in story points could easily be working with the same productivity.

Software Complexity and Technology Flexibility

Software complexity and technology flexibility are not characteristics of software development that impact business value directly because they should be hidden from the end users. However, both characteristics impact business value at one point, because they impact the cost and time to market for incremental improvements to existing software. Put simply, complicated code and/or an inflexible development or production environment means small changes take longer to implement. I described the long-term effect of this problem in Chapter 1 (see Figure 1.3).

Unfortunately, increasing software complexity over time is almost unavoidable as incremental improvements are made. This problem is not unique to software—try comparing the electrical wiring of an old house with that of a new one—but the challenge of complexity in software is that it tends to be invisible. Hence, it is important to have metrics that make software complexity visible.

There are a number of candidates for this metric, such as McCabe's cyclometric complexity number and Halstead's effort metric. Kafura and Reddy (1987) looked at these complexity metrics and several others in a simple study. Their research tallies with my experience in that the most value comes from addressing outliers on these metrics. Put another way, I have often found it to be the case that a large application can have relatively low complexity on average, but always seems to contain one or two components with unreasonably high complexity. These tend to be the "core processing engines" of the application through which most of the "traffic" flows. A small improvement in complexity in these hubs can return lots of value. However, the opposite is also true. Small detriments to complexity in these hubs can seriously degrade the application's performance. I once ran an organization of about 250 developers mostly focused on the same small set of software products. There was one part of our flagship product that was so complex that only three developers were allowed to touch it!

The real solution for measuring software complexity is to use a static code analysis tool* to automatically generate the complexity metrics and to embed this tool into the daily routine of software development. This will enable developers to get early, actionable feedback on the complexity of the software that they are working on. Unnecessary complexity in software is often referred to as *technical debt* (introduced in Chapter 4). Some of the static code analysis tools report the unnecessary software complexity as technical debt, and some even attempt to estimate the time and cost of fixing the technical debt. While the core complexity metrics of such tools are sound and have an indirect impact on long-term business value, care is needed when considering effort and cost for the fixes because these numbers can only be rough approximations at best.

Software Quality/Reliability

Software quality and reliability has a direct impact on business value because it can impact the *fitness for purpose* of the software and customer satisfaction. If the software quality means that it is not completely fit for purpose, then presumably some or all of the planned business value is not being delivered. For example, an otherwise fully functional financial system that cannot produce reports for the company's accountant will generate extra work and cost for the accountant. Similarly, if a customer (end user) perceives that the software quality is poor or the software is unreliable, it will affect their willingness to use the software and, ultimately, might cause them to switch to different software.

One of the challenges to measuring software quality as it relates to business value is that the relationship between severity of quality issues and business value impact is non-linear. That is, a few severe quality issues will have disproportionately more impact on business value than many trivial quality issues. While static code

---

* Examples of static code analysis tools are Sonar and CAST software.

analyzers can be used to assess code quality (as well as complexity—as discussed earlier), one of the challenges is that they tend to view all defects as having equal impact. Indeed, the differentiator between strong and weak tools is their ability to report different levels of severity of issues.

Better software quality comes from better design and coding. One important way to improve design and coding is to provide designers and coders with fast feedback through *in-line* testing of the software that they are producing. In practice, that means integrating daily testing into the software development life cycle through at least one, and ideally more, of the following steps:

- Co-located testers and developers: Manual testing (or test-script writing for automated tests) is carried out in parallel with the code being written by testers and developers on the same team.
- Test-driven development: Tests are written in code like format before any code is written. Just enough code is written to pass the tests, and then more tests are written for the next piece of code.
- Automated testing: Test scripts are run automatically and regularly (ideally daily or more frequently) to ensure that new code works and does not break any previous code. Automatic test-script suites that include all or most previous tests can provide in-line regression testing, as well as covering code written today. Hence, developers get feedback that their new code not only works, but that they didn't break any of the old code.

While all of the previous simple steps are applicable to Waterfall environments, they have become most associated with Agile.

The process-oriented metrics associated with these quality improvement techniques do have impact on business value delivered. For example, the percentage of code coverage of the automated tests is essentially a business risk metric.

Customer Collaboration

The customer collaboration metrics proposed in Figure 8.2 are all related to minimizing business risk, and that does have real business value. While I personally have some difficulty in understanding how I would measure things like customer trust and customer loyalty in the context of software development alone (in my experience they tend to be functions of the broader business relationship), these are clearly influential metrics for ensuring that the feedback loop to the development teams is fast and clear.

Customer satisfaction must be measured. This one is non-negotiable, especially for Agile development organizations, given that one of the primary drivers for the transformation to Agile is closer collaboration with the customer. This brings me to a pet peeve. In the early days of Agile, we always talked about having the customer involved in the Scrum sprint reviews and getting direct feedback for the customer. Over the years, the difficulty of this, for practical reasons or due to customer disinterest, has led to the customer's direct role diminishing and the model depending on customer proxies, such as the *product owner* or *product manager*, for feedback. In my opinion, while I concede the practical challenges, this can be a dangerous step away from core principles. This change is the only justification that I can see for including metrics, such as *interaction frequency* and *communications quality*. To my mind, these are not business value metrics but process deficiency metrics. That said, the risk is there so they should both be measured.

Customer satisfaction metrics must come from real customers not proxies.

Individuals and Interactions

These metrics all relate to the ability and desire of the team to do a good job. They are not business value metrics directly, but to the extent they affect the productivity and sustainability of the development teams, they do impact the long-term ability of the organization to maximize the flow of business value.

These are subjective metrics that can only really be measured through survey and analysis. The subjectivity of the metrics makes them easy to game if individuals feel that they will be rewarded or punished for their responses. Hence, these metrics must be decoupled from individual performance reviews. In Waterfall, these metrics are very difficult to implement, to the point of being a waste of time because individuals have little control over the work they are assigned or the process they follow. In Agile, the driving principle of self-organizing teams allows the potential for the team to take ownership of their own surveys for these metrics and their plans for continuous improvement. I have seen this work very well, but the metrics generated are team-driven and team-owned, not organizational metrics. Hence, it is debatable whether they are really metrics at all from the organization's perspective. Personally, I support any metrics that drive positive behavior and give the organization a sense of the way performance is trending. It is still true that if you can't measure, you can't manage. Hence, I generally promote the visibility of these metrics at levels above the team, provided the organization understands their limitations and has, or is working toward, better aggregate metrics.

Clearly, Agile teams can develop their own surveys and do their own analysis, but one approach that I have used successfully is a process and tool called the AgilityHealth[SM] Radar (AHR) Team Health Assessment.* All Agile teams should be performing a retrospective at the end of each sprint (iteration) to review their sprint and identify opportunities for improvements. I tend to refer to these as *tactical* retrospectives. The AHR is more of a *strategic* retrospective performed once per quarter or every 6-12 sprints. It is designed to look at all the metrics, defined in Figure 8.2, for individuals and interactions and some others as well.

---

* More information on AgilityHealth Radar is available at http://bit.ly/2qzDWip.

Each AHR Team Health Assessment takes the form of a 3-hour, 3-step workshop:

1. A trained facilitator works with the Agile team members to complete an individual survey covering the five key dimensions of a healthy Agile team (clarity, performance, leadership, culture, foundation).
2. The facilitator generates the survey results in the form of two radar plots: an overview showing average scores and a detailed plot of all scores against their respective survey question categories to allow teams to see the diversity of scores in each category. The survey system also captures the team members' notes on the answers. The facilitator engages the team in a healthy and open discussion around analyzing its radar results and reviewing its strengths, improvements, and top impediments to growth.
3. The team then works together to produce a *growth plan* with key outcomes that the team wants to achieve within the next few months.

In my experience facilitating these sessions for teams, some of the key outcomes can include

- Understanding of the key areas that affect this team's health and performance
- Providing a point of comparison for the future positive or negative evolution of the team
- Identifying different perspectives within the team, such as an individual being left out or an unrecognized split in understanding between the old hands on the team and the newbies
- Reviewing the team's strengths—celebrate success!
- Reviewing the team's improvements and opportunities
- Performing targeted just-in-time coaching on top gaps for the team
- Developing a *team growth plan* with actionable deliverables for the next quarter
- Facilitating open and honest conversations in a non-judgmental environment (if the facilitator is good enough) to help the team get past any current roadblocks and develop a clear plan of action for getting their performance and health to the next level

Responding to Change

Many business heads would put responding to change close to the top of a list of desirable characteristics that they want to see from their software developers, but this often means they are seeking the ability to "get what I want when I want it." Having been on both sides of the software development fence, I can relate to that emotion, but I can also relate to the practical challenges of working out what exactly is meant by "when" and "it," and which should be prioritized above the other. I would also like to coin a phrase by suggesting that *flexibility is the enemy of delivery* when it comes to software development. Interestingly, most people would acknowledge that Agile is much more flexible than Waterfall in its ability to deal with change. Yet the driving imperative to deliver incremental chunks of working software in Agile tends to generate more inefficient code (technical debt) than the more deliberate, more high-level, design-oriented Waterfall does. More technical debt means more complex, less flexible code. Hence, flexibility in process has a trade-off against flexibility in design and/or technology.

While there is clearly business value in flexibility, the business must prioritize between the different types of flexibility to identify those that are most valuable in the business context.

Agile Governance Metrics Maturity Evolution

The biggest objection to measuring value delivered by software development is that it is just too difficult. I am often told that software development teams can't map the details from business cases to their work once details are broken down. This issue becomes even more cumbersome if business cases are not shared with development (or there are no business cases at all). The VVF shows that using value for decision-making can be relatively simple, and the business can be involved in a way that's simple for them, too. That said, there is no need to attempt all of this at once. Agile governance metrics can and should evolve over time. Figure 8.3 provides an evolutionary path from traditional Waterfall metrics to full Agile governance through the three levels of organizational metrics maturity.

Why start with traditional Waterfall metrics? Most organizations have a mix of Waterfall and Agile projects, and so there needs to be a basis of comparison for reporting at the senior management level. Even organizations that take a big-bang approach and convert all of their software development to Agile need comparisons to what they were doing before to ensure that the transformation is delivering the promised benefits (yes, you should even measure the business value of software development process change!). We have helped one of our clients measure their Agile transformation over the past few years and the metrics yielded some useful information that made them change their approach in a number of ways. Essentially, they found that while most teams achieved the expected gains in productivity (measured in hours per function point), time to market, and customer satisfaction over the "before" Waterfall metrics, a significant minority did not. Analysis of the differences between the performing and non-performing Agile teams yielded a number of potential drivers for the difference, the most significant of which was co-location. At this point, any Agile champions reading this will throw up their hands in horror that the Agile teams were not co-located from the start. Unfortunately, that ignores the reality of most large corporations today, where teleworking and offshoring preceded Agile as, let's be blunt here, ways to save money. The "before" and "after" metrics that we were able to help our client

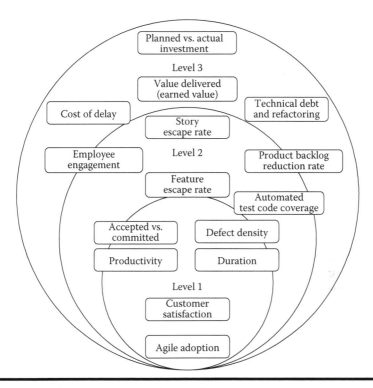

Figure 8.3   Agile governance metrics roadmap.

capture and analyze made the business case for investing in different ways of working predicated on co-location.

The relative positions and level boundaries of the metrics in Figure 8.3 are certainly debatable and may be different depending on the organization. Also, some of the metrics, such as velocity and size, are fundamental to team performance and do not lend themselves to being aggregated because they are almost always team-specific.

These metrics represent a comprehensive set of measurements for Agile governance. The levels are intended to support the increasing maturity of the Agile teams, so level one metrics, such as Agile adoption (percent of projects using Agile) and customer satisfaction, can be measured and used for governance in the early stages of Agile project implementations.

Some of the metrics in Figure 8.3 are obvious or have been covered elsewhere in this book but some are introduced here for the first time:

Duration

We have already touched on *duration* implicitly earlier in this chapter when we referred to the traditional Waterfall metric of timeliness. Strictly, duration refers to the elapsed time from the start of the project (e.g., initial concept, start of requirements definition, approval of funds) to the time that the project is *live* in the hands of the customer.

Often in the Waterfall world, duration is largely fixed (assuming a particular feature stays in scope) because organizations try to lock into a cycle of requirements, to design, to code, to test, to production, over a fixed time period to allow releases to be *pipelined* in parallel. Pipelining means that there is a fixed duration for each of the requirements, design, coding, and so on. When design, say, is finished with release X and passes it on to coding, then that event is always synchronized with requirements being finished with release X+1 and passing it on to design. Any variances in parts of the work that cannot be finished by the synchronization deadline are dealt with by dropping that part of the work back to be completed in the next release. In this sort of implementation of Waterfall, duration is less meaningful and timeliness is more important.

In Agile, duration is usually referred to as a *lead time* or *cycle time*. This is the time that a feature or story takes to get from concept (or funding approval) to cash (being used by a live customer). Rather than being related to a specific piece of functionality, cycle time is a statistical metric, which presumes that all features and, to a greater extent, stories are similar in size and small enough to transit the development life cycle frequently and in a reasonably short time. In theory, all stories should transit the development life cycle in a certain number of sprints. The distribution and variation in that number of sprints over a group of many stories tells the team what the most likely cycle time of the next story will be and how much confidence they can have in that time. A high variance in cycle times could be indicative of several process issues. The most obvious issue could be that stories have a high variance in size. From the lean perspective of maximizing flow, a high variance in story size is undesirable and so more work should be done on breaking up stories into their smallest reasonable size. Another reason for a high variance in cycle time could be due to queues developing in the process. Queues usually develop in front of over-utilized (i.e., under-resourced) steps in the process. For example, Agile teams could be creating working software faster than DevOps can deploy it, or testing may be backed up by an unusual level of defects (perhaps caused by new team members).

Value Delivered (Earned Value)

Value delivered is certainly a higher-maturity metric, but it is no less important for Agile implementations and Agile governance for reasons that we have covered elsewhere in this book; but *earned value* is a new term that merits some explanation. Federal government and federal contractors will be familiar with the term earned value as it is applied to federal software development contracts. Hence, it needs to be mentioned in the context of our not-for-profit lens. Whole books,* and contracts the size of whole books, have been written on earned value management (and I will revisit it in Chapter 9). For now, I will simplify it down to something manageable, on the understanding that interested readers will do more research before taking my words as definitive. Simply then, earned value management is a project management technique for recognizing completed work in otherwise incomplete projects. For example, in a Waterfall project, the work to be done is often broken down into a series of dependent and independent tasks presented in the form of a *work breakdown structure* (WBS). As each task in the WBS is completed, the project earns value. For example, a project in which 43 of the 100 tasks on the WBS were complete could be said to have an earned value of 43%. Typically, this would be related to the project value and some interim payments might be directly or indirectly linked to the earned value.

Earned value is included in Figure 8.3 because it is a helpful bridge for government-driven organizations to start to think about measuring value delivered. It is not the best value-delivery metric in the medium term because it measures activities completed, not working software in the hands of the end user. For example, it is quite possible, and some might say common, to complete more that 50% of the tasks in a typical Waterfall project without having any working software. The earned value might be greater than 50% but the value delivered is zero (note the emphasis on working software metrics in Figure 8.2). That said, hopefully, readers will see that a simple tweak to earned value management, to define it in terms of working software in the hands of users, will be an easy first step along the path to truly measuring value delivered for the many government agencies that use earned value.

Accepted versus Committed

As we have seen, while Waterfall is primarily a *push* workflow, Agile is primarily a *pull* workflow with work in the form of stories, decomposed from epics or features, being pulled by the Agile teams from a backlog. Most of the time, mature Agile teams will have a good idea of what they can accomplish in a given, short time and "commit" to completing the work they pull off the backlog on that basis. But, it is not a precise science and the work can take more or less time than expected. Sometimes, the team may believe that they have completed the work as required, but the *product owner* may disagree and not "accept" the finished result, especially if the acceptance criteria have not been fully met.

The *accepted-versus-committed* metric is a measure of how good the teams are meeting their commitments once they pull work off the backlog. It is a level 1 maturity metric on Figure 8.3 because it should be a transitional metric. Mature teams should be hitting over 90% on a consistent basis. The accepted-versus-committed

---

* For example, *Practice Standard for Earned Value Management*, 2nd edition, Project Management Institute, 2011.

metric is not a great business value flow metric because the easiest way to get a high score is to under-commit!

Feature and Story Escape Rate

The feature and story escape rate metrics allow Agile teams to identify the features or stories that have been committed for the upcoming release and then account for those that "slip" from plan. The feature escape rate metric at the product/program-level monitors the overall predictability of an Agile team's ability to commit and deliver functionality (estimate and plan). This is especially useful at the product/program level, because it informs the likelihood that the product roadmap will be fully or partially executed so it can be adjusted to have a higher probability. Ultimately, the feature escape rate is a measure of the difference between planned and actual business value flow. However, like the team-level, accepted-versus-committed metric, escape rate metrics are good value flow management metrics, but not good value flow optimization metrics, because the easy way to minimize escape rate it to under-commit.

Figure 8.4 shows an example of how feature escape rate might change across a series of releases. I have assumed that each release could contain multiple sprints. At the start of Release One, on the left of the diagram, the teams commit to features A and B for Release One. Feature A is complete, but feature B is incomplete so the feature escape rate is ½ or 50%. It should be noted that this is a simple example and the actual feature escape rate would be aggregated across many teams. In Release Two, the teams commit to completing feature B and features C and D—three features in total. However, during Release Two, it becomes evident that feature D needs to be split into two separate features: D1 and D2. This means a total of four features have been committed for Release Two. At the end of Release Two, features B, C, and D1 have been completed, but D2 is incomplete. Sometimes it is a good idea to split a feature if useful functionality can be delivered by the part that can be completed. At the end of Release Two, one of the four committed features is incomplete, so the feature escape rate is ¼ or 25%.

Benchmarking Business Value

At the risk of stating the obvious, benchmarking is the collection of software metrics in a standardized form so that results can be compared between different entities for example, different organizations or different business units in the same company. Typically, the goal is to compare organizations that are similar in one or more ways such that there is a reasonable expectation of similar benchmark results (e.g., two similar sized banks) or a plausible explanation for differences (e.g., small and large government departments). Hunter and Westerman (2009) wrote,

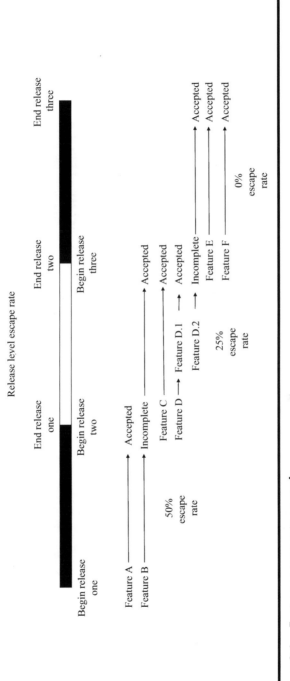

Figure 8.4   Feature escape rate example.

Almost every one of the highly effective CIOs we interviewed for this research benchmarks IT cost and quality of service against peer companies every twelve to twenty-four months.

Important exceptions to this rule

- If the CIO and executive team are satisfied that unit costs and quality are competitive, then benchmarking those factors may not be the best use of IT's time and attention.
- If it is difficult to find comparable peers
- If specific areas are obviously in need of improvement

For some software metrics, such as development productivity, a few companies around the world, such as my own—Premios*—have historical project databases from which they can extract comparative benchmarks. Other companies with development productivity benchmark data include Namcook Analytics,† LedaMC,‡ TI Metricas,§ and Quantimetrics.¶ There is even a not-for-profit organization, the International Software Benchmarking Standards Group (ISBSG)** that accepts software project data from third parties in a standard format and sells the aggregate benchmark data. I have to mention that while we all use this excellent resource, it needs to be used with care because it is almost impossible for the ISBSG team to validate the incoming data as they did not do the measurements themselves. There is also a fear that companies will only submit the data that makes them look good and not include projects with poor metrics.

To help with the challenges of standardizing development productivity and in an effort to provide some industry leadership, three of the aforementioned companies with benchmarking data, Premios, LedaMC, and TI Metricas have recently published a "Benchmarking Guide for Software Development and Maintenance Projects"†† to enable organizations to collect their own data in a standard form. It is hoped that this initial version of the guide will provoke comments and questions from the industry, such that a second edition can be published with wider industry support.

The attentive reader will be asking themselves what these sources of *software development productivity* benchmarks have to do with business value benchmarks. The answer, of course, is "not much." At best, productivity benchmarks inform *value for money* decisions. To be fair, as we have seen, business value is hard to standardize because it is so specific to each organization. That said, business value

---

* http://www.premiosgroup.com
† http://www.namcook.com/
‡ http://leda-mc.com/en/index.html
§ http://www.metricas.com.br/en/
¶ http://www.quantimetrics.net/
** https://isbsg.org/
††http://bit.ly/2qt6H34

benchmarks based on some of the standard approaches described in this book are an aspiration of mine, a "twinkle in my eye" but not yet a reality.

To consider the impact that software development productivity benchmarks can have on value for money, an important component of business value, it is worth considering some analysis of software productivity data that Rafael de la Fuente, CEO of LedaMC, used in announcing the benchmarking guide to the Spanish press in November 2016. LedaMC have presented similar benchmarks in various conferences over the past few years.*

LedaMC's clients in Spain outsource their software development to a variety of outsourced vendors. LedaMC's role is to help their clients analyze the performance of their outsourced providers over a number of metrics including productivity. To demonstrate the value of benchmarking, each year LedaMC analysts look at the productivity of the various "pairings" of their customers and their customers' vendors. For example, customer A might have three outsourced software development vendors, X, Y, and Z, which would represent three "customer pairs." Customer B could have a single outsourced vendor, which would represent one customer pair. For the purpose of the annual presentation, as opposed to the benchmark information provided to individual customers, LedaMC compare each customer pair by rate (€ per hour—see Figure 8.5) and price or FP cost (€ per delivered function point—see Figure 8.6), which, as we will see, may be an indicator of value for money.

It should be noted that for Figure 8.5 the customer pairs have been ranked by rate with highest hourly rate on the left. Figures 8.6 through 8.8 preserve the same chart position on the horizontal axis for any given customer pair as dictated by Figure 8.5. In all the charts, all vertical axis values are percentages relative to the highest value, which is set to 100%.

We can immediately see from Figure 8.6 that, for this data set, there is no correlation between hourly rate and cost per function point. This may be appropriate because function points are just a measure of software problem size and different solutions to the same problem could have different costs. For example, if we have a problem with a size of 100 FP it will be significantly less expensive to hire a Java programmer to solve the problem in Java than to hire an Assembler programmer to solve the problem in Assembler. It will inevitably take longer in Assembler even if the programmers are employed at the same rate (which they probably would not be).

Figure 8.7 puts the previous two charts together and, subject to the caveat about comparing like-for-like development environments, offers a stark lesson that the lowest hourly rates do not necessarily mean the best value for money! Indeed, some of the lowest rates have some of the highest costs per function point.

Another way to look at Figure 8.7 is to compare the wide variation of rates for different customer pairs with broadly the same cost per function point. Rates for a

---

* http://www.bfpug.org/eventos/metricas2015/dacilcastelo.pdf

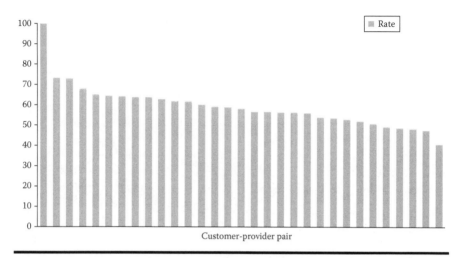

Figure 8.5   Benchmark of customer pairs by rate.

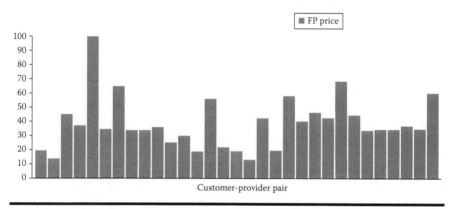

Figure 8.6   Benchmark of customer pairs by price.

cost per function point at about the "35" level, range between roughly the "65" rate level and the "45" rate level—a potential saving of about 30%. Figure 8.8 demonstrates this value for money benchmark in a slightly different way by highlighting the cost per function point for the same vendor at three different customers.

In this case, the range of cost per FP is about "30" to about "100"! Again, with such extremes we must be careful that we are comparing similar development environments but the usefulness of good benchmarking data should be becoming clearer.

Finally, a chart that provides the data to back up common sense. In Figure 8.9, the customer pairs are reordered by cost per function point with the highest on the left. Those customer pairs that represent single vendor situations, that is, the

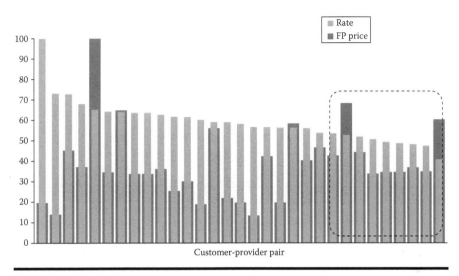

Figure 8.7   Comparison of customer pair rate and FP cost.

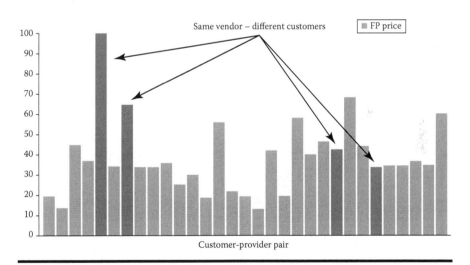

Figure 8.8   Comparison of one vendor FP costs for different customers.

customer only uses one vendor for its outsourced software development, are marked in a darker color. All four customer pairs that represent single-source scenarios are the most expensive in terms of cost per function point.

A final word of caution on this chapter from Hunter and Westerman (2009), "Be especially careful about soft benefits whose quantification depends on metrics that have never been baselined."

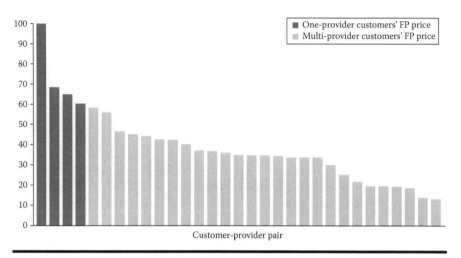

Figure 8.9   Costs of using on vendor and multiple vendors.

Summary

In this chapter, we have referenced some of the main business value metrics described in previous chapters and dived deeper into some other metrics that impact business value directly or indirectly. We have seen that some Waterfall metrics can and need to be carried over to Agile, while Agile has brought in some new metrics that can be applied beneficially to Waterfall. Finally, we looked at the possibilities for improving value for money through benchmarking.

Most of the metrics we have discussed are "hard" objective measures, but some are necessarily "soft" and we have looked at ways to address those metrics.

In the next chapter, we will look at an administrative structure to measure, manage, and act upon all these metrics, the *software value management office*.

Chapter 9

The Software Value Management Office

In a McKinsey article* published in July 2016, "Adapting your board to the digital age," Hugo Sarrazin and Paul Willmott reported that "less than one in five directors fully understand how the industry dynamics of their companies are changing." They quote Marc Andreesen's light-hearted but pertinent observation that, "Software is eating the world." They also reported an expectation among one in three McKinsey clients that their business model will be disrupted in the next 5 years. Sarrazin and Willmott go on to assert that, "Board members need better knowledge about the technology environment, its potential impact on different parts of the company, and its value chain." Hunter and Westerman (2009) point out that, "Ensuring that value is delivered is a process, and a process must be managed. After IT solutions are delivered and business change is complete, the project steering group is replaced by a harvest steering group."

I suggest that what the board and the company need is a software value management office (SVMO), responsible for measuring and monitoring the value delivered by information technology (IT) and specifically software development. Why specifically software development? Because IT is increasingly a utility—it needs to be properly designed, implemented, and managed, and technical expertise is needed to do all of that well—I suggest that most of the company's differentiated IT value will come from its software.

---

* http://www.mckinsey.com/business-functions/business-technology/our-insights/adapting-your-board-to-the-digital-age

Where Does the SVMO Fit in the Organization?

The concept of a *value management office* (VMO) is not new. Before I explain where the SVMO fits in the organization, I want to consider some of the other concepts for VMOs so that we can see if the SVMO would fit within an existing VMO. I have chosen a small, representative sample of VMO ideas that are out there.

In September 2015, Tom Pisello* wrote a blog post about his ideas for a VMO to be "the center of excellence aligning value marketing, selling and consulting,—with the mission of proposing, proving and improving value to customers." Pisello is following a similar thought process to me (or actually I to him) insofar as he is focusing on the importance of delivering value to customers. Hence, the philosophy of Pisello's VMO is well-aligned with the SVMO, but I'm guessing that Pisello's VMO would prefer not to engage with software development. That being said, Pisello's VMO would make an excellent customer for the SVMO. Therefore, while I believe that there are definite organizational benefits that need to be considered in Pisello's ideas, I don't recommend including an SVMO within Pisello's VMO.

Kaplan et al. (2015), writing in the *Harvard Business Review* in 2015, floated the idea of a VMO in the context of health-care organizations,

> A 'value management office' can greatly enhance an institution's ability to improve outcomes and costs across the enterprise. At a minimum, it can serve as a center of excellence to assist decentralized clinical units in outcomes and cost measurement and management, set priorities for continuous improvement projects, facilitate the creation of value-based payment models with insurers and employers, and ensure that new information technology platforms are aligned with the value agenda.

This description is much closer to my idea of an SVMO in that it is a center of excellence that considers the end-to-end value delivered by the organization both in terms of models and measurement. It recognizes the needs of multiple stakeholders—insurers and employers in this case. It even takes responsibility for ensuring that the IT activities are aligned, which reinforces my position that the business units and IT organizations need to collaborate to drive the greatest value from their software.

Kaplan's article gives two examples of health-care organizations that have implemented VMOs. I think that the SVMO could be easily accommodated in Kaplan et al.'s VMO, but more specificity about the role of the SVMO is needed. That is the purpose of this chapter.

The Office of Budget and Management (OBM) of the State of Ohio in the United States has a VMO with an excellent explanation of its motivation, which is noted as follows:[†]

---

* http://blog.alinean.com/2015/09/the-rise-of-value-management-office-vmo.html
[†] http://www.obm.ohio.gov/vmo/faq.aspx

What Is Value Management?
A structured approach similar to project management. Value management

- Extends across the life cycle of an initiative, from conception to implementation and evaluation
- Helps organizations achieve the intended outcome of a program or an initiative
- Measures financial and non-financial benefits of initiatives
- Looks across agencies and silos to identify enterprise results and efficiency

What Value Management Is Not
Value management is not an "add on" to the business process.

- It is integrated and aligned with other change initiatives
- It requires a results focus

Value management is not a quick fix or a silver bullet.

- It involves sustained change over the long-term
- It entails changes in perceptions, relationships, management principles, and actions

Value management is not "one size fits all."

Why Did (Ohio) OBM Create a Value Management Office?
Enterprise programs should be able to demonstrate achievement of expected benefits

- Process improvements and cost savings have not been captured to demonstrate benefits
- Some benefits have not been realized
- Future enterprise programs could improve cost recovery and savings for Ohio tax payers and agency constituents

While Ohio is clearly talking about the whole range of services that the state government delivers to its citizens, I would be happy to see all of the previously mentioned in a charter for any SVMO. Note that Ohio's OBM sees the VMO as a project management function.

In February 2015, Andy Gill floated the idea on his blog* of a VMO to replace the project management office (PMO) in organizations under the title, "The PMO is dead! Long live the VMO!" Gill's VMO would be:

---

* https://www.linkedin.com/pulse/pmo-dead-long-live-vmo-value-management-office-ally-gill

■ A business function, designed to oversee corporate governance, organizational change, quality, compliance and process management. The VMO is permanently staffed with a small core of value champions to co-ordinate, act as gatekeepers and maintain continuity of the function but the ideas, requirements and solutions come from Value Action Teams from within the body of the organization. These are virtual teams created from the people closest to the work, brought together to address real issues within their scope of expertise.

■ A supporting function, providing genuine assistance to the wider business. VMO staff should look at every activity they are involved with and be able to clearly articulate why they are doing it, who they are doing it for, what value it brings, and whether it is genuinely a business necessity.

■ A single conduit for all organizational change where it can evaluate the impact of change and how changes align with each other (or not) and prioritize accordingly. This helps to minimize the risk of change overwhelming the business, and the problem of multiple changes competing for the same resources.

Gill's VMO concept is organizational rather than focused on software development and, even though this book is narrowly focused, Gill's concept is consistent with my view of the SVMO because, as I have often repeated in this book, the value of software development can only be evaluated in an organizational context. Gill sees a functional VMO as a good replacement for dysfunctional PMOs and some of Gill's ideas—business function, small core team enhanced with short-lived virtual teams—are included in my vision of the SVMO. The title of his blog post implies that Gill believes that VMOs can and should arise from the ashes of PMOs.

It is not clear if he intends the same people to transition from PMO to VMO. While I know many project managers whose interpersonal skills and analytical capabilities would make them excellent candidates for the VMO, in many organizations today the role of project manager has been downgraded to basic project administration. People in these roles may be important to support the VMO function, but they will not be capable of driving the work, especially in the early days, because of the need to challenge assumptions and produce creative ways to measure value.

Gill's article includes some stark criticism of PMOs, which I have not repeated here. PMOs have been in existence in most large organizations for a long time. They were established to help standardize processes to ensure projects are executed efficiently and effectively and to measure that execution and effectiveness. PMOs and project managers have played an important role in streamlining organizations, but they are often disliked. Interestingly, they are often disliked equally among executives and staff. Executives see the PMO as always delivering bad news about missed deadlines and hold project managers accountable, or at least responsible, for those missed deadlines. The staff perceives the PMO as parasitic—someone always looking over their shoulder to ensure the proper boxes are checked without taking into consideration the challenges these workers face in accomplishing the task at hand.

The big question is whether the PMO is actually driving business value or if it's more focused on monitoring whether projects are on time and on budget. From a lean software engineering perspective, for maximum flow of value on a software development project, waste needs to be removed. In the *lean* world, waste means any activity that doesn't add value.

In a Waterfall organization, the PMO is justified because it has become the oil that keeps the software development engine moving. But even in Waterfall organizations, the PMO is becoming increasingly commoditized. The PMO has an opportunity to transform from a group that standardizes processes to improve efficiency and measure compliance, to an SVMO that optimizes processes to maximize value flow and measure value.

Since Agile organizations tend to inherit a PMO of questionable value from Waterfall or not use one at all, the SVMO would be a new function. In Agile organizations, the function of the SVMO would be to get the business units to collaborate with the technical team on assigning value to features and epics and making that value visible so everyone is focused on driving value for the project.

What Is the Mission of the SVMO?

To make software value visible and to maximize end-to-end software value flow to customers.

What Are the Functions of the SVMO?

With thanks to Pisello, Kaplan et al., the State of Ohio, and Gill, I propose the key functions set out in Figure 9.1.

Like Gill, I believe that the SVMO is a business function, which needs to be permanently staffed with a small core of value champions to coordinate, act as gatekeepers, and maintain continuity of the function. I believe the only way that this can be done is if some of the permanent staff in the SVMO have respectable business credentials and some have respectable software development credentials. I further agree with Gill that the SVMO should be supported by virtual *value action teams* from within the body of the organization so that ideas, requirements, and solutions come from the "coal face" of the business and software development. By way of example, BT in the United Kingdom has something they call *CIO offices*. These CIO offices are part of the business units and sit at the interface between the business and software development. They tend to be staffed by respected former

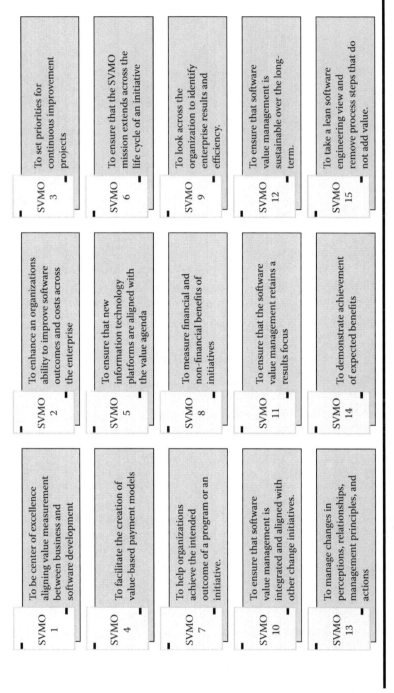

Figure 9.1 Key functions of the SVMO.

SVMO 1
To be center of excellence aligning value measurement between business and software development

SVMO 2
To enhance an organizations ability to improve software outcomes and costs across the enterprise

SVMO 3
To set priorities for continuous improvement projects

SVMO 4
To facilitate the creation of value-based payment models

SVMO 5
To ensure that new information technology platforms are aligned with the value agenda

SVMO 6
To ensure that the SVMO mission extends across the life cycle of an initiative

SVMO 7
To help organizations achieve the intended outcome of a program or an initiative.

SVMO 8
To measure financial and non-financial benefits of initiatives

SVMO 9
To look across the organization to identify enterprise results and efficiency.

SVMO 10
To ensure that software value management is integrated and aligned with other change initiatives.

SVMO 11
To ensure that the software value management retains a results focus

SVMO 12
To ensure that software value management is sustainable over the long-term.

SVMO 13
To manage changes in perceptions, relationships, management principles, and actions

SVMO 14
To demonstrate achievement of expected benefits

SVMO 15
To take a lean software engineering view and remove process steps that do not add value.

members of the software development team seeking a temporary or permanent insight into the workings of the business as part of their career development. Their recent experience of the software development organization makes them invaluable for translating across the interface.

Software Value of People

In Figure 9.1, SVMO function #2 is, "To enhance an organization's ability to improve software outcomes and costs across the enterprise." I want to make explicit here an important point about where some, or most, or all of the software value resides in organizations. It is in people's heads. This software value in people's heads needs to be managed explicitly, because it represents a risk to the organization's ability to improve software outcomes. The SVMO is a good place to manage this risk because they can operate with some detachment from the personal relationships in teams and between teams and their managers.

Identifying the risk of loss of software knowledge is relatively easy. At the team level, the SVMO needs to address the question of whether there are any parts of the software that only one (two, three) people understand sufficiently well to be trusted to make changes. At the product/program level and portfolio level, this question might be applied to outsourced vendors. One of our clients reached a point in their long-term outsourcing strategy where they realized that they no longer had the internal knowledge to validate the estimates that their vendors provided for enhancing some of their applications. They quickly started to recruit people with the right skills to redress the balance.

Managing the risk of software knowledge contained in people's heads is not easy. Even the most dedicated and loyal employee understands that being the only person to understand a piece of software (or any other organizational asset) represents leverage. Why should they share when doing so potentially reduces their usefulness and value to the organization? A "brute force attack" to this challenge never works. Instead, the right incentives need to be set up. These will be different for each individual, but many in software development will respond to the offer of passing on routine chores in return for more interesting work. Incidentally, the *Agilists* are right—documenting the scarce knowledge is not sufficient and will probably not work in most cases. You need to have at least two practitioners who are knowledgeable about each piece of code—this is a little-mentioned benefit of the practice of pair programming (now claimed by Agile).

How Should the SVMO Itself Be Measured?

The mission of the SVMO is, "To make software value visible and to maximize end-to-end software value flow to customers." It should be measured against this mission, which I will break up into its two constituent parts.

	Portfolio	**Product/program**	**Team**
Software value information available	Yes/No	Yes/No	Yes/No
% of individuals with access to software value data	0–100%	0–100%	0–100%
% of individuals using software value data to inform decisions	0–100%	0–100%	0–100%
Software value flow increase versus last quarter	%	%	%

Figure 9.2   Dashboard for measuring SVMO success at software value visibility.

How do we measure if the SVMO is making software value visible? The success criteria here is whether or not software value is visible throughout the organization. If we invoke the Scaled Agile Framework® (SAFe) model for software development again, there are four levels for assessing this: portfolio, value stream, product/program, and team. There are also two perspectives: Is the appropriate information available? Are individuals making decisions based on that data?

We can present the success criteria for this first set of SVMO metrics on the simple dashboard shown in Figure 9.2.

Portfolio, Product/Program, and Team Measurement

Each of the metrics for the performance of the SVMO in Figure 9.2 needs to be measured for each level: portfolio, product/program, and team because the nature of the software value information required will be different. Certainly, some of the data can be aggregated in Agile implementations. However, just because all stories have software value data associated with them for all teams in the program, it doesn't necessarily follow that all epics at the portfolio level have software value data. In fact, this is probably close to the best-case scenario today—all the product owners of all the teams in a mature Agile organization are assigning local value sizes. As I have said earlier in this book, I have no complaints about this scenario, because it is better than nothing. It represents a sort of local maximum, though, because those local value sizes should be derived in some way from business value data at the portfolio level. Put another way, the method for assigning value sizes at the team level will have to change before it can get better. There may be some resistance to this change among the teams.

Software Value Information Available

The first of the four success metrics for the SVMO, as described in Figure 9.2, is determining the software value information that is available. This is an entry-level metric for the SVMO—something to work on immediately. In a fairly stable organization, it should be quite easy to "switch on the lights" for these binary input metrics and keep them on. In a more volatile organization, perhaps with lots of new initiatives or in an outsourcing scenario, keeping these metrics positive will require ongoing diligence and training of new staff.

Percentage of Individuals with Access to Software Value Data

The second success metric is the assessment of the percentage of individuals with access to the software value data. This is an input metric and provides more granular data than the "information available" metric, because all individuals must have access if the software value data is to influence their decision-making.

Percentage of Individuals Using Software Value Data to Make Informed Decisions

The next metric is the percentage of individuals who are using the software value data to make more informed decisions. I consider this to be an output metric, but I concede that it is a "soft" metric because the only way to gather the metric data is by surveying the individuals, perhaps quarterly. Like all surveys, it is reasonable to expect that some individuals will not be entirely truthful, especially when the desired behavior is so obvious. However, I believe this metric is worthwhile because, as a soft metric, it has the purpose of encouraging the right behavior rather than imposing it—always a good change management tactic.

Software Value Flow Increase versus Last Quarter

Measuring the software value flow increase compared with the last quarter is the final metric. This is the ultimate "hard" output metric for the SVMO—Is the SVMO making a difference to the flow of value? I would strongly recommend normalizing the underlying value flow metric here for reasonable comparison of historical data.

One simple normalizing approach could be to use a return on investment (ROI) type methodology by measuring software value delivered per $100 thousand of budget spent on software development in that quarter.

Another simple normalizing approach that might be useful at the portfolio and product/program levels (and team level for Waterfall) is to measure software value delivered per function point of software functionality delivered.

While the ROI approach represents the bottom line, it can hide nuances in the *software value productivity* of different parts of the software development team or vendors because of differences in hourly cost rates in different geographic regions. Executives reading this (including me!) might initially say that the ROI is "the bottom line," but exchange rates and local hourly rates can change, so I would recommend using both metrics. For example, it would be wrong to credit the SVMO with the 10% improvement in ROI-based value productivity for U.K. teams that was a result of the drop in that country's exchange rate after the Brexit vote.

SVMO and Earned Value Management

As we talk about SVMO metrics, *earned value management* (EVM) comes to mind. As mentioned in Chapter 8, EVM is a specialized discipline that is most often used in the context of long-running U.S. federal government projects to enable the measurement of progress and, in some cases, enable stage payments based on that progress. The Project Management Institute (PMI) has published a simple, *Practice Standard for Earned Value Management*—Second Edition," (as a complement to the PMBOK® Guide), which provides an accessible introduction to earned value management that allows me to summarize (and oversimplify) here. EVM consists of

- Building a project plan by decomposing the high-level project activities into a set of dependent and independent work tasks, usually called the *work breakdown structure* (WBS).
- Each work task in the WBS has planned scope, duration, resources and, hence, cost (usually called *planned value* even though it isn't really value—see the Rodrigues quote at the end of this chapter). From this data, a curve of planned value can be plotted on a cost versus time chart (See Figure 9.3) by calculating the number of WBS line items that are planned to have been completed by the chosen date and the amount of planned value associated with each item. In its simplest form, the planned value is simply the number of WBS line items due to be delivered by the chosen date (i.e., each WBS line item has an assumed value of one).
- Each WBS item has a planned or budgeted cost. Hence, there is a total cost associated with the planned value curve, which is known as the *budget at completion* (BAC).
- Once work has commenced, the cumulative *earned value* can be tracked by calculating the number of completed WBS line items and their cumulative value. As can be seen in my example (Figure 9.3), there is often variance between the planned value and the earned value. In my example, the earned value is less than the planned value. This is a scope delivery problem because less scope has been delivered than was planned by the report date. This suggests a possible schedule overrun. It is worth noting here that there are different opinions about what counts as a "completed" WBS line item. I prefer the straightforward binary interpretation, it is either done or it isn't. The Agile concept of *definition of done* can be helpful here. However, I have seen

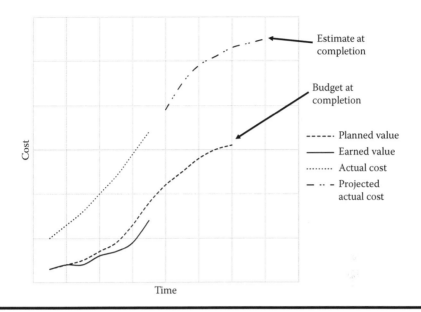

Figure 9.3   Example EVM chart.

projects in which the project managers ask the teams for "percent complete" on their WBS line items and use those numbers to calculate a "rough" earned value. As a manager, I have heard "90 percent complete" from too many software development teams to trust anything based on percent complete.

▪ In addition to, but separate from, the earned value calculation, the cumulative *actual cost* incurred to date can be calculated. It might be expected that with earned value running behind schedule, actual cost might be less than planned. It can be seen in my example (Figure 9.3) that this is not necessarily a valid assumption. The project in Figure 9.3 is behind in schedule and overrunning in cost. Indeed, the forward projection of cost for the project suggests a significant difference between the BAC and the current *estimate at completion*. Figure 9.3 is a project in trouble! Of course, that information is extremely valuable for project management, but not a useful contribution to measuring the software value of the organization or even the contribution to be expected from this project.

For organizations that use EVM, the SVMO would be a great place for EVM to be monitored and managed but, at face value, it is hard to see how value information could be gathered unless each WBS line item has a true or relative value metric associated with it. Based on value metrics described in previous chapters, the granularity of a typical WBS does not really lend itself to separate value metrics for each line item. A typical WBS line item is too detailed and small to sustain an independent value. For readers with an Agile rather than Waterfall background,

WBS line items are typically as small as or smaller than user stories. Clearly, trying to assign even relative independent value to individual line items in a WBS would be difficult, time-consuming, and ultimately counter-productive.

Is there any way that an SVMO can work with a requirement for EVM and use it to build good value data? Perhaps. The key is to remind ourselves that if we have built a process to maximize value flow, then we only need to establish relative value for decision-making. We can assume (somewhat heroically) that the project (for which we are doing EVM based on a WBS) has already been prioritized against other projects for maximum value delivery. How, then, can we develop an algorithm or process for translating the relative value of the project into values for each WBS line item? I have set out one possible solution in Figure 9.4.

Clearly, the assignment of 100 "earned value points" to each project is arbitrary, but my thinking was to drive toward some sense of the percentage value of different parts of the WSJF. Additionally, I recommend striking a pragmatic compromise between the huge WBSs that exist in many government projects and time that could be wasted subdividing value when the subdivisions are increasingly unjustifiable and meaningless.

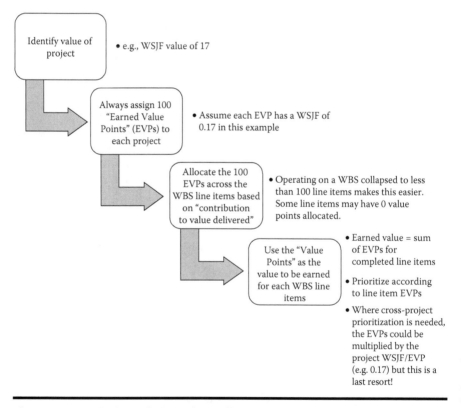

Figure 9.4   Assigning relative value to line items in an EVM WBS.

The PMI quotes Alexandre Rodrigues,* and I'm happy to leave him with the last word in this section:

> The EVM method was developed to measure scope accomplishment and cost and schedule performance. The term 'earned value' actually refers to 'scope accomplished.'
>
> However, the term 'earned value' is often interpreted by managers to mean 'realized benefits' or 'produced economic value.' In most cases for projects, the budget value of the scope accomplished does not equate to the value of business benefits achieved, nor economic value produced.
>
> For that to be the case, EVM concepts would have to be applied at the program and portfolio level, to measure the performance of programs based on benefits realization and the performance of portfolios based on the creation of organizational values.

Summary

In this chapter, I have focused on why and how to set up an SVMO. We have considered the relative value to the organization going forward of a PMO and an SVMO. We have seen that EVM and software value management are different, but could be made to work together where EVM is a required process.

In the next chapter, I will switch gears and look at the value of software estimation—essentially planning value delivery. Arguably, software value delivery planning could be a function of the SVMO, but I have excluded it intentionally because I believe in the lean-Agile principle of "responding to change over following a plan." I think there is a risk that the SVMO would revert to being a traditional PMO without adhering to that principle and I don't want that to happen.

---

* Rodrigues, A. quoted in Project Management Institute, *Practice Standard for Earned Value Management*, 2nd edition. Project Management Institute, 2011.

Chapter 10

The Business Value of Software Estimation

Estimation as a topic is often a synthesis of three related, but different concepts: budgeting, estimation, and planning. These concepts are typical in a normal commercial organization; however, they might be referred to differently depending on your lens (see Figure 1.2) or business model.

Immediately, it should be clear that software estimation impacts *business value* because it impacts business planning—what we think we can do to improve the business in the future—and budgeting—how we can pay for our plans to improve the business in the future. While the three concepts to which estimation contributes are often conflated, I have a bigger problem with those senior managers, including some chief information officers (CIOs), who don't understand or choose to ignore the role that good software estimation should play in their business.

All too often, I see organizations where estimation is left to "expert knowledge." That is, if the organization wants to know how much something will cost or how long it will take, they ask an expert, who pulls a number out of their head (or some other part of their anatomy). At best, the expert does a back-of-the-envelope calculation (sometimes on a spreadsheet to make it look precise) using a few parameters that have worked in the past. Unfortunately, and it's not the expert's fault, this approach has very little chance of consistent success.

There is a whole field of research on cognitive bias* telling us that estimates based on expert knowledge are prone to all sorts of human biases. For example,

---

* A good starting point is Tom Cagley's presentation to the STAREast conference, "The Impact of Cognitive Biases on Test and Project Teams", at http://bit.ly/2pG5kv3.

as humans, we often have a limited capacity to separate our last project estimate from the details of what actually happened on that project—we tend to base the new estimate on the old estimate, not the old actuals. We tend to be overly optimistic about our ability to complete work; or, as experts, we assume we can apply our own productivity and knowledge of the problem to our team, some of whom will certainly be less productive or knowledgeable than us. This overoptimism is particularly true if we are not busy—the same project will have a lower estimate if we are lightly loaded than if we are very busy. And so on.

Too often, I have witnessed annual budget planning sessions where executives squeeze a budget to get all the projects in that they want by "slicing and dicing" the individual programs or projects *in the budget meeting*. It goes something like this:

> Business executive: So, you're telling me that I can't get all eight of my programs in the budget for next year?
> Senior software development manager: Yes, that's right.
> Business: Well, what do I need to cut out of the requirements to get them all in?
> Software: I don't know. We were told that all of the requirements were essential.
> Business: Well, how about if we drop requirement A from program 1 and requirement C from project 3? My guess is that should bring us easily under budget.
> Software: I don't know. Maybe. I will have to go back to the experts and check.
> Business: Who is running the software development? You or the experts? Don't you know roughly how these estimates are built?
> Software: Well, yes, but ...
> Business: So will these two changes, at a high level, get us under budget?
> Software: I suppose they probably will.
> Business: Good. Settled. Next item on the agenda.

I'm sure that some readers will be smiling in recognition of having heard something similar. If not, I'm sorry if I have shattered some illusions or confirmed some worst fears. As you noticed, *business value* was not mentioned in any of these discussions—the focus was all about fitting the projects into a financial constraint. Of course, mature lean-Agile companies will be managing their budgets according to my suggestions in Chapter 5, which concentrates on lean software development that drives business value. Unfortunately, there aren't enough of those around…yet.

As I have said, the concepts of estimation are often conflated so it is important to understand the relationship between the three. An estimate is a finite approximation of cost, effort, and/or duration based on some basis of knowledge (this is known as a basis of estimation). The flow of activity conflated as estimation often runs from budget (which usually includes some high-level estimates), to project estimation (more detailed estimates), to planning (specific activities are allocated resources based on estimates). In most organizations, the act of generating a finite approximation typically begins as a form of portfolio management in order to generate a budget for a department or group.

The budgeting process helps make decisions about which pieces of work are to be done. Most organizations have a portfolio of work that is larger than they can accomplish, therefore they need a mechanism for prioritization. Most portfolio managers, whether proponents of an Agile or a classic approach, would defend using business value as a key determinant of prioritization. Business value requires having some type of forecast of cost and benefit of the project over some time frame. Once a project enters a delivery pipeline in a classic organization, an estimate is typically generated. The estimate is generally believed to be more accurate than the original budget due to the information gathered as the project is groomed to begin.

Software Development Estimates

The information and process needed to generate a software estimate is fairly standard and Figure 10.1 shows a generic approach.

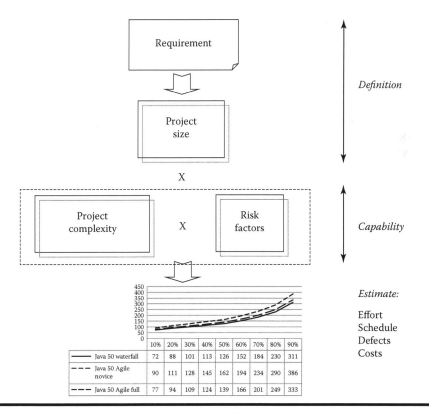

Figure 10.1   Components of a software estimate.

It should be noted that a good estimate, generated with an estimation tool, should not generate a *point estimate* such as, "this project will be completed in 1000 person hours." Instead, the estimate should be a probability distribution such as, "there is a 50% likelihood that this project will be completed in 800 person hours and an 80% likelihood that it will be completed in 1100 person hours." This is a true reflection of the effect of the estimation *cone of uncertainty** and is usually presented in a chart as shown at the bottom of Figure 10.1. Point estimates, especially early in a software development project, are notoriously poor because they do not communicate any sense of the uncertainty of the estimate. It has to be said that executives hate proper, range estimates because they are forced to decide what probability, and risk, they want to commit to in the planning for the project. Some organizations actually standardize the risk they will build into their plans; for example, "all of our estimates have an 80% likelihood of becoming actuals." I prefer to take a project-by-project approach to the risk I'm willing to take on that project. It's fair to say here that I will very rarely choose to plan based on the 100% likelihood estimate because it represents the absolute worst-case scenario, if everything goes wrong.

Where Is the Business Value?

Figure 10.2 shows how the estimation cone of uncertainty changes over time for a hypothetical project.

The classic estimation cone of uncertainty around the *working estimate* starts wide at the start of the project. It may begin at ±100%, because there is uncertainty around the requirements (no matter how much work has been put into defining them) and, hence, the *size* of the problem. Size, ideally measured in function points at this high-level start point of the project (story points have their value at the detailed, team level), is the main driver for estimating effort and duration on most software projects. The development team probably has not been assigned at this point and so there is uncertainty around their capabilities (another key driver for effort and duration estimates), and the technology for the project may or may not have been fixed at this point. As decisions are made and the team discovers some of the hidden challenges that the project presents, then the cone of uncertainty starts to shrink toward the final estimate. The final "estimate" is exactly the same as the "actual" and can only be made with 100% confidence when the project is complete.

From a business value perspective, the cone of uncertainty is important because of the impact that the rigid adoption of early estimates can have on the budgeting and planning processes, especially if the software development is outsourced.

---

* https://en.wikipedia.org/wiki/Cone_of_Uncertainty

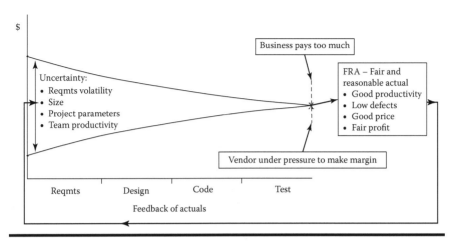

Figure 10.2   Estimation cone of uncertainty.

As an aside, it is tempting to use language here about the challenges presented when estimates are "wrong." That is a misconception. Estimates are rarely wrong, rather they are communicated without the necessary information about that particular estimate's cone of uncertainty. Alternatively, the cone of uncertainty may be communicated but ignored. It is often seen as the software development group "hedging their bets," instead of what really is—a fact of life.

Returning to the business value, I have shown a range of estimates at the end of the project in Figure 10.2. These represent the range of estimates that could have been adopted at different times in the project based on the cone of uncertainty. With a strong parametric estimation process based on historic data from the development group doing the work, there is a good chance that a fair and reasonable estimation of effort could have been achieved at the start. Alternatively, with a weaker process, the early estimate could be too high or too low. In an outsourced environment, too high an estimate would mean the business could end up paying too much for a fixed-price project. Similarly, too low an estimate could result in the vendor swallowing a loss on the project or, worse for the buyer, being driven to maintain a target profit margin by assigning lower-cost developers to the project with a potential reduction in quality. This will need fixing, which will make the project overrun even if it doesn't actually cost the buyer more financially.

There is a more fundamental business value problem with poor estimation processes even when the financial impact is hidden by the development being done internally. Put simply, an overestimate hurts the budgeting process most, and an underestimate hurts the planning process most.

Let's take the underestimate first. An underestimate tends to be avoided at all costs by development organizations because it embarrasses the development team and managers alike in the eyes of their customers. It makes them look incompetent as the projects overrun or blow through their budgets. Project and budget overruns impact planning significantly as inter-project dependencies blow up or resources aren't available when they should be. Past experience of this embarrassment has led many "successful" software development leaders to base their career advancement on careful overestimating. They also develop skills in negotiating project scope reduction when even the overestimates were missed. Unfortunately, it's arguable that in many organizations, the difference between successful and unsuccessful software development leaders pivots on these skills. I knew of one organization that managed this to the point that all the management received their bonuses every year even though they consistently under delivered against their original commitments but over delivered against the (smaller) commitments they ended the year with, after manipulating the change control process. Their business colleagues (internal customers) assumed they were wildly successful. Their external customers were not so sure and the business suffered over time.

This leads directly to the problem with overestimating. A culture of overestimating to avoid planning problems (and team embarrassment) can significantly impact budgeting. If the estimates for the set of projects needed or desired in a given budget window (usually annual) are all higher than necessary, then the total cost estimate will be higher than necessary and there is a strong chance that some projects will not make the cut imposed by the available budget. For example, if there are 10 projects needed or desired for next year with an overall budget of $10 million, and the fair and reasonable estimate for each project is $1 million, then all 10 should be feasible. However, if all 10 are overestimated by 10%, then each will be estimated at $1.1 million and only 9 will be chosen for the coming year's development. Assuming that the projects have different business values and the project with the least business value is dropped (hey, I can dream!), we can assume that the business value delivered next year will be at least 5% less than it could or should have been. Interestingly, this loss of business value usually goes unnoticed, because it is not visible and doesn't carry the same level of "in the moment" embarrassment as the project overrun. Hence, overestimating dominates as the safest course of action for estimating in organizations that don't make value visible or don't use modern lean-Agile techniques for portfolio management.

Returning to the outsourced software development lens, I have shown in Figure 10.3 how the estimation cone of uncertainty can sometimes be disrupted when part or all of the software development is outsourced to a software development vendor.

Referring to Figure 10.3, we can assume that the early part of the cone of uncertainty is unchanged because, generally, the requirements definition and some or all of the design are done in-house. I say "generally" because I know of one organization that had outsourced to the extent that it didn't have sufficient expertise left in-house to specify requirements and do design, so it had to rely on its vendors to perform those activities, as well as doing the development. All the while, they cling to the illusion that they were only outsourcing coding and testing! To be fair, our client had already realized the problem with this set-up before we arrived on the

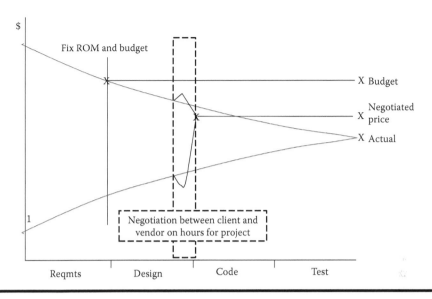

Figure 10.3   Impact of uncertainty on outsourced estimates.

scene and were implementing a build-up of in-house expertise. The disruption to the cone of uncertainty in Figure 10.3 occurs because there comes a point in the project when the client and vendor must agree on an estimate for the effort and duration. Usually, the client establishes a budget for the outsourced part of the project fairly early on (as shown on Figure 10.3).

In long-standing outsourcing relationships, as opposed to one-off development contracts, the client and vendor typically establish a *rate card* that specifies the hourly rates to be paid for different development skills and levels of skill. Hence, the effort and duration estimate simply becomes a proposal for what people (at what rates) will deliver the work in how many hours each. Inevitably, that proposal becomes a negotiation, which may or may not result in an estimate in the "fair and reasonable" range. As we can see in Figure 10.3, the client has "won" the negotiation by getting a negotiated price that is less than they budgeted. But have they really "won" if the vendor's price is still above the "actual" at the end of the project?

It is reasonable to assume that "wins" and "losses" in this scenario tend to balance out, but there are real risks for the client and the vendor if this balance does not occur. The impacts of imbalanced trends in estimating and negotiating between client and vendor are summarized in Figure 10.4.

It is important to note that the most likely causes of an imbalanced trend are lack of information and a culture of aggressive negotiation on either side. Of the two, the former is more important to address. Good information in the form of good estimates based on defensible choices of estimation parameters and parameter values can, usually, disarm the most aggressive negotiator (even if an appeal to a higher authority is required).

Trend for ...	... Budget greater than	... Negotiated price greater than	... Actual price greater than
Budget		Budget overrun (budget waste)	Scope cut and/or budget overrun (planning waste)
Negotiated price	Budgeting waste		Excess vendor loss and/or low cost resources applied to project (planning waste)
Actual price	Budgeting waste	Unnecessary cost (budget waste) and excess vendor profit	

Figure 10.4   Impact of over- and under-estimating trends when outsourcing.

#NoEstimates*

In a chapter about the business value of software estimates, it is perhaps a little strange to include a discussion about a movement that seeks, to a greater or lesser extent, to do away with software estimates. Readers may already be aware of the #NoEstimates movement within the Agile community and, if not, they are sure to be made aware of it if they discuss estimating with Agile colleagues. The basic premise behind the idea is that estimates are a form of planning. It follows that if software development is a learning process that will always involve discovery and be influenced by rapid external change, then detailed, up-front plans are a waste of time (not good lean practice). The #NoEstimates advocates argue that without detailed, up-front plans, detailed up-front estimates will be inaccurate and also a waste of time. Since we are keen to maximize value flow and avoid waste, we must take the #NoEstimates philosophy seriously.

Over the past few years, the concept of #NoEstimates has emerged and has become a movement within the Agile community. #NoEstimates has several camps revolving around a central concept of not generating task-level estimates. The newness of the movement also means that there are no (or very few) large project examples that can be used as references.† Further, at the time of writing, there are no published quantitative studies of results comparing the results of work performed using #NoEstimates techniques with other methods. To better understand the thinking behind #NoEstimates, we need to begin by establishing a shared context and language

---

* My colleague, Tom Cagley, has written extensively on #NoEstimates and some of his work is included in this chapter with permission. See https://tcagley.wordpress.com/2015/04/16/noestimates/

† The C3 Project was used to hone and prove many of the Agile techniques (eXtreme Programing and WIKIs for example) and acted as a training ground for many luminaries of the early Agile movement.

across the gamut of estimating ideas, whether Agile or not. Without a shared language that includes #NoEstimates, we will not be able to compare the concept to the classical estimation concepts, which were described earlier in this chapter.

There are two main camps of thought leaders in the #NoEstimate movement (the two camps probably reflect more of a continuum of ideas rather than absolutes). The first camp argues that a team should break work down into small chunks and then immediately begin completing those small chunks (doing the highest value first). The chunks would build up quickly to a *minimum viable product* (MVP) that can generate feedback, so the team can hone its ability to deliver value. This camp leverages continuous feedback and re-planning to guide work, and luminaries like Woody Zuill* often champion this camp. A second camp begins in a similar manner—by breaking the work into small pieces, prioritizing on value (and perhaps risk), delivering against an MVP to generate feedback—but they measure *throughput*. Throughput is a measure of how many units of work (e.g., stories or widgets) a team can deliver in a specific period of time. Continuously measuring the throughput of the team provides a tool to understand when work needs to start in order for it to be delivered within a period of time. Average throughput is used to provide the team and other stakeholders with a forecast of the future. This is very similar to the throughput measure used in *Kanban*. People like Vasco Duarte† champion the second camp who practice #NoEstimates from a lean or Kanban perspective. Both camps in the #NoEstimates movement eschew developing story- or task-level estimates. The major difference is on the use of throughput to provide forecasting, which is central to bottom-up estimating and planning at the lowest level of the classic estimation continuum.

To the extent that planning is done in Agile teams, teams breakdown stories into tasks based on personnel assigned and by estimating the effort required at the task level. These estimates are combined into higher-level estimates for the work that can be completed in a sprint. Any of these steps can (but should not) be called estimation. This process, if misused, can cause several team and organizational issues. Proponents of the #NoEstimates movement often classify these issues as estimation pathologies. Jim Benson, author of *Personal Kanban*, established a taxonomy of estimation pathologies‡ that includes

- Guarantism: A belief that an estimate is actually correct
- Swami-itis: A belief that an estimate is a basis for sound decision-making
- Craftosis: An assumption that estimates can be done better
- Reality blindness: An insistence that estimates are prima facie implementable
- Promosoriality: A belief that estimates are possible (planning facility)

---

* http://zuill.us/WoodyZuill/about/
† https://www.infoq.com/articles/book-review-noestimates
‡ http://herdingcats.typepad.com/my_weblog/2015/03/five-estimating-pathologies-and-their-corrective-actions.html 4/27/15 or http://moduscooperandi.com/blog/modus-list-3-our-five-estimate-pathologies/ 4/27/15

Estimates by definition are imprecise and can only be accurate within a range of confidence; however, these facts are often "forgotten" in lieu of the single number contract, for example, we will do 17 tasks in this sprint. Acting as if one or more of these pathologies are true has generated the anger and frustration needed to fuel the #NoEstimates movement.

When done correctly, both #NoEstimates and classic estimation are tools to generate feedback and create guidance for the organization. In its purest form, #NoEstimates uses functionality to generate feedback and to provide guidance about what is possible. The less absolutist "Kanban'er" form of #NoEstimates uses both functional software and throughput measures as feedback and guidance tools. Classic estimation tools use plans and *performance to the plan* to generate feedback and guidance. The goal is usually the same, it is just that the mechanisms are very different.

#NoEstimates Scenarios

Standard Corporate Environments

Organizational budgeting (strategy and portfolio): Continuous flow or other #NoEstimates techniques don't answer the central questions most organizations need to answer, which include

- How much money should I allocate for software development, enhancements, and maintenance?
- Which projects or products should we fund?
- Which projects will return the greatest amount of value?

While most budgets are "scientific guesses," there is a need to understand at least some approximation of the size and cost of the work on the overall backlog.

High-Level Estimation (Product and Release)

Release plans and product road maps could easily be built from forecasts based on teams that have a track record of delivering value on a regular basis. The idea of #NoEstimates can be applied at this level of planning and estimation IF the right conditions are met. Conditions include

- Stable teams
- Agile mindset (both team and organizational levels)
- Well-groomed stories

The classic questions of "when?", "what?", and "how much?" can be answered in this environment for work done by single teams or by scaled Agile programs.

It should be noted that the example used by Woody Zuill, which uses the most frequently referenced form of #NoEstimates (start, deliver, get feedback, and then do more), is a reflection of an environment where all of these factors are favorable.

Task-Level Estimation (Iteration and Daily)

Task-level planning is the sweet spot for #NoEstimates discussions. Stable teams that are able to consistently accept and deliver what is expected do not have any need to plan effort at a task level.

Commercial/Contractual Work

Raja Bavani, senior director at Cognizant Technology Solutions, stated in a recent conversation with my colleague Tom Cagley that he thought that #NoEstimates was a non-starter in a contractual environment. Where one party is buying something from another, there is always a need to specify what that "something" is in order to ensure reasonable value for money!

Budgeting, Estimation, Planning, #NoEstimates, and the Agile Planning Onion

There are many levels of estimation including budgeting, high-level estimation, and task planning (detailed estimation), and this is the key to understanding where the #NoEstimates philosophy is applicable. We can link a more classic view of estimation to the *Agile planning onion*, popularized by Mike Cohn (2005) (see Figure 10.5).

In the Agile planning onion, strategic planning is on the outside of the onion and the planning that occurs in the daily sprint meetings is at the core of the onion.

Figure 10.5   Agile planning onion.

Budgeting is a strategic form of estimation that most corporate and governmental entities perform. Other than in its most extreme form, budgeting is generally not a practice being considered by #NoEstimate proponents. Estimation exists in the middle layers of the Agile planning onion (product and release layers). In classic estimation, these estimates are often developed using top-down techniques, such as analogy or parametric estimation using function points, story points, or T-shirt sizing. #NoEstimates proponents leveraging Kanban techniques perform this level of estimates as forecasts using average flow rates and queuing theory (an application of Little's law). The resistance at this level has generated the perception that size-based estimation at this level (and later, planning at the task level) generates several pathological behaviors within organizations. The final layers of the planning onion, iteration and daily planning, are generally the areas of highest concern to the #NoEstimates movement. While tasks may be identified, effort is not assigned.

It should be noted that while effort estimates are not done at the planning layers or generally at the estimation layer, most teams adopt rules to break work down into predictable units. Rules or guidelines are often established that affect story and task size. The use of rules to govern granularity is one of the reasons flow measures can be used to forecast when work needs to begin in order to meet date or dependency requirements. Johanna Rothman stated in her article "The Case for #NoEstimates," that "when you deliver small, valuable chunks of work every day or more often" that you can avoid estimation. The critical words being small and every day, which require the team to understand how to groom stories to the desired granularity. Whether through the use of rules or feedback, using these techniques to groom stories could easily be construed as a crude form of estimation.

Summary

In this chapter, I have argued that the business value of software estimation is derived from the fact that estimation is both a form of planning and an input to the business planning process. Planning is considered an important competency in most business environments. I have considered the Agile aversion to planning and the evolution of the #NoEstimates philosophy. But, using #NoEstimates techniques does not help organizations to budget. Using #NoEstimates techniques requires breaking down stories into manageable, predictable chunks so that teams can predictably deliver value. The ability to predictably deliver value provides organizations with the tool to forecast the delivery. #NoEstimates really isn't eliminating estima … it is just estimating differently.

In the next chapter, I will investigate a different perspective of estimating the business value of the software of a business that is a target for a merger or acquisition. How much of the target's software is a real or potential asset to the mergers and acquisitions (M&A) deal and how much is a real or potential liability?

Chapter 11

Mergers and Acquisitions: Software Value and Risks

In this chapter, I will take a different perspective on software value by considering the business value of the software of a company that is a target for a merger or acquisition. How much of the target's software is a real or potential asset to the *mergers and acquisitions* (M&A) deal and how much is a real or potential liability?

In some respects and for one set of stakeholders in particular—the investors—this is the "acid test" of software value. Many venture capitalists, investors, and managers have experienced unforeseen and unnecessary losses due to hidden challenges in a target company's software. Excessive enhancement requirements stemming from the size and/or complexity of a software asset can lead to significant upgrade and maintenance costs—or worse—non-performing functionality. These, sometimes large, issues can remain unidentified until very late in the transaction.

Those who have unexpectedly dealt with these problems often face a loss of clients as they struggle to adapt to the new demands placed on their software development departments by their acquirers. Pressured to meet sometimes unrealistic budgetary and release constraints, perhaps due to excessive transaction savings expectations, they find themselves understaffed and incapable of getting their software development back under control.

The questions that I set out in this chapter are not so much about what the management of the organization thinks their software is worth, but how much will the market pay for it? As such, it is reasonable to apply some of the ideas in this chapter to an organization's software value metrics even if there is no merger or acquisition on the table. A periodic *mark to market* or fair value accounting of the accrued software value will have the useful side benefit of tightening up the value models in use in the day to day, or perhaps more realistically, monthly, or quarterly assessments of value delivered and value flow from software development.

Why is risk important with the software value assessment? The risk I am referring to in this chapter is almost always a risk that can be mitigated. For example, if the target company's software has a lot of defects, these can be fixed, but at a cost. In an M&A scenario, the trick is to establish a mitigation cost for each risk and include that in the transaction cost negotiation.

While M&A valuation skills are widely available in the general sense to assist with my proposed periodic mark-to-market exercise, my experience has been that the vast majority of practitioners in the M&A valuation space are unskilled and/or inexperienced in identifying the opportunities and challenges presented by the software portfolios of their target companies. Sometimes, this is not an issue because software just isn't that important to the purchasing company or the purchased company. More and more though, the unique value of the target company is embodied in their business processes, which are enabled in or dependent on their software.

This chapter is intended to help organizations (including investment bankers) to structure their assessment of the business value of a target organization's software and the risk associated with continuing to use it. Readers who work for not-for-profit organizations might be tempted to skip this chapter. Please don't. While not-for-profits are unlikely to be "acquired" in the traditional sense, they are sometimes merged with other not-for-profit agencies or organizations and this chapter is very relevant to that scenario. While it is an extreme example, the U.S. Department of Homeland Security was formed in 2002 from 22 existing federal agencies.* On a smaller scale, some local government authorities in the United Kingdom are merging their information technology (IT) departments and capabilities to try to save money.†

Prioritizing the Software Value and Risk Assessment Based on Business Functions

As we think about the structure of the acquirer's valuation and risk assessment process, we should start by separating out the business functions of the target company (and their associated software) into those functions that are similar to the acquiring company and those that are different. Put another way, the merger or acquisition is usually happening either to grow the acquirer's capabilities and/or customers in a business that it already operates or to diversify the acquirer's capabilities outside of the business that it already operates. Similar functions might include, for example, finance and human resources (HR), but could also include other, more specialized

---

* https://www.dhs.gov/history
† http://www.techmarketview.com/ukhotviews/archive/2016/09/22/sopra-steria-shared -service-shares-after-seven-years

business processes if the target is operating in the same business. Different functions are most likely to appear when the acquirer is diversifying. Probably there will be a mix of similar and different functions. While an apparently trivial exercise, this first step is important, because it starts to prioritize the evaluation of the target's software for value and risk.

Software for Common Functions

By way of an example, both companies will have some sort of financial software. It is highly unlikely that the acquirer will adopt the target's financial software so a detailed evaluation of the value associated with the target's financial software is not a high priority—essentially the target's financial software has no value. There may be some risk associated with the target's financial software and/or data integrity, but the challenge is usually an accounting one—mapping accounts and working out appropriate data transition plans to ensure compliance with financial regulations.

If the target has some functions that overlap or compete with the acquirer then it is possible or even likely that there are two sets of software that perform broadly the same function, but possibly embody different business processes to achieve the same end result. For example, I have advised on a number of potential acquisitions in the "collections" industry in the United States. The collections industry is all about calling and e-mailing people who are behind on their payments for goods or services. It sounds like tough work and, indeed, it can often be challenging, but in my experience in the industry, the people doing the calling are highly trained, highly regulated, and mostly pleasant, hard-working people who are trying to help others in a difficult predicament. Returning to my example, the basic processes are broadly the same for all collections companies: data on people to be called needs to be stored, calls need to be scheduled and then dialed, and actions need to be recorded—especially money flows. That said, each form of collections has its own special characteristics, and while some standardized software has become available in recent years as online *software-as-a-service* (SaaS), most of the industry is using highly customized versions of old desktop software or they have developed their own code. In my experience, even for companies with such apparently similar, narrow functions, perhaps 30–70% of the software used is different between any two companies. In this scenario, it is important to prioritize a comparison of the business value of the two different sets of software performing the same function where *business value* means value to the joint business that will survive the merger or acquisition.

Software for New Functions (New to the Acquirer)

This can be the most difficult scenario for the acquirer because the target company is conducting business functions that the acquirer may not fully understand. Also, the acquirer may have limited exposure to or experience with the software options available. Evaluating the business value and risk associated with the target's software for these business functions must be a high priority even though the default strategy will be to leave the existing software in place after the merger or acquisition. It is possible that the value of the enabling software will be a consideration in the overall value of the target company, particularly if it has been developed or customized by the target company and/or embodies unique business processes. The risk associated with the software becomes a bigger consideration in this scenario. If the target company has done or commissioned development or customization, there is a risk that the acquirer will not be able to maintain or extend the software if the developers are not available for any reason.

At two of the collections agencies where I advised, most of the working software was developed in-house and tightly integrated with the ancillary software for telephone dialing, printing, and so on. This made for very efficient operations, but in both cases, only two people were available who understood and could modify the code, and neither of these people actually worked for the target company! In one case, the risk was retirement of the key people and in the other it was the extortionate prices of the subcontractor who knew that the target company had nowhere else to go. To be fair to the subcontractor, from their perspective they were charging a reasonable price for two highly skilled developers with only one customer to fund them.

In both cases, while the default immediate post-acquisition scenario was clear—keep the existing software in place—it was equally clear that the pro forma budget for the combined entity for the next 3 years post-acquisition needed to include the cost of converting the target company to a new software platform.

Note that the custom-built software sitting on the target company's balance sheet as an asset became a liability in the eyes of the acquirer because of the money they needed to set aside to do the software platform conversion. Interestingly, in one of the transactions, the acquirer decided to convert both the target and its own existing software to a new platform to achieve operating efficiencies that would quickly pay back the investment. The risk became an opportunity!

Prioritizing the Software Value and Risk Assessment Based on Lenses

It is also useful to remind ourselves of the lenses I defined in Chapter 1 (summarized in Figure 1.2), because they form a good starting point for sub-dividing the target's software portfolio:

- Build-buy lens: In-house or *commercial off-the-shelf* (COTS)
- End-client lens: In-house or external
- Profit lens: For-profit organization or not-for-profit organization

Build-Buy Lens

Of the three lenses, the build-buy lens, is the most important for prioritizing the software value and risk assessment. Software that has been built in-house (including that built by sub-contracted vendors) can have significantly higher value to the acquirer than COTS software if the target's in-house software contains significant intellectual property in the form of unique knowledge or implemented or enabled business processes. However, the in-house software generally carries higher risk because, prior to the due diligence process, the acquirer has no knowledge of how "good" the in-house source code is.

What do we mean by "good" software in the context of an M&A? As with all considerations in an M&A situation, the most important first consideration is financial predictability. Once financial predictability for the software is established, or not, then a decision can be made about whether or not the future financial implications of the software, and the degree to which that is certain, represents good value in the context of the deal. For example, I was involved in an acquisition where the target company had written and extended its own in-house software for its core business processes over many years. The software was fit for purpose and served the business well, but it was all the work of one developer who had been a subcontractor for years using an obscure database technology. The target company had attempted to mitigate their risk on the software by getting another third-party developer involved, but with minimal effort and a corresponding lack of success. Future challenges had started to manifest themselves as difficulties (tricky coding, more time, more money) in interfacing to software for ancillary services based on modern technology. My advice was that the acquirer should continue the existing arrangement in the short term (short-term financial predictability), but post-acquisition, immediately start to move the target company onto a new software platform—ideally SaaS—for medium-term financial predictability.

For existing in-house software, in most cases, historic data on the cost and productivity of the development and maintenance teams will indicate how costly the target company's software is likely to be to maintain and extend. If such data is not available and the risk is felt to be high, static code analysis can generate some useful metrics that will give a good indication of the sustainability of the code. For example, the Application Intelligence Platform from CAST Software is a sophisticated static code analysis tool that can provide a number of different metrics* on the code of an application, including

- Complexity: Software complexity is a key driver of the level of effort it takes to enhance or maintain an application.
- Changeability: A software characteristic that measures how flexible and adaptable the application is when it is getting enhanced. If an application has

---

* http://www.castsoftware.com/products/what-cast-measure

low changeability that probably means it has a lot of spaghetti code, it's not very well structured, it's not well documented, and it's overly complex.

- Transferability: A health factor that evaluates the ability for new teams or members of new teams to quickly understand and begin working with an application. Code that has high transferability exhibits good modularity, clarity, testability, and reusability.
- Efficiency: A measure of potential performance and scalability bottlenecks in software.
- Robustness: An indication of the likelihood that an application will incur defects, corrupt data, or completely fail in production.
- Technical debt: The accumulated amount of rework needed to correct or recover from mistakes made and short cuts taken during the development process. Not only an indication of cost and effort, technical debt also represents the level of risk of experiencing post-production issues and increased cost of ownership within applications.

For COTS software, it is reasonable to presume that the target company's COTS software has enough other users to be stable, with any outstanding issues being well known or easily discoverable from the user community. This presumption should be validated. COTS software has the benefit of being used by many people and seen by many eyes, so problems surface and are solved quickly. There are some caveats to this:

- Today's popular or new and exciting COTS software can be tomorrow's forgotten relic. If the target company has COTS software that falls into the forgotten relic category, then maintaining and extending functionality are likely to be more expensive. Skills may be scarce or impossible to find if the source company has gone out of business or if the skill sets have "aged out." This can also happen to programming languages.
- The ability to customize COTS systems to tailor the functionality of the software to the business processes of the purchasing organization was often touted as a valuable feature of the COTS software. Indeed, in many *enterprise resource planning* (ERP) implementations in the 1980s and 1990s, extensive customization was almost a requirement. Predictably and unfortunately, lots of purchasers took advantage of this flexibility to build, or have built by third parties, extensive customizations that quickly became unmanageable. At a certain level of change or extension, COTS software customizations must be considered as in-house developed software. The additional challenge is that understanding of, and ability to change, the underlying COTS software may be limited.
- COTS software must be fully licensed for the number and type of users currently in the target company and, sometimes, for the type of use. For example, the target company may be using the COTS software as part of,

or to build other software, that it then sells or passes on to its customers. This "commercial use" may not be permitted under the terms of the COTS license—understandably because the COTS software supplier could be losing out on license sale opportunities.

A special case that bridges in-house and COTS software under the build-buy lens is open-source code. Open-source code can generally be accessed and used by private individuals for their own purposes for free. Like COTS software, it often comes with the benefit of having been used by many people and, even better, enhanced by other developers. Most developers understand that open-source code carries a programmer's "health warning" in that it could have been deliberately compromised by a bad actor. Different types and sources of open-source code build their own reputations. Sometimes, the risk is worthwhile to save time and money. However, some developers are not aware that the terms under which open-source software is licensed for commercial use (e.g., included the open source in code that is intended for anything other than personal use) vary considerably. It is entirely possible that in-house developed software could include open-source software that is being used in contravention of its original license. Finding such software in a target company's in-house software is virtually impossible, but it is still worth asking the question about any known open-source software, and any controls in place to prevent such software getting in, as part of the due diligence.

End-Client Lens

The end-client lens is very useful in an M&A situation because, frankly, there is more reputational risk associated with changing software that is used by or visible to external customers than there is in changes to the software that the staff uses. In most M&A scenarios, keeping revenue flowing from existing customers is important to the value proposition of the deal. This is particularly true in deals involving customer-visible software, where a change in software due to an M&A event could motivate the customer to change to a different vendor. From the customer perspective, if they are forced to change software anyway (and endure the pain of transition), why not look for a better/cheaper alternative? Clearly, this is a risk to be considered and mitigated in the M&A value proposition. My company went through an M&A-driven change of time reporting software some years ago. At the time, we were a pure consulting company so billable hours were our life blood. The vendor of the new software offered to do the transition free of charge and grandfather in our old, lower costs for 5 years to keep us on board. Clearly, this risk mitigation has a financial consequence for an acquirer.

Staff software cannot be ignored completely in the risk equation. First and foremost, any transition of accounting software needs to be fast and smooth so that invoices continue to flow seamlessly to customers. Again, the flow of money is the most important continuity risk in these transactions. In a similar vein, any software that staff uses to enable the business to draw in revenue needs to be carefully considered. An example here would be the software used by the collections agents at a collections agency. Calls, promises of money, and actual money flows through the collections agency keep the lights on, so these flows cannot be interrupted for more than a few days and, ideally, no more than a few hours in an M&A transition.

Profit Lens

From the perspective of the profit lens, it would be easy to assume that the focus on financial predictability only applies to for-profit organizations. However, most not-for-profits provide services that users depend on as part of their daily lives. Interruption of these services is the worst-case scenario for not-for-profits, and the most likely cause of this in a merger scenario is a disruption, however temporary, in the flow of funds to pay for services. This can be a particular problem if it creates a backlog. The restoration of a steady, sometimes just sufficient, flow of funds may be insufficient to undo the accumulated backlog quickly.

Figure 11.1 summarizes the default integration strategies and top-level priorities under each of the lenses for two scenarios where the acquirer is buying or merging with a target company in the same business line or where the acquirer is diversifying.

Approach to Assessing the Software Value and Risk of a Business

Having set out the priorities in Figure 11.1, Figure 11.2 recasts them as a process under the assumption that the target company represents a new, different business function for the acquirer—somewhat the best-case scenario for potential added software value and the worst-case scenario for added software risk. What steps do we need to take to evaluate the risk?

Generally, there can be four distinct tasks in the acquisition process as it relates to the target company's software:

- Software asset due diligence (ADD): A profile of how the target organization relies on its software.
- Software asset risk management (ARM): An assessment of the risk involved in transitioning the target organization's software.
- Software asset maturity analysis (AMA): A profile of the return on investment (ROI) for the acquired software, with an eye on the future.
- Software asset integration management (AIM): An analysis of how to integrate the acquired software into the current environment.

Challenges occur for the surviving IT department if all of these tasks are not done or if they are not done by software experts.

Consideration for assessment	Default integration strategy	Priority to assess software value	Priority to assess software risk
Acquirer and target function: Same	Use acquirers software	Medium	Low
• Target build-buy lens: In-house	Use acquirers software	Medium (may be better than acquirers)	Low
• Target build-buy lens: COTS	Use acquirers software	Low (unique value unlikely)	Low
• Target end-client lens: In-house	Use acquirers software	Low (target's staff can be retrained)	Low
• Target end-client lens: External	Not clear –client retention may be important	Medium (What do clients value?)	Medium (Clients may leave)
• Target profit lens: For-profit	Use acquirers software	Low (single platform likely to be less cost)	Low
• Target profit lens: Not-for-profit	Use acquirers software	Low	Low
Acquirer and target function: Different	Use targets software	High	High
• Target build-buy lens: In-house	Use targets software	High (What is software worth?)	High (How much will risk mitigation cost?)
• Target build-buy lens: COTS	Use targets software	Low	Low
• Target end-client lens: In-house	Use targets software	Low	Low
• Target end-client lens: External	Use targets software	High (Is this a unique selling point?)	High (Could software lose existing clients?)
• Target profit lens: For-profit	Use targets software	High (Will be included in valuation)	High (Will be included in valuation)
• Target profit lens: Not-for-profit	Use targets software	Low (least cost more important)	Low (least cost more important)

Figure 11.1   M&A software value assessment priorities.

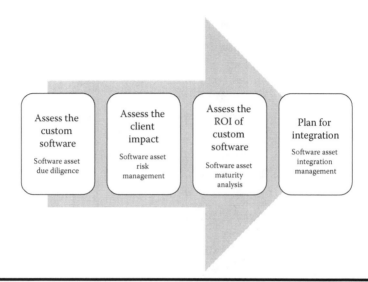

Figure 11.2   Assessment priorities for acquisition of target with different functions.

Software Asset Due Diligence

The prospect of capital losses or unplanned expenditures in a targeted company, due to their software, rarely generates much concern in the M&A team. It rarely affects deal pricing and structure as much as it should. However, anyone who has experienced the challenges of unexpected software project costs, schedule overruns, integration management problems, or source code failure can imagine the potential for unforeseen damage to the value of an asset.

Both the balance sheet and the profit and loss (P&L) statements are affected by a target company's dependence on its software. In particular, if custom software is the embodiment of the target company's unique business model and value, then there is a real risk of unplanned capital requirements if the software is unduly expensive to maintain or extend.

Acquirers should be informed about the potential pitfalls or the hidden asset value in any target company that depends on software. Investors will appreciate the thorough nature of the software due diligence and the enhanced quality of performance for the ongoing management teams.

The initial due diligence examination of a targeted asset's software provides the M&A team with an evaluation of the current state of the targeted asset's software and internal operating structure. This information can produce substantial gains for the M&A team, either via negotiation for a more advantageous position in the targeted asset or via a much more thorough understanding of financial statement impact. In some cases, we have identified hidden asset value for our clients, thereby substantially enhancing returns for investors. In all cases, the benefit has far outweighed the cost of the initial software due diligence.

Software ADD is designed to shed light on the impact that software can have on a merger or acquisition. Other benefits include

■ Improved confidence in the profitability associated with a merger or acquisition
■ Identification of hidden asset value
■ Early recognition of post-acquisition risks, including software maintenance and upgrade fees
■ Identification of undue dependency on selected individuals in the development team

In practical terms, there is often little time for software ADD when the time is right—the initial due diligence. Figure 11.3 shows a typical list of contents for a short software due diligence exercise.

Software ADD should provide recommendations on how to move forward with the technological piece of the merger or acquisition—or not!

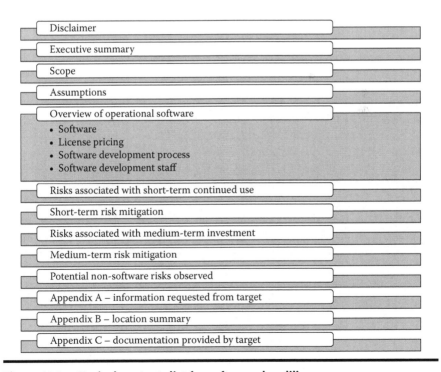

Figure 11.3   Typical contents list for software due diligence.

Software Asset Risk Management

Software ARM should identify post-acquisition risks. One of the more intangible risks is often the quality of the source code in any custom applications. Venture capitalists, investors, and managers have been subject to unforeseen and unnecessary losses too often due to hidden challenges in the target company's software. These, sometimes large, capital exposures can remain unidentified until very late in the investment life cycle. Excessive operating expense due to the size and/or complexity of software applications leads to large enhancement requirements and maintenance costs, or worse, non-performing functionality. Some acquirers who have experienced these problems have endured losses of credibility and market share.

One way to manage risk in the target's custom software is to identify the code that presents the biggest risks, and then use source code analysis tools to build up a picture of each custom application's strengths and weaknesses. The source code analysis can then inform the investment decision at hand to evaluate the potential financial impact. Source code analysis can provide an appraisal of the source code's maintainability, its ability to support growth, and a risk profile defining issues embedded within the custom software, actionable for mitigation.

Of course, the acquirer will require access to the source code for this service. This may be difficult to arrange during due diligence and may need to be deferred to the post-acquisition implementation phase.

Software ARM outlines the risks involved in transitioning a target company's software into your portfolio. Other benefits include

■ The ability to avoid unnecessary losses due to hidden issues in the target's custom software
■ The identification of potential IT team constraints—and enough time to mitigate them
■ An improved transition timeline based on a comprehensive understanding of the software-related issues involved

Software Asset Maturity Analysis

The software comes with its own unique growth cycle. Unfortunately for most M&A teams, it can be difficult for an outsider to spot the signs that a particular custom software application is reaching the point where its maturity is becoming a liability rather than an asset.

Typically, new software platforms and applications evolve through several stages of maturity, each with their own set of capital, personnel, strategy, and support requirements. Dependent on the nature and size of software functionality, most growth entities will see a consistent pattern of increased resource requirements through the first stages of the maturity curve. If business growth continues, there will come a point where large influx of resources will be a necessity to allow the software asset to perform to match the business growth and maximize opportunity profit. Put more simply, the more complex an application becomes, the harder it is to make even small changes. I discussed this point in more detail in Chapter 1 and illustrated it in Figure 1.3.

The difficulty comes in defining where you are on the curve and, hence, the resources necessary to maintain consistency in performance going forward. Should management not be aware of (or be misinformed about) these metrics, implosion may be on the horizon. Many target assets have appeared to be wonderfully performing with respect to market penetration, quality of provision, and profitability until the bubble bursts. Such organizations can enter a period of stagnation due to their inability to be responsive to market demands, and in doing so, severely damage their brand.

The key to success is understanding whether the custom software behind the business processes is up to the task of supporting the business model in the future and what future investments might be required. Undetected and unplanned development or maintenance expenditures can be devastating to the transaction business case if substantial efforts are required. Management may be forced into unplanned software asset acquisitions in order to meet future needs.

As more and more seemingly successful organizations fall victim to the expansion bubble, many investment management entities now want to identify and avoid software asset–related capital losses and unplanned expenditures. To that end, software AMA provides a clear understanding of exactly where your custom software asset sits on the maturity curve.

Software Asset Integration Management

Venture capitalists, M&A firms, and private equity investors all have target metrics they use to evaluate transactions including (ROI) and return on equity (ROE). Substantial amounts of money and time are invested in potential targets to determine whether these metrics meet or exceed prescribed limits, both now and during the tenure of the investment. When the stars align, the completed transaction becomes another asset in inventory requiring ongoing financial reporting, planning, and management. Should management meet or exceed pro forma (essentially a financial plan for the joint entity) in the ensuing years, balance sheets can balloon from the increase in retained earnings. That being said, an inadequate software asset integration plan or an adequate plan based on insufficient information about the custom software will cause unexpected roadblocks on the path to value creation. Existing customers may risk the loss of functionality or may simply choose other alternatives if the integration plan is not well-defined. Clearly, this could impact ongoing revenue.

Most M&A experts understand capital, marketing, sales, and HR requirements as defined in painstakingly generated pro forma. Unfortunately, most do not consider the impact of weakness in operational systems and/or individual custom software applications. Even fewer plan for these requirements, producing too many examples of non-performing assets with pro forma of great promise. Understanding if, and how, the custom software should be integrated into a new parent company's software asset portfolio can be the difference between substantial capital losses and financial health.

For a successful merger, it is necessary to document a clear understanding (via analysis and in the form of a plan) of how each target software asset should be integrated (or not) with the parent company's software asset portfolio in order to achieve the pro forma savings targets. This provides operating and management efficiencies and early identification and management of software integration and scaling problems.

The first step in the integration plan is to decide which applications duplicate the same functionality (e.g., HR software) and which provide unique value to the acquiring or target companies. Generally, the decisions over duplicated functionality applications will be decided in favor of the acquiring company, which will want to retain its existing HR, finance, and so on software unless there is a compelling reason not to do so (e.g., cost). For these applications, the integration is an operational, people problem. For the target's custom applications with business value to add to the combined entity, the integration plan should cover the following information for all affected applications:

- *Development and testing*—for example, a description of methodologies and techniques used for software development and testing
- *Maintenance*—for example, current defect backlog by severity and age, and staff assigned to maintenance
- *Software*—for example, a list of purchased and developed software and the authors and other creators, including information on whether the author/creator made their contribution as a company employee under their employment contract, outside their employment, as a consultant, or as an independent contractor
- *Application(s)*—for example, components within an application, including third-party software embedded (especially open source) and the schedule of all ongoing or planned software, databases, and related systems development projects that affect the application or its environment
- *Partners*—for example, a list of other companies, partnerships, individuals, or other entities who are stakeholders in the application
- *Customers and users*—for example, a list of the application's largest customers or users in terms of sales or activity
- *Employees, other staff, and subcontractors*—for example, a list of key employees or contractors who work on the application for development, testing, operation, or security and an organization chart showing line management and functional relationships.

- *Legislation, codes of practice, and standards*—for example, list any mandatory compliance requirements in which the application must comply and evidence of most recent compliance audit
- *Risk mitigation*—for example, a copy of the business continuity plan and data backup and verification policies and procedures with a schedule of tests undertaken

Summary

If your company is acquiring another company, you should plan to integrate their software by working with the M&A team as early as possible to gather information about the risks and challenges you are likely to face during the due diligence process.

It is sensible to focus on the target's custom software that is part of their unique business proposition. It is likely that your existing software will replace any software where there is duplicate functionality. The custom software is more likely to be risky and difficult to integrate than any COTS software they have in use.

Having identified the riskiest, most difficult applications to integrate, gather as much information about them as you can and plan accordingly. Measure twice and cut once!

In the next chapter, I will look at some applications of the software value concepts described in this book that are somewhat tangentially related to my focus on software development.

Chapter 12

Broader Impact of Software Value Management

In my first book, co-written with David Herron and Stasia Iwanicki (Harris et al. 2008), we made the point that, like beauty, value is in the eye of the beholder. In this book, the emphasis on setting up processes involving the business implicitly repeats that theme. That said, this has been a practical and, hopefully, pragmatic book so far. I have intentionally rejected "fuzzy" interpretations of value because, in my experience, these can be used to justify doing nothing at all to measure value—an inexcusable equivocation. However, there are "fuzzy" issues around assessing software value and so, in this last chapter, I want to take a look at some of these broader issues.

Business Value of Cybersecurity

Like it or not, as I write this, software is causing one of the biggest headaches to organizations large and small because it is the source of risks associated with cybersecurity. Indeed, there is probably a chief executive officer (CEO) (or possibly a politician) somewhere in the world right now who can't think about the business value of software because of the potential liability to which a software breach is exposing them.

In 2014, Gartner* reported that 84% of security breaches occur at the application layer and there has been a 68% increase in mobile application vulnerability disclosures. In their 2016 Cybersecurity Trend Report,† UBM Tech, a division of United Business Media LLC, reported that organizations spent more per breach in 2015 than in 2014, with an annualized cost to detect, respond to, and mitigate a breach globally of around $7.7 million. This is the downside of the ubiquity of software. Enterprise software is like an enormous dam holding back hugely valuable reservoirs of water and/or generating valuable electricity, one small hole can bring down everything.

Readers might reasonably respond that, with good engineering, the risk of the dam succumbing to that one small hole before it is taken out of service is small, and dams are continuously monitored for indications of structural problems. That's true, but can we say the same of our enterprise software systems? On the engineering side, historically, in our rush to push out more functionality, there has been little training for developers on building or testing for secure code. That is changing now, but only slowly. Indeed, some critics have argued that the incremental nature of Agile software development can lead to weak security. After all, they argue, what is technical debt if not substandard code? On the monitoring side, there are a number of tools and systems that can do static analysis of code to identify security risks. While many organizations use these, I believe that significantly less than half of the software organizations in the world have these tools built into their code development, deployment, and maintenance processes.

Often the blame for cybersecurity problems gets shifted through risk categorization. For example, the current breach is an information security, data security, or network security problem not an application security problem. Maybe. Often it's true that a breach requires the cooperation of a malicious or unknowing insider. However, there would be no cybersecurity risk without software. Almost invariably, a hacker hacks a network router by hacking the software not the hardware.

This is not a book about cybersecurity and how to implement it so let's return to our main theme, what is the business value of cybersecurity? Specifically, having established that most cybersecurity issues involve software, I will focus on the business value of *application security* (as opposed to network or endpoint security), which is generally considered to mean writing code that does not have security vulnerabilities and fixing code that does have security vulnerabilities.

Some diverse examples might help to establish the breadth of the challenge in identifying the business value of investing in application security:

---

* https://blogs.sap.com/2014/08/12/bringing-security-to-the-forefront-of-application-development-with-sap-fortify/

† http://techbeacon.com/resources/cybersecurity-2016-trend-report-ubm-ponemon-study

- In their "Application Security Buyer's Guide," TechBeacon* offers the example of Adobe patching more than 300 security vulnerabilities in their Flash Player product in 2015. This product is used by many websites to enable interactivity and multimedia. Each of these 300 patches cost Adobe money. So what business value did they receive in return? It's all about risk avoidance. They are seeking to avoid the reputational risk of a major attack based on one of their vulnerabilities, which could result in hard revenue loss and the consequential risk of lawsuits if Adobe Flash Player users can prove loss of actual or reputational value through suffering an attack based on a security flaw in the flash player. Adobe's investment has business value in the same way that buying business insurance has business value. The monetary cost is small compared with the potential monetary losses. More and more businesses are buying *cyber insurance* designed specifically to insure against some of the risks that fall into this category. My own business is being required to buy cyber insurance by some of our clients as part of the overall package of insurances that they expect their vendors to hold.
- In the same guide, TechBeacon describes another example from 2015 in which pirates boarding a ship traveling near Singapore toward the Indian Ocean knew which containers to open and where to find the most valuable items. How? Apparently, the shipping firm "used a homegrown content management system (CMS) to manage inventories," and the pirates had used hackers to attack a vulnerability in the CMS to get access to the bills of lading (the ship's inventory). So what's the cost-benefit equation for this cybersecurity investment? It is the cost of rigorous application security reviews of the apparently innocuous, low-risk, in-house code versus the reputational damage (loss of future business revenue) and increased shipping insurance premiums. Not an easy set of costs and benefits to predict, especially not in advance.
- As I was writing this chapter, news broke that money was taken from 20,000 accounts of Tesco Bank in the United Kingdom. The bank's CEO reported the halting of online payments for current account customers. The number of accounts affected suggests that this was a systemic failure of security around Tesco's core database. Peter Roe of TechMarketView† reported, "Bank customers will be refunded any losses, but account holders will be expected to leave the bank in droves, probably reverting to the perceived 'safe houses' among the bigger banks. People's enthusiasm for new-generation banks had already been pretty half-hearted, as seen by the relatively low levels of utilisation of the new account switching service. This latest episode will further drain confidence."

---

* http://techbeacon.com/resources/application-security-buyers-guide-sample-rfp
† http://www.techmarketview.com/

■ The University of Santa Cruz IT Services Group reports a number of security breach incidents,* but this one caught my eye because it sits on the boundary between bug and cybersecurity issue:

An error in the Texas Women's University degree auditing program allowed anyone accessing the system to view the names, courses and grades of the 12,000 students enrolled at the university.

To me, this feels like a functional defect has caused a disproportionate business value risk. The business value derived from the original functionality for staff use. The bug introduces a risk of liability—*negative business value* if you will—that would be very hard to consider or calculate during planning because there is an infinite range of answers to the question, "What damage could the software do if it does things that were not specified?"

Cigital has produced an "Agile Security Manifesto,"† which is a manifesto document in form ("we value the phrases on the left over those on the right"), but with none of the industry weight of the original Agile Manifesto. The document contains a nugget of wisdom that is relevant here: "Mitigate risks more than fix bugs." A preliminary evaluation of the risks can be done using the value visualization framework (VVF) technique and weighted shortest job first (WSJF) described in Chapter 7, but with different risks being considered and the resulting prioritization being used to decide which risks need to be addressed first.

Value of Unused Software

Most of this book has focused on the business value of software under the reasonable assumption that the software that has been developed or purchased is being used. However, my experience has been that there is a lot of software in organizations that is not being used (and still may be on the books). It may not be used because its usefulness has past, more licenses were purchased than are being used or people who could use it, don't know it's available. I run across the latter two cases often in our consulting business through more than one of our partners who provide software products to support software development, such as estimation or code analysis tools.

All too often, our partners have new clients that are persuaded of the value of the software development support tool; they buy the licenses and then have a group of people go through the training. The active use might last a year or two, but then when our partners go back to the same client, they find that only one person or nobody at all is still using the tool. I could write another book on why this happens,

---

* http://its.ucsc.edu/security/breaches.html
† https://www.cigital.com/resources/ebooks-and-whitepapers/agile-security-manifesto-principles/

and there are many scenarios, but the short version is that software development organizations are just not good at sustaining value-added functions that are not on the critical path of churning out code—irrespective of the value of the code they are developing. Quantity and delivery date are kings in most software development organizations, with quality coming third and value rarely being considered. Hence, when resources are constrained (as they invariably are) software development managers and their teams start asking, "Why do we have to use tool 'x' when it isn't directly benefitting us as individuals?"

Of course, it's not just software development tools that suffer this fate, but also other commercial off-the-shelf (COTS) software used across the business and even in-house developed software.

A company called 1E publishes an annual "Software Usage and Waste Report."* In the report, 1E defines software waste as, "any piece of software that has been deployed to a desktop but is not being run by the user." A desktop application is defined as "unused" if it has not been run within the past 90 days and "rarely used" if it has not been run in the past 30 days. "Total waste" is the sum of unused and rarely used. The 2016 version of the report estimates that 30 percent of desktop software is unused and 8 percent is rarely used. In the United States and the United Kingdom combined, 1E estimates a total waste of $34 billion of software with an average waste per user of $247. Some of this waste is certainly coming from bundled applications that cannot be unbundled, such as Microsoft Office where certain users might never use, say, Excel. However, a lot of the wastage is coming from a few users who are not using highly specialized and expensive software that they have on their desktop. 1E provides details of the 10 most wasted enterprise applications, summarized in Figure 12.1.

The key message here is that the ongoing business value of software in the business needs to be continually monitored. I'm sure that many of the users of the applications listed in Figure 12.1 would think they are so valuable that they would fight to keep them, and they may be right. However, there are real opportunities to increase the value to the business by decreasing the cost as a result of taking away the applications from those that never use them. Of course, the vendors would argue, with some justification, that the lapsed users would get more value from actually using their applications rather than removing them and that the appropriate training could release hidden value for some, if not all, of the lapsed users.

Hardware and Software Value

In previous chapters, I have mentioned the lean principle of taking an end-to-end systems view when trying to maximize the flow of value through a product development or manufacturing system. Of course, this principle applies to the business value

---

* https://www.1e.com/resource-center/software-usage-report/

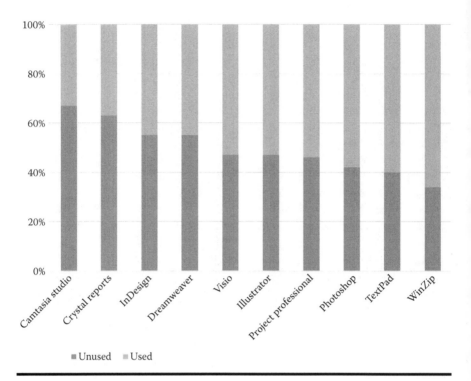

Figure 12.1 1E's 2016 top 10 most wasted enterprise applications. (Adapted from 1E. Software usage and waste report 2016. 1E, London, 2016. https://www.1e. com/resource-center/software-usage-waste-report-2016/)

of software, which is dependent on the hardware system through which it is delivered, and therefore, it is important to take an end-to-end systems view of the business value.

Let's consider one piece of software to illustrate this point. The game Grand Theft Auto: San Andreas by Rockstar Games is downloadable from Google Play on my Samsung smartphone for $6.99, as I write this in November 2016. If I look online from my laptop,* I can see the same game is available on five (six?) alternative hardware platforms: Xbox 360, PS3, Xbox, PS2, and PC/MAC (I had to smile—too much history to consider this the same hardware!). From a business value perspective, which configuration has the most value to the customer (the end user is "the business" in this example)? Well, if I don't have a smartphone, the mobile version has no value to me. If I have an Xbox, but not an Xbox 360, the production of a compatible version for my current machine is clearly valuable but it provokes the questions, "What extra value could I get if I upgraded my hardware?" and "Would the extra value justify the cost?" More likely these days, is the scenario in which I have a smartphone, one of the game hardware devices, and a laptop

---

* http://www.rockstargames.com/sanandreas/

(personal computer [PC] or Mac). Which hardware option offers the most value for money? Would purchasing the same software for two out of the three options generate disproportionate extra value compared with the extra cost (e.g., play it at home and on the bus/train to work/school)?

In the case of this example, the software producer has clearly recognized the nuances in their value proposition because they have incurred the additional investment of producing and testing the additional versions.

Some readers may consider the game example trivial or unrepresentative of the business world. I would disagree and cite the revenue involved and the increasing digitalization of the workplace, which involves more and more business software being used on non-traditional devices. Nonetheless, let's think about a business example. Let's assume that we are an internal software development group in a national plumbing supplies company. The task at hand is to build a business-to-business portal to allow our distributors to order, and track delivery of, items from our catalog. In this case, the business value will accrue to our internal customers and ultimately the CEO of our company as our system increases revenue from the distributors and cuts down our costs of manually handling distributor inquiries. We have quite a few software choices to make, but we also have some hardware options. Here are some examples:

- Are we going to require the distributors to install some software on their systems (e.g., applications on their laptops) or are we going to provide browser access?
- How will security be provided—simple user name and password or some sort of identity verification device?
- Will we host the application ourselves or put it in the cloud? Public or private cloud?
- Is there any value in enabling mobile access (e.g., do we expect actual plumbers or maybe large-scale contractors to order from job sites)? Do we want them to?
- How will we close and confirm transactions? Is a signature required? Is a paper trail necessary or optional as a business benefit?
- If our software is installed on distributors' hardware then what operating systems will we support? This may seem like a software question, but in practice, it is often tied to the end-user's hardware replacement strategy. Some large businesses can control when/if they move all their in-house PCs from one Windows version to the next. However, in smaller organizations, it is the hardware wearing out that dictates the operating system, so three or more generations of Windows could be operational in the same business at the same time.
- If our software is browser based, which browsers will be supported? Again, this seems like a software issue, but default browsers for Apple, Windows, and Android devices will be different. Can we ask the end user to install a particular browser?

One final example of the hardware/software end-to-end business value challenge that exists today, but is predicted to grow in the future—the so-called *Internet of things*. Just as the economic business models of the Internet itself took a while to evolve and are still working themselves out, it will take a while for the economics of the Internet of things to do so as well. One key factor here is that the business value is often derived from the existence of a critical mass of users. A useful analogy might be to compare the business value of me setting up a table selling lemonade outside my house in suburbia versus setting it up at my local farmers market among many stallholders selling different items, or outside the local railway station during rush hour. Essentially, my business model depends on a certain amount of traffic, and I am more likely to be successful when and where there is more traffic.

The Internet of things challenge from a business value of software perspective is creating software that can access a critical mass of simple devices, presumably simple or intelligent sensors, in a plethora of hardware forms, old and new, to generate business value. There are challenges, such as hardware types, hardware capabilities, communication, addressing, and security, which to the typical software developer are simple configuration problems after the completion of the software that can store and process all these parameters. For example, we recently installed a security system in our small office in Colorado. The system is integrated and has motion sensors for open spaces like the open plan office, window and door sensors, a wall-mounted key pad, and so on. To us, the end users, the software alone is without value (well, almost). The business value is only derived when the software is configured to our office or, more precisely, the security system vendor's hardware in our office. Frankly, the set-up was easy, but it could have been more difficult (or even impossible) if we had wanted to add, say, one third-party sensor like a carbon monoxide detector; or even two third-party sensors—the carbon monoxide detector and a flood warning detector on the basement sump pump.

The point of this section is, of course, that the business value of the software will almost always be enhanced or constrained by the hardware through which it interacts with the user's environment.

Software and People

It is a central proposition of this book that software has value. In this section, I want to introduce the concept that the people associated with a piece of software affect the value of the software. Manage the people around the software correctly and you can increase the value of the software, mismanage them and you risk destroying the value of the software. In this context, I propose three different types of software value that are dependent on people, as shown in Figure 12.2.

Let's start with an example. A couple of years ago, I was engaged to perform a software due diligence evaluation for a company that was considering buying an

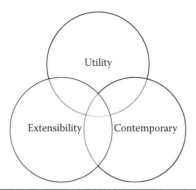

Figure 12.2   Software value and people: three types.

operational branch of a larger company. The operation was basically a call center set-up that provided outbound calling services for various different financial services clients. The software used by employees of the call center for scheduling, recording, and capturing the data from their calls was highly customized to their needs and contributed significantly to operational efficiency. My client wanted to know if the software was worth the proposed price (as a component of the overall deal), what risks were associated with it, and what the alternatives might be. To cut a long story short, I found that the value of the software was significantly impacted by people issues. First, the high level of customization to the users' needs meant that although the business process was tightly aligned with the software, new employees coming from other similar jobs had an unusually long learning curve. This is not necessarily a problem in all scenarios, but there is a high level of staff turnover in call centers so training delays hurt the business. Second, the software developers did not work for the target company, but rather for the vendor who had supplied the original software many years ago. Worse, because of the high level of customization carried out on behalf of the target company over the years, only two of the vendor's developers had enough knowledge of the customized software to work on the target company's version of the software. Some of you will have already guessed the next problem, the vendor could pretty much charge whatever they liked for the two developers' services for maintaining and extending the software. Interestingly, in this scenario, the vendor had seemingly increased the value of their software because their revenue from maintenance was higher. This view represents the mistake of local optimization—simply because I walk to the highest point in my neighborhood, it does not necessarily mean it's the highest point in my country or the world. The customized version of the software represents a value dead-end to the vendor because the software has just one customer who will, presumably, only accept being fleeced for a limited time. By the same argument, the customer (the target company in this example) had made some decisions about the people (the developers) associated with the software that significantly diminished the value of the software when seen through the eyes of my client.

More generally, if we consider a self-contained piece of software, which might be an application, then some proportion of the value of that software is in its utility. That is, the software has value because of the job it does—whether that job is taking someone's information for a mortgage application, guiding a missile, driving a washing machine, or some other equally important task. While there is always some loss (or, occasionally, gain) of value in the software based on loss (or gain) of value of its utility, generally we can view this as the "stable" (or perhaps "steadily declining") part of the application's value. People can influence the steady, utility component of the application's value through the way that they use it.

Facebook as a global phenomenon (today) is much more valuable than Facebook as a dorm room gimmick (when it started). This is the "going viral" that all software entrepreneurs dream of, but it is much easier to identify in retrospect than to plan for it.

In the early days of the PC, there were several disk operating systems (DOSs) to choose from before IBM bet on MS-DOS. For my younger readers, "MS" stands for Microsoft, which you would not have heard of if not for this "small piece of luck." People drove the success of the IBM PC and, hence, Microsoft.

Another component of software value is much more transient—let's call it the "contemporary" or "current" value of software. I would argue that the "utility" value of computer games is very low, but they have great value because people want them, pay for them, and enjoy them. Generally, while older games have some retro or collector value, most value comes from very up-to-date or contemporary games. The established industry norm of releasing new versions of sports games every year is evidence of this.

Beyond the simple utility, software has value in its potential to be extended and used for other things—let's call this the software's *extensibility* value. The ease by which software can be extended to do more than it does today is dependent on its design and implementation. Generally speaking, both design and implementation are things that people do. Most software does not have the best documentation in the world, in the code or outside the code. My personal expectation for software documentation (including Agile source code) quality is a grade of about C+, but even that may be unduly optimistic. The point is that some percentage of the critical knowledge about how the software works, why it works, and where it works is always exclusively in the heads of a few people connected with the software. If you want to ensure the continuing extensibility value of the software, then you need to make sure that there is no critical knowledge in the head of only one person and that you treat the few people as well as you can. In short, the total value of the software depends on having the right team of knowledgeable people around it.

Now, I do not want to minimize the skills of some people and the capabilities of some tools to reverse engineer code, to learn how it works, and to find ways to extend it. These are valid options, but my point is that they cost more money than keeping the right people around the code in the first place.

Holistic Value

This section is included to provoke the reader into considering other ways to think about the business value of software. In earlier chapters in this book, I have been careful not to raise questions for which I cannot offer a practical approach to a solution. However, I would be remiss if I did not admit that there are questions out there in or around the field of value measurement and management that don't have good solutions yet.

In an article in October 2016,* Shane Greenstein of Harvard Business School asked, "Ten open questions for techno-optimists." Greenstein suggests that, "A techno-optimist appears to be somebody who has blind faith in the power of technology to cure all ills and, in particular, to create economic growth." Greenstein's questions are shown in Figure 12.3

My first reaction to reading Greenstein's list was that these are all social questions—interesting but not particularly applicable to my work on software value. But, then I realized that most, and arguably all, of the questions relate to the value of different software projects. Just what is the business value of Google? Or, more to the point, what did the founders think the business value was going to be when they started coding? Of course, there is much mythology and urban legend around this question so I will simply hazard a guess that the founders did not think about business value, but about personal utility. Their code was going to make their lives easier in the short term (and, OK, possibly other people's lives easier in the long term too). In the case of Google, business value was partly intangible, but it was also emergent. The way to make the software valuable and more valuable to business emerged or became apparent as the software was used. This ability to identify and reinforce emergent value of software is a key capability of Agile software development. The existence and importance of emergent business value certainly challenges the notion that we can plan to build software that has the highest business value, but it does not destroy the idea. It simply reminds us that for business value, as for software functionality, we must build mechanisms for fast feedback into our processes.

Based on the value of function points as a normalizing denominator for measurements of software productivity, quality, and so on, Capers Jones† has suggested a number of new, similar metrics, such as risk points, security points, and so on. One of these new metrics would be a *value point* metric that would assign weights to both financial and business value, but also to intangible value such as that provided by medical devices and national security software. Jones' ideas go much further than the business value metrics for software that I have discussed in this book. The overall idea is to be able to do integrated estimates and economic studies of hybrid products that include hardware, software, and service components.

---

* Greenstein, Shane, "Ten Open Questions for Techno-Optimists," October 2016. Available at www.computer.org/computing edge
† In correspondence with the author, July 2016.

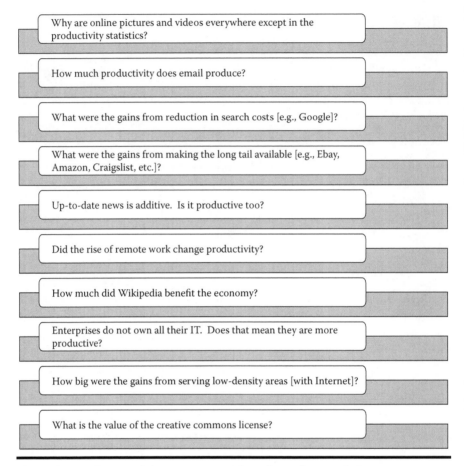

Why are online pictures and videos everywhere except in the productivity statistics?

How much productivity does email produce?

What were the gains from reduction in search costs [e.g., Google]?

What were the gains from making the long tail available [e.g., Ebay, Amazon, Craigslist, etc.]?

Up-to-date news is additive. Is it productive too?

Did the rise of remote work change productivity?

How much did Wikipedia benefit the economy?

Enterprises do not own all their IT. Does that mean they are more productive?

How big were the gains from serving low-density areas [with Internet]?

What is the value of the creative commons license?

Figure 12.3   Greenstein's 10 open questions for techno-optimists.

To quote Jones:

> One of the major weaknesses of the software industry has been in the area of value analysis and the quantification of value. All too often what passes for 'value' is essentially nothing more than cost reductions or perhaps revenue increases. While these are certainly important topics, there are a host of other aspects of value that also need to be examined and measured: customer satisfaction, employee morale, national security, safety, medical value, and a host of other topics.

Jones brainstormed a list of considerations that might be included in a hypothetical comprehensive value point metric, and I have captured these in Figure 12.4.

The list in Figure 12.4 illustrates how quickly a holistic consideration of software value could become very difficult. How do you apply the same scale to staff

More tangible

- Safety improvement
- Health and medical improvement
- Patents and intellectual property
- Risk reduction
- Cost reduction
- Revenue increases
- Market share increases
- Schedule improvement
- Customer satisfaction increase
- Staff morale increase

Less tangible

- Military and defense value
- National security improvement
- Competitive advantages
- Mandates or statutes
- Synergy (compound values)

Figure 12.4   Jones' hypothetical contributors to a comprehensive value point metric.

morale and national security considerations? Jones notes that although cost reduction and revenue increases are both tangible value factors, a host of other less tangible factors also need to be examined, weighted, and included in a value point metric. In Figure 12.4, I have arbitrarily separated the factors into "more tangible" and "less tangible" groups to reinforce this point.

Jones continues:

> Intangible value is the current major lack of today's methods of value analysis. There is no good way to quantify topics such as medical value, security value, or military value. For example medical devices such as cochlear implants improve quality of life. Military devices such as a ship-board gun control system improve crew and vessel defenses. Better encryption algorithms in software improve security of classified and all kinds of private information.

For readers like me who are looking for practical tools and techniques, discussion of some of these intangible contributors to our assessment of value may seem fanciful. However, the boundaries of what can be done are constantly being moved forward. For example, in *Nature in the Balance: The Economics of Biodiversity*, Helm and Hepburn (2014) present a set of chapters by authors who are pragmatically trying to find economic metrics to help us understand what biodiversity is worth to us (the human race) beyond our general sense that pandas and butterflies "look nice." Clearly, Helm and Hepburn are not writing about software, but I recommend their book to readers who still, at the end of this book, believe that it is too hard to measure the business value of software.

Other Applications of Value Visualization, Cost of Delay, and WSJF in Information Technology

In this book, I have described various techniques for assessing the business value of software either economically or relatively as a basis for prioritizing the flow of value. I have been asked if the techniques are only applicable to software development. Of course, they are not. Many of the ideas came from manufacturing despite the software development environment being very different.

The criteria for deciding the applicability of the ideas in this book (vs. say, lean manufacturing) are

- Is the work flowing through a multistep process?
- Is each item of work more unique rather than less unique at different levels of scale?
- Does each item of work, at some level, have a different business value (or are all parts necessary before any value is delivered)?
- Can a small group of stakeholders decide on relative value and duration for each task?
- Do the practitioners have discretion over the order in which they tackle work?
- Can the work be organized as a pull system rather than a push system?

Based on these criteria, the following areas could be potential applications:

- Information technology (IT) (as opposed to software) projects
- Some construction projects
- Some engineering projects
- Certain business processes that have different problems continuously flowing through (e.g., a car repair garage)

The following areas probably would not be good applications:

- Public transport systems—tend to be push rather than pull systems.
- Certain business processes that are highly repetitive with very homogeneous inputs (e.g., processing mortgage applications).

Summary

In this book, I have tried to take a hard-headed view of the business value of software, seeking monetary metrics wherever possible and relative metrics to enable value-maximizing choices where hard monetary metrics are not available without a high level of effort or uncertainty. In this chapter, I have looked at different areas where the business value of software impacts and is impacted by the way that the software is used in other parts of the business. I have also considered the more intangible types of value that can be considered in a holistic approach to value measurement and management. The pragmatist in me looks for solutions that can be used today, but it is fair to recognize that today's solutions would not be available if researchers and thinkers did not look over the horizon. In other words, assessment of value that seems intangible today may not seem so difficult in the future.

Appendix: Waterfall and Agile Software Development Methodologies

This appendix is intended as a brief overview of the *Waterfall* and *Agile* software development methodologies for readers who have never come across these terms before or whose exposure to one or both is limited. Many books have been written on both methodologies with the author of each adding their own small tweaks and ideas to the simple underlying concepts. Readers who want a starting point through the maze of literature on these topics may want to start with the following:

- For Waterfall: A good starting book under $100 is difficult to find. Why the high price? It's difficult to be sure, but I think it's a combination of the low demand for books on Waterfall these days and the inclusion of the topic into large tomes that cover many other areas of software development and act as undergraduate text books. So, for the beginner seeking some deeper insight at a reasonable price, I recommend Steve McConnell's (1997) *Software Project Survival Guide*, which is intended for this audience.
- For Agile: The original "Agile Manifesto" (Beck et al. 2001) (be sure to read the 12 principles as well as the 4 leading assertions) and Schwaber and Beedle's (2001) original book on *Scrum, Agile Software Development with Scrum*.

Waterfall Development

The name *Waterfall development* is used because a visual representation of this method resembles a stream flowing over a series of Waterfalls, as shown in Figure A1.

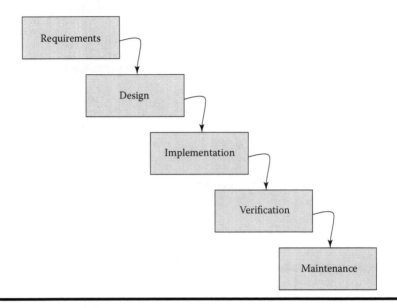

Figure A1   Waterfall.

The implication of the name Waterfall is that software projects (difficult to define, but essentially small to large chunks of software development work) flow through a series of discrete steps. The discrete steps are given different names by different organizations, but the functions performed are broadly understood to be

- *Requirements definition*: A process by which certain specialized members of the development team and the customer(s) agree on exactly what functional (e.g., what it will do) and non-functional (e.g., how fast it will do it) requirements are to be delivered.
- *Design*: A process by which certain specialized members of the development team document a high-level solution to implement the prescribed requirements. This historical attribute of Waterfall development—attempting to design the full system at the beginning—can be contrasted with the Agile approach of having only a rough approximation of the full system and doing formal designs at the beginning of each sprint.
- *Implementation or coding*: A process by which certain specialized members of the development team implement the high-level solution AND the detailed requirements in the form of programs written in source code in one or more languages. Typically, coding also includes *unit testing* of the developed code in the environment in which it was developed. This development environment may or may not reflect the eventual testing and user environments.

■ *Verification or testing*—A process by which certain specialized members of the development team apply a series of manual and/or automated tests. These tests ensure that the functional and non-functional requirements are fulfilled in an environment as close as possible to the environment in which the software will be deployed for users.

Despite the name Waterfall, in real life the Waterfall phases are not actually completed before the next phase begins. For example, requirements are usually only about 50% complete when design starts; design is only about 60% complete when coding starts; and coding is only about 35% complete when testing starts. These overlapping phases make project planning and estimating tricky because the sum total of the phases is not equal to the sum total of the project schedule. Also, the simple diagram of Figure A1 does not acknowledge the real-world flow backward up the Waterfall. This backflow is usually caused by problems down the line (e.g., ambiguity in requirements or design documents, defects discovered in testing). The inevitable result is rework, which causes more overlap of the steps.

Management of Waterfall is predicated on the assumption that the inputs (the requirements) and the processes (requirements definition, design, coding, and testing) can be fixed and controlled. From this assumption (which Agile advocates argue is misguided at best), the amount of work that can be crammed into a project and delivered by a given sized team (sometimes hundreds of developers) is a simple function of careful planning and monitoring by project managers. The planning usually consists of the breakdown of the work into smaller chunks that require different resources (or the same resources at different times) together with capturing dependencies between the smaller chunks of work. This plan is usually known as the *work breakdown structure* (WBS). The WBS most often takes the form of a *Gantt chart* and/or spreadsheet—usually captured in a suitable project management software tool.

Historically, a number of major systems were developed using the Waterfall approach, so it does have some proof of success. In today's world, Waterfall is regarded as something like an antique that is slowly fading from use, despite many current usages in many countries. For large systems, the more popular replacements to Waterfall include the *Rational Unified Process** (RUP) and the *Team Software Process*† (TSP). For smaller projects, the more popular replacements to Waterfall include Agile, DevOps, and Extreme Programming (XP).

For those companies and projects that still use Waterfall, it can be augmented by modern tools and approaches, such as static analysis and automated testing. Formal inspections of key deliverable topics, such as requirements, design, and code inspections are also useful in a Waterfall context.

---

* https://www.ibm.com/developerworks/rational/library/content/03July/1000/1251/1251_best-practices_TP026B.pdf

† http://www.sei.cmu.edu/tsp/

The venerable Waterfall approach is often criticized today. But, it provided over 30 years of continuous service and was used to successfully develop hundreds of major applications. In fact, Waterfall is still used today for many large applications (e.g., in the 10,000-function point size range).

Waterfall has been the default methodology assumed for the CMMI®* approach for software development process improvement, appraisal, and certification.

The main criticism of Waterfall, which seems to be justified, is that Waterfall tries to accomplish too much too soon, such as the development of full requirements before starting design. In real life, requirements are seldom more than about 50% firm when design starts.

In any case, Waterfall is supported by all parametric estimating tools and has more valid benchmark data than any other methodology. This means that estimating and measuring Waterfall projects is fairly easy to do.

Agile Development

Currently, Agile with Scrum (Schwaber and Beedle 2001) is the top development method in the world. Agile is among the best software methodologies for small projects below 500 function points. In its implementations to date, Agile effectiveness has declined as applications and customer numbers grow larger, but different frameworks for scaling Agile are now available that are seeking to address this issue (e.g., *Scaled Agile Framework* [SAFe] [Leffingwell 2011] and the *Disciplined Agile Delivery* [DAD] [Ambler and Lines 2012]). Similarly, Agile has presented challenges for projects needing certification by government agencies, such as the Food and Drug Administration (FDA), the Federal Aviation Administration (FAA), or the Sarbanes–Oxley legislation—although I am starting to see examples of approval of Agile methods by some certification authorities at some of our clients.

Agile is partly an evolutionary method based on iterative development and partly a new approach based on the famous "Agile manifesto" (Beck et al. 2001). In 2001, some 17 well-known software experts met at the Snowbird resort in Utah to discuss software development problems and the potential of solving the problems. The result of this meeting was the Agile Manifesto published in February 2001. The main principles of the Agile Manifesto are

- Individuals and interactions are better than formal processes and tools.
- Working software is better than comprehensive documentation.
- Customer collaboration is better than comprehensive contracts.
- Responding to change is better than following a rigid plan.

---

* http://cmmiinstitute.com/

Far and away the most popular implementation of Agile, and most people's first experience of it, is the Scrum methodology described by Ken Schwaber and Mike Beedle (2001) and illustrated in Figure A2.

In Scrum, work is carried out in *sprints*, now more often called *iterations*, of 2–4 weeks. A core principle is that software developed in a sprint must be completed to the point that it can be demonstrated and, if acceptable, released to users at the end of the sprint. The short duration of the sprint combined with a limited development team size (seven people plus or minus two) means that functionality is developed incrementally, which avoids large investments in misunderstood requirements or requirements that have been superseded by external events. It also means that the small team has to include all development skills sets: requirements definition, design, coding, and testing.

If we revert to a Waterfall viewpoint briefly, this incremental approach suggests that requirements from customers must be described in advance in great detail at a highly granular level. In fact, the opposite is true—customers' requirements are captured at a high level in a *product backlog*, which is a prioritized list of potential future requirements sometimes in the form of *user stories* or *epics* (large user stories) or *features* (larger requirements that might include several user stories or epics). At the start of each sprint, during a sprint planning meeting, the development team works with the *product owner* (generally considered to be a member of the Scrum team) to select items to work on from the product backlog and decompose them into appropriately sized tasks (less than 2 effort days) for the team to work on during the next sprint. The list of tasks for the sprint is known as the *sprint backlog*.

Management of Scrum is different from the classical project planning, monitoring, and reporting associated with Waterfall in that the teams are required to be self-organizing. Essentially, this boils down to a commitment from the team

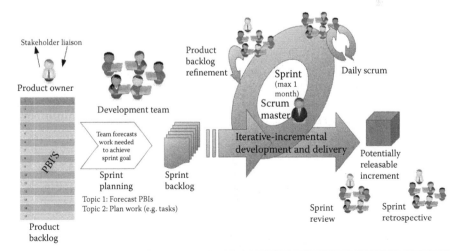

Figure A2   Agile—Scrum.

to complete the work that they take on in the sprint backlog in return for a commitment from management not to interfere with (e.g., change requirements or resources) or micromanage the team during a sprint. In practice, management and customers can change or better define the contents of the product backlog at any time during a sprint—a process known as *product backlog refinement*—but they cannot change the working sprint backlog other than by providing more detail in response to questions from the Scrum team.

Communication is valued very highly within Agile and ideally Scrum teams that are co-located. In any case, Scrum teams meet every day for a 15-minute "stand up" meeting (sometimes called *the daily Scrum*) to report work completed yesterday, work planned for today, and any impediments to completing committed work in this sprint. The daily standup is facilitated by a Scrum master (one of the team or someone responsible for a few teams) whose job is to remove impediments reported by the team.

At the end of the sprint, the team demonstrates the working code and any other completed artifacts (e.g., an architectural design for the next sprint) in a *sprint review* to the product owner and sometimes the customers, for approval or adjustment. After the sprint review, the team always conducts a *sprint retrospective*, which is a time for the team to reflect on any improvements they might want to make to their activities or processes in the next sprint—an informal, but real implementation of a continuous improvement philosophy.

While many, if not most, practitioners are unaware of the fact, Scrum is designed to implement many theoretical principles of maximizing the flow of value through a system learned from lean manufacturing. This is not a straightforward translation because while manufacturing systems can maximize business value *throughput* by controlling the variability of the process and of the inputs, software development can only control the variability of the processes. One way to achieve this, learned from manufacturing, is to keep "batch sizes" small. Clearly, Scrum achieves this by limiting the duration of sprints and the size of teams.

Other Agile Methodologies

Another technique co-opted as Agile is *Kanban*. Traditionally, Kanban is the implementation of a series of steps, such as workstations in manufacturing or Waterfall development phases in software with *work in progress* limits on each step. If work is *pushed* into a flow system like Waterfall (as has been the custom over the years), it is easy for bottlenecks to develop if the steps are not perfectly matched in capacity to the workload or if difficulties arise at a particular step. Such bottlenecks have a disastrous impact on flow. Work in progress limits reduce the likelihood and soften the impact of bottlenecks by limiting the number of tasks that can be present at or between workstations. Work is *pulled* from the end of the Kanban line (i.e., the end closest to completion) whenever the work in process or waiting is less than the work in progress limit. This maximizes flow and ensures that any issues can be recognized and dealt with quickly. For more information on the theory, Reinertsen's (2009) book, *The Principles of Development Flow* is unbeatable.

While, today, Agile is the world's most popular software development method, it has come to include (apparently by osmosis) a number of practices and techniques beyond the "original" Scrum methodology that in some cases predated the use of the term *Agile*. Examples include Extreme Programming (XP) (Beck and Andres 2004), test-driven development (Beck 2002), crystal development, Kanban, and the older iterative development methodology and spiral development methodology, which all have some common characteristics with Agile. Broadly, all these methodologies share some or all of the characteristics associated with the principles of lean software engineering (Poppendieck and Poppendieck 2006)—an attempt to apply lean manufacturing principles to software development—and the term *lean-Agile* has been coined to recognize the tight relationship between all of these approaches. At a lower level, hybrid approaches have been implemented by various organizations under names such as *Scrumban*. The existence of so many Agile variations shows that Agile is not a panacea that works equally well with all sizes and types of software applications. Frankly, from my perspective, many organizations "cherry pick" parts of the lean-Agile spectrum that they like or can implement easily and often end up with suboptimal implementations that are worse than their original Waterfall methodologies.

References

Ambler, Scott W., and Mark Lines. 2012. *Disciplined Agile Delivery: A Practitioner's Guide to Agile Software Delivery in the Enterprise*. Boston, MA: IBM Press.

Beck, Kent. 2002. *Test-Driven Development: By Example*. Boston, MA: Addison-Wesley Professional.

Beck, Kent, and Cynthia Andres. 2004. *Extreme Programming Explained: Embrace Change*, 2nd Edition (The XP Series). Boston, MA: Addison-Wesley.

Beck, Kent, Mike Beedle, Arie van Bennekum, Alistair Cockburn, Ward Cunningham, Martin Fowler, James Grenning, et al. 2001. Manifesto for Agile Software Development. http://www.agilemanifesto.org/. Accessed January 31, 2016.

Bell, Gertrude. 2016. *The Desert and the Sown*. Taurus Parke Paperbacks. First published in 1907 by Willian Heinemann, London.

Christensen, Clayton M. 1997. *The Innovator's Dilemma*. Cambridge: Harvard Business School Press.

Cockburn, Alistair. 2004. *Crystal Clear: A Human-Powered Methodology for Small Teams*. Boston, MA: Addison-Wesley Professional.

Cohn, Mike. 2005. *Agile Estimating and Planning*. Upper Saddle River, NJ: Prentice Hall.

Garmus, David, and David Herron. 2001. *Function Point Analysis: Measurement Practices for Successful Software Projects*. Boston, MA: Addison-Wesley.

Harris, Michael D.S., David Herron, and Stasia Iwanicki. 2008. *The Business Value of IT*. Boca Raton, FL: Auerbach Publications.

Helm, Dieter, and Cameron Hepburn. 2014. *Nature in the Balance: The Economics of Biodiversity*. Oxford, UK: Oxford University Press.

Hunter, Richard, and George Westerman. 2009. *The Real Business of IT: How CIOs Create and Communicate Value*. Boston, MA: Harvard Business Review Press.

Kafura, Dennis and G.R. Reddy. 1987. The use of software complexity metrics in software maintenance, *IEEE Transactions on Software Engineering*, SE-13(3).

Kaplan, Robert S., Catherine H. MacLean, Alexander Dresner, Derek A. Haas, Thomas W. Feeley. 2015. Health care providers need a value management office. *Harvard Business Review* December 2. https://hbr.org/2015/12/health-care-providers-need-a-value-management-office

Leffingwell, Dean. 2011. *Agile Software Requirements: Lean Requirements Practices for Teams, Programs, and the Enterprise*. Upper Saddle River, NJ: Addison-Wesley.

McConnell, Steve. 1997. *Software Project Survival Guide (Developer Best Practices)*. Redmond, WA: Microsoft Press.

Moore, Geoffrey A. 2014. *Crossing the Chasm, 3rd Edition: Marketing and Selling Disruptive Products to Mainstream Customers*. New York: HarperBusiness.

Ohno, Taiichi. 1988. *Toyota Production System: Beyond Large-Scale Production.* Portland, OR: Productivity Press.

Parkkola, Mikko. 2010. Product management and product owner role in large-scale agile software development. Master's thesis, Aalto University.

Poppendieck, Mary, and Tom Poppendieck. 2006. *Implementing Lean Software Development: From Concept to Cash.* Boston, MA: Addison Wesley Professional.

Poppendieck, Mary, and Tom Poppendieck. 2007. *Implementing Lean Software Development.* Boston, MA: Pearson Education.

Reinertsen, Donald G. 2009. *The Principles of Product Development Flow: Second Generation Lean Product Development.* Redondo Beach, CA: Celeritas Publishing.

Rico, David F., Hasan H. Sayani, and Saya Sone. 2009. *The Business Value of Agile Software Methods: Maximizing ROI with Just-in-Time Process and Documentation.* J. Ross Publishing.

Ries, Eric. 2011. *The Lean Startup: How Today's Entrepreneurs Use Continuous Innovation to Create Radically Successful Businesses.* New York: Crown Business.

Schwaber, Ken, and Mike Beedle. 2001. *Agile Software Development with Scrum.* Pearson.

Simmons, Chad. 2002. *Business Valuation Bluebook.* Tempe, AZ: Facts on Demand Press.

Stewart, G. Bennett. 1999. *The Quest for Value: A Guide for Senior Managers.* New York: HarperCollins.

Weinberg, Gerald M. 1992. *Quality Software Management, Volume 1: Systems Thinking.* New York: Dorset House.

Index